IAPP® CIPM
Certified Information Privacy Manager
Study Guide

IAPP® CIPM
Certified Information Privacy Manager
Study Guide

Mike Chapple, PHD, CIPP/US, CIPM

Joe Shelley, CIPP/US, CIPM

SYBEX®
A Wiley Brand

Acknowledgments

Even though only the authors' names appear on the front cover, the production of a book is a collaborative effort involving a huge team. Wiley always brings a top-notch collection of professionals to the table, and that makes the work of authors so much easier.

In particular, we'd like to thank Jim Minatel, our acquisitions editor. Jim is a consummate professional, and it is an honor and a privilege to continue to work with him on yet another project. Here's to many more!

We also greatly appreciated the editing and production team for the book, including Kristi Bennett, our project editor, who brought great talent to the project. Our technical editors, Joanna Grama and John Bruggeman, provided indispensable insight and expertise. This book would not have been the same without their valuable contributions. Magesh Elangovan, our production editor, guided us through layouts, formatting, and final cleanup to produce a great book. We would also like to thank the many behind-the-scenes contributors, including the graphics, production, and technical teams who made the book and companion materials into a finished product.

Our agent, Carole Jelen of Waterside Productions, continues to provide us with wonderful opportunities, advice, and assistance throughout our writing careers.

Finally, we would like to thank our families, who supported us through the late evenings, busy weekends, and long hours that a book like this requires to write, edit, and get to press.

About the Authors

Mike Chapple, Ph.D., CIPM, CIPP/US, CISSP, is the author of the best-selling *CISSP (ISC)² Certified Information Systems Security Professional Official Study Guide* (Sybex, 9th edition, 2021) and the *CISSP (ISC)² Official Practice Tests* (Sybex, 3rd edition, 2021). He is an information security professional with two decades of experience in higher education, the private sector, and government.

Mike currently serves as a teaching professor in the IT, Analytics, and Operations Department at the University of Notre Dame's Mendoza College of Business, where he teaches undergraduate and graduate courses on cybersecurity, data management, and business analytics.

Before returning to Notre Dame, Mike served as executive vice president and chief information officer of the Brand Institute, a Miami-based marketing consultancy. Mike also spent four years in the information security research group at the National Security Agency and served as an active duty intelligence officer in the U.S. Air Force.

Mike is technical editor for *Information Security Magazine* and has written more than 35 books. He earned both his B.S. and Ph.D. degrees from Notre Dame in computer science and engineering. Mike also holds an M.S. in computer science from the University of Idaho and an MBA from Auburn University. Mike holds the Certified Information Privacy Manager (CIPM), Certified Information Privacy Professional/US (CIPP/US), Cybersecurity Analyst+ (CySA+), Security+, Certified Information Security Manager (CISM), Certified Cloud Security Professional (CCSP), and Certified Information Systems Security Professional (CISSP) certifications.

Learn more about Mike and his other security and privacy certification materials at his website, CertMike.com.

Joe Shelley, M.A., CIPM, CIPP/US, is a leader in higher education information technologies. He is currently the vice president for Libraries and Information Technology at Hamilton College in New York. In his role, Joe oversees central IT infrastructure, enterprise systems, information security and privacy programs, IT risk management, business intelligence and analytics, institutional research and assessment, data governance, and overall technology strategy. Joe also directs the Library and Institutional Research. In addition to supporting the teaching and research mission of the college, the library provides education in information sciences, digital and information literacy, and information management.

Before joining Hamilton College, Joe served as the chief information officer at the University of Washington Bothell in the Seattle area. During his 12 years at UW Bothell, Joe was responsible for learning technologies, data centers, web development, enterprise applications, help desk services, administrative and academic computing, and multimedia production. He implemented the UW Bothell information security program, cloud computing strategy, and IT governance, and he developed new initiatives for supporting teaching and learning, faculty research, and e-learning.

Joe earned his bachelor's degree in interdisciplinary arts and sciences from the University of Washington and his master's degree in educational technology from Michigan State University. Joe has held certifications and certificates for CIPM, CIPP/US, ITIL, project management, and Scrum.

Contents at a Glance

Contents

Introduction

If you're preparing to take the Certified Information Privacy Manager (CIPM) exam, you'll undoubtedly want to find as much information as you can about privacy. The more information you have at your disposal and the more hands-on experience you gain, the better off you'll be when attempting the exam. We wrote this study guide with that in mind. The goal was to provide enough information to prepare you for the test—but not so much that you'll be overloaded with information that's outside the scope of the exam.

We've included review questions at the end of each chapter to give you a taste of what it's like to take the exam. If you're already working in the privacy field, we recommend that you check out these questions first to gauge your level of expertise. You can then use the book mainly to fill in the gaps in your current knowledge. This study guide will help you round out your knowledge base before tackling the exam.

If you can answer 90 percent or more of the review questions correctly for a given chapter, you can feel safe moving on to the next chapter. If you're unable to answer that many correctly, reread the chapter and try the questions again. Your score should improve.

Don't just study the questions and answers! The questions on the actual exam will be different from the practice questions included in this book. The exam is designed to test your knowledge of a concept or objective, so use this book to learn the objectives behind the questions.

The CIPM Exam

The CIPM certification is designed to be the gold standard credential for privacy professionals who are either currently working in management roles or aspire to become leaders in the field. It is offered by the International Association of Privacy Professionals (IAPP) and complements its suite of geographic-based privacy professional certifications.

The exam covers six major domains of privacy knowledge:

1. Developing a Privacy Program
2. Privacy Program Framework
3. Privacy Operational Life Cycle: Assess
4. Privacy Operational Life Cycle: Protect
5. Privacy Operational Life Cycle: Sustain
6. Privacy Operational Life Cycle: Respond

These six areas include a range of topics, from building a privacy program to understanding the full privacy operational life cycle. You'll find that the exam focuses heavily on scenario-based learning. For this reason, you may find the exam easier if you have some real-world privacy experience, although many individuals pass the exam before moving into their first privacy role.

The CIPM exam consists of 90 multiple-choice questions administered during a 150-minute exam period. Each of the exam questions has four possible answer options. Exams are scored on a scale ranging from 100 to 500, with a minimum passing score of 300. Every exam item is weighted equally, but the passing score is determined using a secret formula, so you won't know exactly what percentage of questions you need to answer correctly in order to pass.

Exam Tip

There is no penalty for answering questions incorrectly. A blank answer and an incorrect answer have equal weight. Therefore, you should fill in an answer for every question, even if it is a complete guess!

IAPP charges $550 for your first attempt at the CIPM exam and then $375 for retake attempts if you do not pass on the first try. More details about the CIPM exam and how to take it can be found in the IAPP Candidate Certification Handbook at http://iapp.org/certify/candidate-handbook.

You should also know that certification exams are notorious for including vague questions. You might see a question for which two of the possible four answers are correct—but you can choose only one. Use your knowledge, logic, and intuition to choose the best answer and then move on. Sometimes, the questions are worded in ways that would make English majors cringe—a typo here, an incorrect verb there. Don't let this frustrate you; answer the question and move on to the next one.

Certification providers often use a process called *item seeding*, which is the practice of including unscored questions on exams. They do this as part of the process of developing new versions of the exam. So, if you come across a question that does not appear to map to any of the exam objectives—or for that matter, does not appear to belong in the exam—it is likely a seeded question. You never really know whether or not a question is seeded, however, so always make your best effort to answer every question.

Taking the Exam

Once you are fully prepared to take the exam, you can visit the IAPP website to purchase your exam voucher:

http://iapp.org/store/certifications

IAPP partners with Pearson VUE's testing centers, so your next step will be to locate a testing center near you. In the United States, you can do this based on your address or your ZIP code, while non-U.S. test takers may find it easier to enter their city and country. You can search for a test center near you at the Pearson Vue website, where you will need to navigate to "Find a test center."

```
http://home.pearsonvue.com/iapp
```

In addition to the live testing centers, you may also choose to take the exam at your home or office through Pearson VUE's OnVUE service. More information about this program is available here:

```
http://home.pearsonvue.com/iapp/onvue
```

Now that you know where you'd like to take the exam, simply set up a Pearson VUE testing account and schedule an exam. One important note: Once you purchase your exam on the IAPP website, you have one year to register for and take the exam before your registration will expire. Be sure not to miss that deadline!

On the day of the test, take two forms of identification, and make sure to show up with plenty of time before the exam starts. Remember that you will not be able to take your notes, electronic devices (including smartphones and watches), or other materials into the exam with you.

Exam policies can change from time to time. We highly recommend that you check both the IAPP and Pearson VUE sites for the most up-to-date information when you begin your preparing, when you register, and again a few days before your scheduled exam date.

After the CIPM Exam

Once you have taken the exam, you will be notified of your score immediately, so you'll know if you passed the test right away. You should keep track of your score report with your exam registration records and the email address you used to register for the exam.

Maintaining Your Certification

IAPP certifications must be renewed periodically. To renew your certification, you must either maintain a paid IAPP membership or pay a $250 non-member renewal fee. You must also demonstrate that you have successfully completed 20 hours of continuing professional education (CPE).

IAPP provides information on the CPE process via its website at

```
http://iapp.org/certify/cpe
```

What Does This Book Cover?

This book covers everything you need to know to pass the CIPM exam.

Chapter 1: Developing a Privacy Program

Chapter 2: Privacy Program Framework

Chapter 3: Privacy Operational Life Cycle: Assess

Chapter 4: Privacy Operational Life Cycle: Protect

Chapter 5: Privacy Operational Life Cycle: Sustain

Chapter 6. Privacy Operational Life Cycle: Respond

Appendix: Answers to Review Questions

Study Guide Elements

This study guide uses a number of common elements to help you prepare. These include the following:

Summaries   The summary section of each chapter briefly explains the chapter, allowing you to easily understand what it covers.

Exam Essentials   The Exam Essentials focus on major exam topics and critical knowledge that you should take into the test. The Exam Essentials focus on the exam objectives provided by IAPP.

Chapter Review Questions   A set of questions at the end of each chapter will help you assess your knowledge and whether you are ready to take the exam based on your knowledge of that chapter's topics.

Additional Study Tools

This book comes with a number of additional study tools to help you prepare for the exam. They include the following.

Go to www.wiley.com/go/Sybextestprep to register your book to receive your unique PIN, and then once you receive the PIN by email, return to www.wiley.com/go/Sybextestprep and register a new account or add this book to an existing account. After adding the book, if you do not see it in your account, please refresh the page or log out and log back in.

Sybex Online Learning Environment

Sybex's online learning environment software lets you prepare with electronic test versions of the review questions from each chapter and the practice exams that are included in this book. You can build and take tests on specific domains, by chapter, or cover the entire set of CIPM exam objectives using randomized tests.

Electronic Flashcards

Our electronic flashcards are designed to help you prepare for the exam. Over 100 flashcards will ensure that you know critical terms and concepts.

Glossary of Terms

Sybex provides a full glossary of terms in PDF format, allowing quick searches and easy reference to materials in this book.

Practice Exams

In addition to the practice questions for each chapter, this book includes two full 90-question practice exams. We recommend that you use them both to test your preparedness for the certification exam.

 Like all exams, the CIPM certification from IAPP is updated periodically and may eventually be retired or replaced. At some point after IAPP is no longer offering this exam, the old editions of our books and online tools will be retired. If you have purchased this book after the exam was retired, or are attempting to register in the Sybex online learning environment after the exam was retired, please know that we make no guarantees that this exam's online Sybex tools will be available once the exam is no longer available.

CIPM Exam Objectives

IAPP goes to great lengths to ensure that its certification programs accurately reflect the privacy profession's best practices. They also publish ranges for the number of questions on the exam that will come from each domain. The following table lists the six CIPM domains and the extent to which they are represented on the exam.

Domain	Questions
1. Developing a Privacy Program	13–17
2. Privacy Program Framework	9–11
3. Privacy Operational Lifecycle: Assess	13–17
4. Privacy Operational Lifecycle: Protect	12–16
5. Privacy Operational Lifecycle: Sustain	5–7
6. Privacy Operational Lifecycle: Respond	9–11

CIPM Certification Exam Objective Map

The objective mapping below takes each of the learning objectives found in the IAPP body of knowledge v3.0 and identifies where in the book you will find coverage of each objective.

Objective	Chapter
I. Developing a Privacy Program	
I.A. Create an organizational vision	1
I.A.a. Evaluate the intended objective	1
I.A.b. Gain executive sponsor approval for this vision	1
I.B. Establish a Data Governance model	1
I.B.a. Centralized	1
I.B.b. Distributed	1
I.B.c. Hybrid	1
I.C. Define a privacy program	1
I.C.a. Define program scope and charter	1
I.C.b. Identify the source, types, and uses of personal information (PI) within the organization and applicable laws	1
I.C.c Develop a privacy strategy	1
I.D. Structure the privacy team	1
I.D.a. Establish the organizational model, responsibilities, and reporting structure appropriate to the size of the organization (e.g., Chief Privacy Officer, DPO, Privacy manager, Privacy analysts, Privacy champions, "First responders")	1
I.D.b. Designate a point of contact for privacy issues	1
I.D.c. Establish/endorse the measurement of professional competency	1
I.E. Communicate	1
I.E.a. Create awareness of the organization's privacy program internally and externally (e.g., PR, Corporate Communication, HR)	1
I.E.b. Develop internal and external communication plans to ingrain organizational accountability	1
I.E.c. Ensure employees have access to policies and procedures and updates relative to their role	1

IAPP occasionally makes minor adjustments to the exam objectives. Please be certain to check their website for any recent changes that might affect your exam experience.

How to Contact the Publisher

If you believe you have found a mistake in this book, please bring it to our attention. At John Wiley & Sons, we understand how important it is to provide our customers with accurate content, but even with our best efforts an error may occur. In order to submit your possible errata, please email it to our Customer Service Team at wileysupport@wiley.com with the subject line "Possible Book Errata Submission."

Assessment Test

1. Max is a freelance database specialist operating in Spain. He helps companies organize their data and clean up legacy databases. From a legal perspective, what role is Max playing when it comes to handling personal information?

   A. Data processor

   B. Business associate

   C. Data controller

   D. Data manager

2. Adrian is reviewing a new application that will be used by his organization to gather health information from customers. The application is now in testing and about to be released into production. After his review, Adrian realizes that the way the software is implemented is not compliant with the organization's HIPAA obligations. What is the root cause of this issue?

   A. Failure to use strong encryption

   B. Failure to integrate privacy into the SDLC

   C. Failure to incorporate customer requirements

   D. Failure to minimize data collection

3. NIST provides an example of which of the following?

   A. Industry self-regulatory framework

   B. Privacy regulation

   C. Privacy program framework

   D. Core privacy principles

4. Which of the following factors is not a primary consideration when developing a privacy program framework?

   A. Compliance with applicable regulations

   B. Scope and scale of the organization's data processing

   C. Technological infrastructure for data storage and protection

   D. Alignment with business objectives

5. Lena runs a mid-sized data analytics company in Paris. She is considering moving her databases to a cloud computing solution. What is she required to do first?

   A. Consult her DPA.

   B. Conduct a vendor assessment.

   C. Conduct a PIA.

   D. Conduct a DPIA.

6. A graph that shows a decrease in privacy incidents over time is an example of which of the following?

    A. Statistical analysis

    B. Compliance metric

    C. Performance target

    D. Trend analysis

7. David is an IT professional responsible for applying, monitoring, and maintaining access controls to a filesystem containing sensitive information used by the human resources department. He works closely with the management of that department to identify appropriate permissions. What term best describes David's role in relation to this data?

    A. Data custodian

    B. Data steward

    C. Data owner

    D. Data subject

8. Harold recently completed leading the postmortem review of a privacy incident. What documentation should he prepare next?

    A. Remediation list

    B. Risk assessment

    C. Lessons-learned document

    D. Mitigation checklist

9. Tamara is a cybersecurity analyst for a private business that is suffering a security breach. She believes the attackers have compromised a database containing sensitive information. Which one of the following activities should be Tamara's first priority?

    A. Identification of the source of the attack

    B. Containment

    C. Remediation

    D. Recovery

10. Brianna is reviewing the dataflows for one of her organization's information systems and discovers that records are not destroyed when they are no longer needed. What privacy by design principle is most directly violated?

    A. Full functionality

    B. End-to-end security

    C. Privacy embedded into design

    D. Visibility and transparency

11. Sally is a new privacy manager at an accounting firm. She decides to get started by evaluating the privacy program currently in place. She notes that processes are well documented and there is a written privacy policy. When she asks for records of the last privacy program review, she learns that the privacy program performance is managed "on the go" and "in real time"; when". If employees find problems with the program, they fix them, so formal reviews and feedback processes just haven't seemed necessary. Since there doesn't seem to be much of a program assessment process in place, where should Sally start?

A. Initiate tabletop drills.

B. Request a program audit to measure performance.

C. Ensure that the training and awareness programs include the need to periodically review procedures.

D. Establish the program's baseline performance.

12. Xavier is a data custodian responsible for maintaining databases with sensitive information, including Social Security numbers. He would like to protect those SSNs from prying eyes but will need to be able to retrieve the original value on occasion. What data protection technique would be most appropriate for his use?

A. Redaction

B. Tokenization

C. Masking

D. Hashing

13. Conducting audits is most closely associated with which part of the privacy operational life cycle?

A. Respond

B. Sustain

C. Assess

D. Protect

14. Paula is a privacy manager at a data management company. She has well documented procedures for executing PIAs when required, but she keeps hearing about planned changes to IT systems when it's almost too late for a PIA. What part of the privacy operational life cycle might help Paula fix this problem?

A. Compliance monitoring

B. Monitoring regulatory changes

C. IT audit

D. Monitoring the environment

15. Marco owns an electronics store in Barcelona, and he's interested in hiring a contractor to help build and manage a new customer database and help him dive into the world of online sales. Marco would prefer an individual contractor to a larger agency so that he can develop a strong relationship with someone who really learns about his business. Thanks to modern cloud technology, Marco thinks that a single individual will be able to do the job just as well as a large company anyway. Why should Marco be concerned about cloud computing technology when selecting a contractor?

A. The cloud computing vendor may profit by selling Marco's customer data to third parties.

B. Cloud computing is less secure.

C. Cloud computing vendors usually comingle the data of multiple customers.

D. Cloud providers may store data outside of the EU.

16. Jasmine is responsible for responding to data subject requests to exercise their rights under GDPR. Jasmine keeps a record of each request and the resolution, even after the requests are fulfilled What is the primary reason for this recordkeeping?

A. To establish ROI for her position

B. For records retention

C. To create an audit trail

D. To establish ROI for her position

17. Which of the following best defines the Monitor phase of the privacy operational life cycle?

A. Sustain and improve a program over time.

B. Measure program effectiveness.

C. Establish outcomes and objectives for the program.

D. Effectively manage incidents when they occur.

18. Norm is reviewing his organization's privacy practices and observes that the privacy notice is not posted on their website in a location that is accessible to customers. What GAPP principle is most directly violated by this action?

A. Notice

B. Choice and Consent

C. Communication

D. Collection

19. Which one of the following ISO standards is not commonly used in the design and implementation of cybersecurity and privacy programs?

A. ISO 9001

B. ISO 27001

C. ISO 27002

D. ISO 27701

20. Marcia runs a boulangerie in Lyon, France. She has a new computer system that allows her to capture data on regular customers. She can record what they ordered, the date and time of their visits, and additional data on their transactions. Marcia is contracting with another company to compile the data and give her insights into customer habits, preferences, and patterns so that she can understand which products she should offer at different times of the day. In this case, Marcia is acting as which of the following?

A. Data processor

B. Data collector

C. Data controller

D. Data owner

Answers to Assessment Test

1. **A.** Since Max is operating in the European Union, his role is defined by the General Data Protection Regulation (GDPR). A data processor manages and manipulates personal information on a data controller's behalf. For more information, see Chapter 1.

2. **B.** While any of these options may be true, we are looking for the root cause of the HIPAA compliance failure in this question. The root issue is that Adrian did not identify the failure to meet HIPAA requirements until the testing phase of the process. These privacy requirements should have been identified during the requirements phase of the SDLC before any software was written. There is no indication that the software fails to meet customer requirements, only that it fails to meet privacy requirements that come from a regulatory (not customer) source. While the system may (or may not) fail to use strong encryption or minimize data collection, those would be symptoms of the same root cause—a failure to integrate privacy into the SDLC. For more information, see Chapter 4.

3. **C.** The National Institute of Standards and Technology (NIST) has published a broadly applicable privacy program framework called the NIST Privacy Framework. The NIST Privacy Framework may be required by some regulations or industry self-regulatory frameworks and used to uphold core privacy principles. For more information, see Chapter 2.

4. **C.** Privacy program frameworks help ensure that a privacy framework achieves all intended outcomes and manages all private information without neglecting any part of an organization's operations. The scope and scale of an organization's data processing, regulatory compliance, and alignment with the organization's business objectives all help to design a comprehensive program. A good program framework should be able to manage privacy regardless of the technology infrastructure in place and should be flexible enough to account for changes in technology. For more information, see Chapter 2.

5. **D.** Since Lena is in France, she is subject to GDPR. GDPR requires her to complete data protection impact assessments (DPIAs) before implementing any change to data processing that might impact privacy protections. For more information, see Chapter 3.

6. **D.** Tracking changes to a given measurement over time gives the audience a sense of whether a given measurement is increasing or decreasing over time. This is known as trend analysis and helps to track metrics that are pegged to a rate of change rather than to an absolute value. For more information, see Chapter 2.

7. **A.** Data custodians, or data processors, are the individuals who actually store and process sensitive information. As an IT professional implementing the directions of the data owners and stewards in the HR department, David is a data custodian. Data subjects are the individuals referred to in these records. Technically, David may also be a data subject because he is likely an employee of the organization and would be in the HR database. However, the question is asking for the role that best describes David, which is his primary role as the data custodian for the entire dataset rather than the incidental fact that he is one of many data subjects described in the records. For more information, see Chapter 1.

8. C. A lessons-learned document is often created and distributed to involved parties after a postmortem review to ensure that those who were involved in the incident and others who may benefit from the knowledge are aware of what they can do to prevent future issues and to improve response if an incident occurs. For more information, see Chapter 6.

9. B. Tamara's first priority should be containing the attack. This will prevent it from spreading to other systems and also potentially stop the exfiltration of sensitive information. Only after containing the attack should Tamara move on to eradication and recovery activities. Identifying the source of the attack should be a low priority. For more information, see Chapter 6.

10. B. The principle of end-to-end security calls for full data life cycle protection. This means that information must be protected from the time it is collected until it is securely destroyed at the end of its useful life. Brianna's organization is failing to complete the end of the life cycle process by securely destroying information. For more information, see Chapter 4.

11. D. Sally must first establish a baseline of performance to find out how well the program is currently doing before she can start to use assessments to measure program improvement. For more information, see Chapter 3.

12. B. Tokenization replaces sensitive values in a table with a nonsensitive token value. Employees with access to the lookup table may use these tokens to retrieve the original value when necessary. Masking, redaction, and hashing are all techniques that destroy the original value, making it impractical to retrieve it. For more information, see Chapter 4.

13. B. Audits are a key tool for sustaining a program through formal monitoring over time. Audits provide accountability to ensure ongoing compliance with the privacy program and ensure that the privacy program itself remains compliant with regulations. For more information, see Chapter 5.

14. D. The process of monitoring the environment includes policies and procedures for planning changes to IT systems in a timely manner so that other processes, such as completing PIAs, can take place as required. For more information, see Chapter 5.

15. D. When evaluating vendors, it is critical to know where private information will be physically located. Marco's business is subject to GDPR and if he unknowingly exports his customer data to another country, it may trigger compliance risks with GDPR. For more information, see Chapter 3.

16. C. Audits look for evidence of compliance. By keeping records of activities related to complying with requests under GDPR, Jasmine can streamline her response to any GDPR audit by having evidence at the ready. This is known as creating an audit trail. For more information, see Chapter 5.

17. A. The Monitor phase is about sustaining a program through ongoing management and alignment activities. Measuring program effectiveness is part of the Assess phase, setting objectives is part of developing the program, and incident management is part of the Respond phase. For more information, see Chapter 5.

18. A. The second GAPP principle, notice, requires that organizations inform individuals about their privacy practices. One of the criteria for this principle includes writing privacy notices in plain and simple language and posting them conspicuously. Norm's organization is not doing this. This does not directly impact the principles of Choice and Consent or Collection. Communication seems like an obvious answer here, but it is not one of the 10 GAPP principles. For more information, see Chapter 1.

19. A. ISO 27001 and 27002 are used in the design of cybersecurity programs. ISO 27701 is used in the design of privacy programs. ISO 9001 is a standard used for quality management programs. For more information, see Chapter 1.

20. C. Marcia's company is subject to GDPR because she is in France. She is acting as a data controller because she collects and determines how customer data are to be used. For more information, see Chapter 2.

Chapter

1

Developing a Privacy Program

THE CIPM EXAM OBJECTIVES COVERED IN THIS CHAPTER INCLUDE:

✓ **Domain I. Developing a Privacy Program**

- I.A. Create an organizational vision
  - I.A.a. Evaluate the intended objective
  - I.A.b. Gain executive sponsor approval for this vision
- I.B. Establish a data governance model
  - I.B.a. Centralized
  - I.B.b. Distributed
  - I.B.c. Hybrid
- I.C. Define a privacy program
  - I.C.a. Define program scope and charter
  - I.C.b. Identify the source, types, and uses of personal information (PI) within the organization and the applicable laws.
  - I.C.c. Develop a privacy strategy
- I.D. Structure the privacy team
  - I.D.a. Establish the organizational model, responsibilities, and reporting structure appropriate to the size of the organization (e.g., Chief Privacy Officer, DPO, Privacy manager, Privacy analysts, Privacy champions, "First responders")
  - I.D.b. Designate a point of contact for privacy issues
  - I.D.c. Establish/endorse the measurement of professional competency

- I.E. Communicate

  - I.E.a. Create awareness of the organization's privacy program internally and externally (e.g., PR, Corporate Communication, HR)

  - I.E.b. Develop internal and external communication plans to ingrain organizational accountability

  - I.E.c. Ensure employees have access to policies and procedures and updates relative to their role.

Organizations around the world find themselves under increasing scrutiny for their privacy practices. Legal and regulatory requirements, consumer pressure, and ethical obligations drive them to identify the personal information that they use and to implement controls to protect the privacy of that information.

As privacy functions flourish within organizations, they need qualified managers and leaders to ensure their success. From top-level chief privacy officers to mid-level managers, demand continues to increase for privacy experts.

Introduction to Privacy

Privacy is one of the core rights inherent to every human being. The term is defined in many historic works, but they all share the basic tenet of individuals having the right to protect themselves and their information from unwanted intrusions by others or the government. Let's take a brief look at the historical underpinnings of privacy in the United States.

In 1890, lawyers Samuel D. Warren and Louis D. Brandeis wrote an article for the *Harvard Law Review* titled "The Right to Privacy." In that article, they wrote:

> Recent inventions and business methods call attention to the next step which must be taken for the protection of the person, and for securing to the individual . . . the right "to be let alone." Instantaneous photographs and newspaper enterprises have invaded the sacred precincts of private and domestic life; and numerous mechanical devices threaten to make good the prediction that "what is whispered in the closet shall be proclaimed from the house-tops." For years there has been a feeling that the law must afford some remedy for the unauthorized circulation of portraits of private persons; and the evil of the invasion of privacy by the newspapers, long keenly felt, has been but recently discussed by an able writer.

Reading that excerpt over a century later, we can easily see echoes of Warren and Brandeis's concerns about technology in today's world. We could just as easily talk about the impact of social media, data brokerages, and electronic surveillance as having the potential to cause "what is whispered in the closet" to be "proclaimed from the house-tops."

The words written by Warren and Brandeis might have slipped into obscurity were it not for the fact that 25 years later one author would ascend to the Supreme Court where, as Justice Brandeis, he would take the concepts from this law review article and use them to argue for a constitutional right to privacy. In a dissenting opinion in the case *Olmstead v. United States*, Justice Brandeis wrote:

> The makers of our Constitution undertook to secure conditions favorable to the pursuit of happiness . . . . They conferred, as against the Government, the right to be let alone—the most comprehensive of rights and the right most valued by civilized men. To protect that right, every unjustifiable intrusion by the Government upon the privacy of the individual, whatever the means employed, must be deemed a violation of the Fourth Amendment.

This text, appearing in a dissenting opinion, was not binding upon the courts, but it has surfaced many times over the years in arguments establishing a right to privacy as that right "to be let alone." Recently, the 2018 majority opinion of the court in *Carpenter v. United States* cited *Olmstead* in an opinion declaring warrantless searches of cell phone location records unconstitutional, saying:

> As Justice Brandeis explained in his famous dissent, the Court is obligated as "[s]ubtler and more far-reaching means of invading privacy have become available to the Government"—to ensure that the "progress of science" does not erode Fourth Amendment protections. Here the progress of science has afforded law enforcement a powerful new tool to carry out its important responsibilities. At the same time, this tool risks Government encroachment of the sort the Framers, "after consulting the lessons of history," drafted the Fourth Amendment to prevent.

This is just one example of many historical precedents that firmly establish a right to privacy in U.S. law and allow the continued reinterpretation of that right in the context of technologies and tools that the authors of the Constitution could not possibly have imagined.

What Is Privacy?

It would certainly be difficult to start a book on privacy without first defining the word *privacy*, but this is a term that eludes a common definition in today's environment. Legal and privacy professionals asking this question often harken back to the words of Justice Brandeis, describing privacy simply as the right "to be let alone."

In their Generally Accepted Privacy Principles (GAPP), the American Institute of Certified Public Accountants (AICPA) offers a more hands-on definition, describing privacy as "the rights and obligations of individuals and organizations with respect to the collection, use, retention, disclosure, and destruction of personal information."

The GAPP definition may not be quite as pithy and elegant as Justice Brandeis's right "to be let alone," but it does provide privacy professionals with a better working definition that they can use to guide their privacy programs, so it is the definition that we will adopt in this book.

What Is Personal Information?

Now that we have privacy defined, we're led to another question. If privacy is about the protection of *personal information*, what information fits into this category? Here, we turn our attention once again to GAPP, which defines personal information as "information that is or can be about or related to an identifiable individual."

More simply, if information is about a person, that information is personal information as long as you can identify the person that it is about. For example, the fairly innocuous statement "Mike Chapple and Joe Shelley wrote this book" fits the definition of personal information. That personal information might fall into the public domain (after all, it's on the cover of this book!), but it remains personal information.

 You'll often hear the term *personally identifiable information (PII)* used to describe personal information. The acronym PII is commonly used in privacy programs as a shorthand notation for all personal information.

Of course, not all personal information is in the public domain. Many other types of information fit into this category that most people would consider private. Our bank balances, medical records, college admissions test scores, and email communications are all personal information that we might hold sensitive. This information fits into the narrower category of *sensitive personal information (SPI)*. SPI tends to designate the type of information that a person might want to keep confidential. SPI can have differing levels of sensitivity and may also be protected by law. For example, General Data Protection Regulation (GDPR) in the European Union (EU) has a listing of "special categories of personal data," which includes:

- Racial or ethnic origin
- Political opinions
- Religious or philosophical beliefs
- Trade union membership
- Genetic data
- Biometric data used for the purpose of uniquely identifying a natural person
- Health data
- Data concerning a natural person's sex life or sexual orientation

GDPR uses this list to create special boundaries and controls around the categories of information that EU lawmakers found to be the most sensitive.

What Isn't Personal Information?

With a working knowledge of personal information under our belts, it's also important to make sure that we have a clear understanding of what types of information do not fit the definition of personal information and, therefore, fall outside the scope of privacy programs.

First, clearly, if information is not about a person, it is not personal information. Information can be sensitive, but not personal. For example, a business's product development plans or a military unit's equipment list might both be very sensitive but they aren't about people, so they don't fit the definition of personal information.

Second, information is not personal information if it does not provide a way to identify the person that the information is about. For example, consider the height and weight information in Table 1.1.

TABLE 1.1   Height and weight information

Name	Age	Gender	Height	Weight
Mary Smith	43	F	5′ 9″	143 lbs
Matt Jones	45	M	5′ 11″	224 lbs
Kevin Reynolds	32	M	5′ 10″	176 lbs

This information clearly fits the definition of personal information. But what if we remove the names from this table, as shown in Table 1.2?

TABLE 1.2   Deidentified height and weight information

Age	Gender	Height	Weight
43	F	5′ 9″	143 lbs
45	M	5′ 11″	224 lbs
32	M	5′ 10″	176 lbs

Here, we have a set of information (or attributes) that are about an individual, but it doesn't seem to be about an *identifiable* individual, making the information *deidentified* and falling outside the definition of personal information. However, we must be careful here. What if this table was known to be the information about individuals in a certain department? If Mary Smith is the only 43-year-old female in that department, it would be trivial to determine that the first row contains her personal information, making the height and weight information once again identifiable information.

This leads us to the concept of *anonymization*, the process of taking personal information and making it impossible to identify the individual to whom the information relates. As illustrated in our height and weight example, simply removing names from a table of data does not necessarily anonymize that data. Anonymized data should never be related back to a specific individual, and the anonymization process is actually a quite challenging problem and requires the expertise of privacy professionals.

Exam Tip

It's important to understand that deidentification and anonymization are similar, but not identical, concepts. Deidentification is the removal of identifying characteristics from data, as was done in Table 1.2. Anonymization is the process of altering information to a point that makes it impossible to tie it back to a specific individual person.

The U.S. Department of Health and Human Services (HHS) publishes a deidentification standard that may be used to render information unidentifiable using two different techniques:

 The HHS deidentification standards cover medical records, so they include fields specific to medical records. You may use them as general guidance for the deidentification of other types of record, but you must also supplement them with industry-specific fields that might identify an individual. You can read the full HHS deidentification standard at www .hhs.gov/hipaa/for-professionals/privacy/special-topics/ de-identification/index.html#standard.

- *Expert determination* requires the involvement of a trained statistician who analyzes a deidentified data set and determines that very little risk exists that the information could be used to identify an individual, even if that information is combined with other publicly available information.
- *Safe harbor* requires the removal of 18 different types of information and indirect links to an individual. These include:
  - Names
  - Geographic divisions and ZIP codes containing fewer than 20,000 people
  - The month and day of a person's birth, death, and hospital admission or discharge or the age in years of a person over 89
  - Telephone numbers
  - Vehicle identifiers and serial numbers, including license plate numbers
  - Fax numbers
  - Device identifiers and serial numbers
  - Email addresses

- Web URLs
- Social Security numbers
- IP addresses
- Medical record numbers
- Biometric identifiers, including finger and voice prints
- Health plan beneficiary numbers
- Full-face photographs and any comparable images
- Account numbers
- Any other uniquely identifying number, characteristic, or code
- Certificate/license numbers

We will cover how this standard fits into the broader requirements of the Health Insurance Portability and Accountability Act (HIPAA) in Chapter 2, "Privacy Program Framework." We only discuss it here as an example of the difficulty of deidentifying personal information.

Closely related to issues of anonymization and deidentification is the process of *aggregation*, summarizing data about a group of individuals in a manner that makes it impossible to draw conclusions about a single person. For example, we might survey all the students at a university and ask them their height and weight. If the students included any identifying information on their survey responses, those individual responses are clearly personal information. However, if we provide the summary table shown in Table 1.3, the information has been aggregated to an extent that renders it nonpersonal information. There is no way to determine the height or weight of an individual student from this data.

TABLE 1.3   Aggregated height and weight information

Gender	Average Height	Average Weight
F	5′ 5″	133 lbs
M	5′ 10″	152 lbs

Why Should We Care about Privacy?

Protecting privacy is hard work. Privacy programs require that organizations invest time and money in an effort that does not necessarily provide a direct financial return on that investment. This creates an opportunity cost, as those resources could easily be deployed in other areas of the organization to have a direct financial impact on the mission. Why, then, should organizations care about privacy?

Privacy is an ethical obligation.   Organizations who are the custodians of personal information have a moral and ethical obligation to protect that information against unauthorized disclosure or use.

Laws and regulations require privacy protections.   Depending on the nature of an organization's operations and the jurisdiction(s) where it operates, they may face legal and contractual obligations to protect privacy. Much of this book is dedicated to exploring these obligations.

Poor privacy practices reflect poorly on an organization.   The failure to protect privacy presents a reputational risk to the organization, which may suddenly find its poor privacy practices covered on the front page of the *Wall Street Journal*. The reputational impact of a privacy lapse may have a lasting impact on the organization.

Consumers demand strong privacy practices.   Today's consumer is increasingly sophisticated and aware of privacy concerns. The modern consumer expects organizations to take appropriate steps to protect their personal information and to transparently disclose their privacy practices.

Emerging technologies create new privacy concerns.   The age of artificial intelligence (AI) and cloud computing creates many new opportunities to collect, store, and process personal information. These practices create new privacy issues that organizations adopting emerging technologies must address.

As the field of privacy matures, different organizations play a role in promoting strong privacy practices. The International Association of Privacy Professionals (IAPP) plays a strong role in developing and certifying privacy experts. Other organizations, including the American Civil Liberties Union (ACLU), the Electronic Frontier Foundation (EFF), and the Electronic Privacy Information Center (EPIC), advocate for strong privacy practices and appropriate applications of those practices to emerging technologies.

Generally Accepted Privacy Principles

Now that you have a basic understanding of the types of information covered by a privacy program and the reasons that organizations pay particular attention to protecting the privacy of personal information, we can start to explore the specific goals of a privacy program. These goals answer the question "What do we need to do to protect privacy?"

The *Generally Accepted Privacy Principles (GAPP)* are an attempt to establish a global framework for privacy management. GAPP includes 10 principles that were developed as a joint effort between two national accounting organizations: AICPA and the Canadian

Institute of Chartered Accountants (CICA). These two organizations sought expert input to develop a set of commonly accepted privacy principles.

The 10 GAPP principles are:

1. Management
2. Notice
3. Choice and Consent
4. Collection
5. Use, Retention, and Disposal
6. Access
7. Disclosure to Third Parties
8. Security for Privacy
9. Quality
10. Monitoring and Enforcement

The remainder of this section explores each of these principles in more detail.

Exam Tip

GAPP is one of many frameworks designed to help privacy professionals articulate the goals of their privacy programs and industry best practices. Other similar frameworks include the Fair Information Practice Principles (FIPPs) and the Organisation for Economic Co-operation and Development's (OECD) Privacy Guidelines.

We present GAPP to you in this chapter as a framework to help you understand the basic requirements of privacy programs. The GAPP principles are not included in the CIPM/US exam objectives, so you shouldn't see exam questions specifically covering them.

You will see many of these principles come up repeatedly in federal, state, and international laws that *are* covered by the exam objectives, so expect to see questions covering these concepts, just not in the context of GAPP.

Management

Management is the first of the 10 privacy principles, and GAPP defines it as follows: "The entity defines, documents, communicates, and assigns accountability for its privacy policies and procedures." GAPP lists a set of criteria that organizations should follow to establish control over the management of their privacy program.

These criteria include:

- Creating written privacy policies and communicating those policies to personnel
- Assigning responsibility and accountability for those policies to a person or team
- Establishing procedures for the review and approval of privacy policies and changes to those policies
- Ensuring that privacy policies are consistent with applicable laws and regulations
- Performing privacy risk assessments on at least an annual basis
- Ensuring that contractual obligations to customers, vendors, and partners are consistent with privacy policies
- Assessing privacy risks when implementing or changing technology infrastructure
- Creating and maintaining a privacy incident management process
- Conducting privacy awareness and training and establishing qualifications for employees with privacy responsibilities

Notice

The second GAPP principle, *notice*, requires that organizations inform individuals about their privacy practices. GAPP defines notice as follows: "The entity provides notice about its privacy policies and procedures and identifies the purposes for which personal information is collected, used, retained, and disclosed."

The notice principle incorporates the following criteria:

- Including notice practices in the organization's privacy policies
- Notifying individuals about the purpose of collecting personal information and the organization's policies surrounding the other GAPP principles
- Providing notice to individuals at the time of data collection, when policies and procedures change, and when the organization intends to use information for new purposes not disclosed in earlier notices
- Writing privacy notices in plain and simple language and posting it conspicuously

Choice and Consent

Choice and consent is the third GAPP principle, allowing individuals to retain control over the use of their personal information. GAPP defines choice and consent as follows: "The entity describes the choices available to the individual and obtains implicit or explicit consent with respect to the collection, use, and disclosure of personal information."

The criteria associated with the principle of choice and consent are as follows:

- Including choice and consent practices in the organization's privacy policies
- Informing individuals about the choice and consent options available to them and the consequences of refusing to provide personal information or withdrawing consent to use personal information

- Obtaining implicit or explicit consent at or before the time that personal information is collected
- Notifying individuals of proposed new uses for previously collected information and obtaining additional consent for those new uses
- Obtaining direct explicit consent from individuals when the organization collects, uses, or discloses sensitive personal information
- Obtaining consent before transferring personal information to or from an individual's computer or device

Collection

The principle of *collection* governs the ways that organizations come into the possession of personal information. GAPP defines this principle as follows: "The entity collects personal information only for the purposes identified in the notice."

The criteria associated with the collection principle are:

- Including collection practices in the organization's privacy policies
- Informing individuals that their personal information will only be collected for identified purposes
- Including details on the methods used to collect data and the types of data collected in the organization's privacy notice
- Collecting information using fair and lawful means and only for the purposes identified in the privacy notice
- Confirming that any third parties who provide the organization with personal information have collected it fairly and lawfully and that the information is reliable
- Informing individuals if the organization obtains additional information about them

While it is not explicitly included in the collection criteria, data minimization is another crucial component of privacy programs. This principle says that an organization should collect the minimum amount of personal information necessary to meet their objectives and discard that information when it is no longer needed for that purpose.

Use, Retention, and Disposal

Organizations must maintain the privacy of personal information throughout its life cycle. That's where the principle of *use, retention, and disposal* plays an important role. GAPP defines this principle as follows: "The entity limits the use of personal information to the purposes identified in the notice and for which the individual has provided implicit or explicit consent. The entity retains personal information for only as long as necessary to fulfill the stated purposes or as required by law or regulations and thereafter appropriately disposes of such information."

The criteria associated with the use, retention, and disposal principle are as follows:

- Including collection practices in the organization's privacy policies
- Informing individuals that their personal information will only be used for disclosed purposes for which the organization has obtained consent and then abiding by that statement
- Informing individuals that their data will be retained for no longer than necessary and then abiding by that statement
- Informing individuals that information that is no longer needed will be disposed of securely and then abiding by that statement

Access

One of the core elements of individual privacy is the belief that individuals should have the right to access information that an organization holds about them and, when necessary, to correct that information. This right to correct information is also known as the right of redress. The GAPP definition of the *access* principle is as follows: "The entity provides individuals with access to their personal information for review and update."

The criteria associated with the access principle are as follows:

- Including practices around access to personal information in the organization's privacy policies
- Informing individuals about the procedures for reviewing, updating, and correcting their personal information
- Providing individuals with a mechanism to determine whether the organization maintains personal information about them and to review any such information
- Authenticating an individual's identity before providing them with access to personal information
- Providing access to information in an understandable format within a reasonable period of time and either for a reasonable charge that is based on the organization's actual costs or at no cost
- Informing individuals in writing why any requests to access or update personal information were denied and informing them of any appeal rights they may have
- Providing a mechanism for individuals to update or correct personal information and providing that updated information to third parties who received it from the organization

Disclosure to Third Parties

Some challenging privacy issues arise when organizations maintain personal information about an individual and then choose to share that information with third parties in the course of doing business. GAPP defines the *disclosure to third parties* principle as follows: "The entity discloses personal information to third parties only for the purposes identified in the notice and with the implicit or explicit consent of the individual."

The criteria associated with the disclosure to third parties principle are as follows:

- Including third-party disclosure practices in the organization's privacy policies
- Informing individuals of any third-party disclosures that take place and the purpose of those disclosures
- Informing third parties who receive personal information from the organization that they must comply with the organization's privacy policy and handling practices
- Disclosing personal information to third parties without notice or for purposes other than those disclosed in the notice only when required to do so by law
- Disclosing information to third parties only under the auspices of an agreement that the third party will protect the information consistent with the organization's privacy policy
- Implementing procedures designed to verify that the privacy controls of third parties receiving personal information from the organization are functioning effectively
- Taking remedial action when the organization learns that a third party has mishandled personal information shared by the organization

Security for Privacy

Protecting the security of personal information is deeply entwined with protecting the privacy of that information. Organizations can't provide individuals with assurances about the handling of personal data if they can't protect that information from unauthorized access. GAPP defines *security for privacy* as follows: "The entity protects personal information against unauthorized access (both physical and logical)."

The criteria associated with the security for privacy principle are as follows:

- Including security practices in the organization's privacy policies
- Informing individuals that the organization takes precautions to protect the privacy of their personal information
- Developing, documenting, and implementing an information security program that addresses the major privacy-related areas of security listed in ISO 27002:
  - Risk assessment and treatment
  - Security policy
  - Organization of information security
  - Asset management
  - Human resources security

- Physical and environmental security
- Communications and operations management
- Access control
- Information systems acquisition, development, and maintenance
- Information security incident management
- Business continuity management
- Compliance

 This list includes the ISO 27002 elements that are relevant to privacy efforts and, therefore, our conversation. ISO 27002 does include other recommended security controls that fall outside the scope of a privacy effort.

- Restricting logical access to personal information through the use of strong identification, authentication, and authorization practices
- Restricting physical access to personal information through the use of physical security controls
- Protecting personal information from accidental disclosure due to natural disasters and other environmental hazards
- Applying strong encryption to any personal information that is transmitted over public networks
- Avoiding the storage of personal information on portable media, unless absolutely necessary, and using encryption to protect any personal information that must be stored on portable media
- Conducting periodic tests of security safeguards used to protect personal information

Quality

When we think about the issues associated with protecting the privacy of personal information, we often first think about issues related to the proper collection and use of that information along with potential unauthorized disclosure of that information. However, it's also important to consider the accuracy of that information. Individuals may be damaged by incorrect information just as much, if not more, than they might be damaged by information that is improperly handled. The GAPP *quality* principle states that "The entity maintains accurate, complete, and relevant personal information for the purposes identified in the notice." The quality principle enforces data integrity.

The criteria associated with the quality principle are as follows:

- Including data quality practices in the organization's privacy policies

- Informing individuals that they bear responsibility for providing the organization with accurate and complete personal information and informing the organization if corrections are required
- Maintaining personal information that is accurate, complete, and relevant for the purposes for which it will be used

Monitoring and Enforcement

Privacy programs are not a one-time project. It's true that organizations may make a substantial initial investment of time and energy to build up their privacy practices, but those practices must be monitored over time to ensure that they continue to operate effectively and meet the organization's privacy obligations as business needs and information practices evolve. The GAPP *monitoring and enforcement* principle states that "The entity monitors compliance with its privacy policies and procedures and has procedures to address privacy related inquires, complaints, and disputes."

The criteria associated with the monitoring and enforcement principle are as follows:

- Including monitoring and enforcement practices in the organization's privacy policies
- Informing individuals about how they should contact the organization if they have questions, complaints, or disputes regarding privacy practices
- Maintaining a dispute resolution process that ensures that every complaint is addressed and that the individual who raised the complaint is provided with a documented response
- Reviewing compliance with privacy policies, procedures, laws, regulations, and contractual obligations on an annual basis
- Developing and implementing remediation plans for any issues identified during privacy compliance reviews
- Documenting cases where privacy policies were violated and taking any necessary corrective action
- Performing ongoing monitoring of the privacy program based on a risk assessment

Developing a Privacy Program

At this point in the chapter, you should have a reasonable understanding of the fact that privacy issues are complex and nuanced. There are no "quick fix" solutions to protecting the privacy of personal information, and organizations developing a privacy program for the first time will need to expend considerable effort designing that program, implementing appropriate privacy controls, and monitoring the program's ongoing effectiveness to ensure that it continues to meet the organization's legal obligations and privacy objectives.

Crafting Vision, Strategy, Goals, and Objectives

At the outset of a privacy initiative, senior leadership should outline the vision, strategy, and goals of the privacy program. These provide the high-level direction that those implementing the program will need to guide their efforts. For example, the U.S. Department of Commerce (DOC) offers the following mission statement for their privacy program:

> The DOC is committed to safeguarding personal privacy. Individual trust in the privacy and security of personally identifiable information is a foundation of trust in government and commerce in the 21st Century. As an employer, a collector of data on millions of individuals and companies, the developer of information management standards and a federal advisor on information management policy, the Department strives to be a leader in best privacy practices and privacy policy. To further this goal, the Department assigns a high priority to privacy consideration in all systems, programs, and policies.

That's a very high-level statement that clearly explains the purpose of the program. Notice that it doesn't contain any specific objectives or measures. The privacy obligations and controls used by the DOC might change over time, but it is very likely that this strategic-level mission statement will remain appropriate (at least through the end of the 21st century!). The program document also contains goals that the DOC has to guide the execution of a privacy program in support of their mission. The four goals of their plan are as follows:

1. Foster a culture of privacy and disclosure and demonstrate leadership through policy and partnerships.

2. Provide outreach, education, training, and reports in order to promote privacy and transparency.

3. Conduct robust compliance and oversight programs to ensure adherence with federal privacy and disclosure laws and policies in all DOC activities.

4. Develop and maintain the best privacy and disclosure professionals in the federal government.

These goals start to get into the details of *how* the DOC will carry out its privacy mission. They provide four key deliverables that privacy officials can then use to align their work with the DOC's strategy.

Beneath each of these goals, the DOC provides a series of specific objectives that will satisfy each goal. These are the activities that the DOC plans to undertake to meet its goal and, therefore, achieve the privacy program's strategic purpose. For brevity's sake, we won't cover all the objectives in this book, but let's take a look at the four objectives that align with the DOC's third privacy goal to conduct robust compliance and oversight programs:

1. Review, assess, and provide guidance to DOC programs, systems, projects, information sharing arrangements, and other initiatives to reduce the impact on privacy and ensure compliance.

2. Promote privacy best practices and guidance to the DOC's information sharing and intelligence activities.

3. Ensure that complaints and incidents at DOC are reported systematically, processed efficiently, and mitigated appropriately in accordance with federal and DOC privacy policies and procedures.

4. Evaluate DOC programs and activities for compliance with privacy and disclosure laws.

These objectives are highly specific, and you might imagine them being handed to a middle manager to execute. They also might change much more frequently than the program's high-level purpose in order to meet the changing needs of the DOC.

 Throughout this section, we draw examples from the Department of Commerce's Privacy Plan. If you'd like to review this plan in more detail, you can download it from `http://osec.doc.gov/opog/privacy/Memorandums/PRIVACY_PROGRAM_PLAN_2017.pdf`.

Obtaining Executive Support

The privacy program will require resources to succeed. Those resources include the time of privacy team members and other stakeholders throughout the organization, funds to cover the direct costs of the program, and authority to enforce new policy directions. Therefore, it's crucial that the privacy program have executive-level support.

The best way for a new program to obtain this support is to have an executive sponsor who will serve as the program's champion with the organization's leadership. The executive sponsor should agree with the vision and strategy for the privacy program, and it is crucial to gain that person's approval before moving forward.

Ensure Business Alignment

While privacy professionals find themselves primarily focused on the world of privacy, they must also remember that they are part of a larger organization with a different mission. The purpose of the organization might be to create software, educate students, govern a nation, or almost anything else imaginable. In order for a privacy program to succeed, it must be able to justify its existence within the context of that broader mission.

This leads to one of the key responsibilities of a privacy manager: ensuring that the privacy program remains aligned with the broader business. It's easy for privacy experts to get lost in the weeds of their work and come to think of privacy as an end in and of itself, but privacy is only effective when it facilitates the achievement of organizational goals and objectives. Privacy efforts must align with the business's goals, objectives, functions, processes, and practices.

There are five key ways that privacy managers can ensure this business alignment:

Finalize the business case for privacy.   Privacy managers must be able to justify the investments of time and money that they expect the organization to make in the privacy program. This requires identifying how privacy supports business goals and clearly articulating the return on investment that senior leaders should expect.

Identify stakeholders.   There are many different stakeholders who play a role in achieving the objectives of a privacy program. These include information security, human resources, marketing, legal, procurement, and other specialists. It's important to bring these stakeholders into the process early and engage them in the privacy program. You'll learn more about effective ways to integrate these business functions with the privacy program in Chapter 4, "Privacy Operational Life Cycle: Protect."

Leverage key functions.   In addition to involving other business functions as stakeholders in the privacy program, privacy managers should leverage the expertise of those functions to achieve privacy objectives. For example, privacy professionals spend much of their time analyzing and interpreting legal requirements. The organization's legal team can play an invaluable role assisting with this work. Similarly, most organizations have communications teams that can assist with communicating privacy messages.

Create a process for interfacing within the organization.   The privacy team will often work closely with other teams in the organization and should have clearly defined processes for these interactions. For example, the information technology team will likely have to carry out much of the technical work of the privacy program. Privacy professionals should understand the IT service management (ITSM) processes used by that team and take advantage of that knowledge to improve their ability to work together.

Align organizational culture and privacy/data protection objectives.   Every organization has a unique culture, and navigating that culture is crucial to the success of internal initiatives. Privacy professionals should understand the culture of their organization and use that knowledge to successfully advance privacy objectives.

Developing Business Cases

The implementation and management of privacy personnel, projects, and tools requires investments of financial and human resources by the organization. Those resources are, of course, finite, and there is normally stiff competition within the organization over their allocation. Other business leaders may want the same resources assigned to initiatives they find to be a higher priority, whereas shareholders may prefer that the resources be returned to them as profit in the form of dividends.

Therefore, privacy managers must be able to make coherent business cases that justify their proposed investments. These business cases outline the rationale for the investment and justify it as the best possible use of the requested resources. Privacy managers should investigate the business case process used by the rest of their organization and adopt it as closely as possible. These formats may vary, but they typically include several core components:

A *scope statement* that concisely describes the proposed initiative

The *strategic context* that demonstrates the need for the initiative and how the investment aligns with the organization's broader strategic goals

A *cost analysis* that outlines the financial and human resource costs of the initiative, on both a one time and a recurring basis

An *evaluation of alternatives* that describes other possible approaches for achieving the strategic goals addressed by this project and explains why the current proposal is the best available option

A *project plan* that describes the detailed implementation plan for the initiative

A *management plan* that describes how the organization will oversee the processes created by this initiative on an ongoing basis in a manner that integrates with the privacy and corporate governance frameworks

Maintain Flexibility

Privacy programs have clearly stated objectives, but at the same time, managers must ensure that the program remains flexible enough to accommodate changing requirements. Leaders must monitor legislative, regulatory, market, and business requirements to ensure that the program remains relevant.

This flexibility should extend to all aspects of your privacy strategy. For example, you may need to adapt your privacy strategy to accommodate different regulatory requirements, business needs, and the cultural norms of the geographic areas where your business operates.

Structuring the Privacy Team

Organizations should appoint a senior leader with overall responsibility for the organization's privacy program. This establishes senior-level accountability for the program's success and provides the privacy program with a seat at the executive table. This role is commonly referred to as an organization's *chief privacy officer (CPO)*, although it may also be implemented using other titles, such as director of privacy or privacy program manager. The CPO also serves as the designated point of contact in the organization for privacy issues, although they may delegate much of the responsibility for handling those issues to privacy analysts or others on their team.

Ethics Officers

Many organizations now have dedicated ethics officers, and in fact, some regulations now require the creation of this office. Ethics officers should work closely with privacy teams to ensure that the organization meets its privacy obligations and acts in a responsible manner. An organization's ethics officer typically has a reporting relationship with the board of directors, allowing them to communicate directly with the board when issues arise that affect senior leadership.

In the DOC Privacy Plan that we have been using as an example in this section, the department identifies a position within the office of the Secretary of Commerce as the DOC's chief privacy officer. The program includes a detailed set of responsibilities for this position. Here is an abbreviated set of those responsibilities, paraphrased for brevity:

- Serve as the senior privacy policy authority
- Develop and oversee implementation of privacy policies
- Communicate the privacy vision, principles, and policy internally and externally
- Ensure the department complies with applicable privacy laws and regulations
- Advocate privacy-preserving strategies for information collection and dissemination
- Manage privacy risks
- Ensure employees and contractors receive appropriate privacy training
- Facilitate relationships with senior DOC leaders, other federal agencies, and private industry

Of course, the DOC is a very large organization and it would be impossible for one person to be involved in all aspects of its privacy program in any type of thorough manner. For this reason, the DOC policy also specifies that each operating unit should have its own CPO and that those CPOs should meet regularly as the Department of Commerce Privacy Council.

This type of hierarchical privacy authority is common in government agencies and other large organizations. It may not be necessary in smaller organizations, depending on the nature of the organization and the scope of its privacy program. Some organizations opt to use the role of "privacy champions" distributed throughout the organization. These liaisons serve as the primary point of privacy contact for their organization and work directly with the CPO office. Depending on the size of the unit they serve, the liaison role may be a full-time position or a secondary responsibility for someone in another primary role.

The composition and structure of the privacy team will vary depending on the size of the organization and the complexity of its privacy requirements. In smaller organizations, a single individual might be appointed as the data protection officer (DPO) for GDPR compliance purposes and also be responsible for the management of the entire privacy program. Larger organizations may have a large team consisting of a CPO, a DPO, several privacy managers, and teams of privacy analysts and first responders who handle emerging privacy incidents.

Measuring Professional Competency

Privacy is a professional discipline, and it is important that privacy leaders take steps to establish and endorse the measurement of professional competency. One of the primary mechanisms they may use to achieve this goal is providing team members with the encouragement and resources necessary to obtain privacy certifications appropriate to their goals. This may include having privacy team members earn the Certified Information Privacy Professional (CIPP) certification(s) appropriate for the regions where they operate and having IT professionals who work on privacy initiatives earn the Certified Information Privacy Technologist (CIPT) credential.

The reporting structure for privacy leaders also varies from organization to organization, and the choice of reporting structure conveys a message about the importance that the organization places on privacy. For example, organizations where the CPO reports directly to the chief executive officer (CEO) may convey the message that they take privacy more seriously than an organization where the CPO reports to the general counsel or chief risk officer.

Creating a Program Scope and Charter

New privacy managers in an organization without a mature privacy function may find themselves developing a program from the ground up. This effort should begin with the development of a privacy strategy that outlines the vision, mission, goals, and objectives of the program.

With that strategy in hand, managers may begin to outline the set of initiatives required to bring the organization from its current state to the desired state of privacy. As they establish the program, they should ensure that its work remains aligned with the privacy strategy that guides their effort.

Defining Program Scope

The first step in developing a new privacy program is creating a clear statement of the program's *scope*. This is the definition of the activities that are (and are not) included in the program's work. There are two important elements to the program's scope:

The Type of Privacy Objectives Included in the Program   Does the program cover all aspects of privacy, or are there exceptions? For example, does the privacy program cover international requirements, or is it specific to one jurisdiction?

The Portion of the Organization Covered by the Privacy Program   A privacy program might cover the entire organization, or its work might be limited to a business unit or other portion of the organizational structure.

In most cases, the scope statement may be concise, communicating the nature of the program clearly to all employees. For example, a broadly defined privacy program might use this scope statement:

> The privacy program is responsible for protecting the privacy of all personally identifiable information stored, processed, or transmitted by the organization in any form: physical or digital.

If the program applies only to a specific area of the organization or excludes a specific area of the organization, this would also be included in the scope statement. For example, many universities have associated health systems and those health systems often have separate privacy functions. In that situation, the university's main privacy program might have a scope statement that describes this scope limitation:

> The privacy program is responsible for protecting the privacy of all personally identifiable information stored, processed, or transmitted by the organization in any form: physical or digital. The program does not apply to elements of the University Health System governed by the UHS Privacy Program.

Developing a Program Charter

With a scope statement in hand, privacy managers may then begin creating the privacy program *charter*. The charter is the organizing document for the privacy program. Building on the scope, the charter outlines the parameters within which the program will function. Common components of a privacy program charter include the following:

- A *scope statement* identifying the scope of the privacy program. This is simply reiterating the scope statement created for the program in a location where all interested stakeholders may reference it.

- A *business purpose* clearly linking the privacy program objectives to business objectives. For example, the University of Pennsylvania uses this business purpose statement in their Information Security and Privacy Program Charter (`www.isc.upenn.edu/ information-security-and-privacy-program-charter`):

> Penn is committed to preeminence in research, teaching, and service. As a result, Penn owns significant assets in the form of information. Penn's informational assets include, but are not limited to, student education records, employment records, financial information, research data, protected health information, alumni and donor information, Penn operational data, Penn intellectual property, and other data relating to Penn's infrastructure, technology resources, and information security. The improper use of such information, the unauthorized or inadvertent disclosure, alteration or destruction of information assets, or a significant interruption in their availability can disrupt Penn's ability to fulfill its mission. Such actions can also result in regulatory, legal, financial, and/ or reputational risk to Penn and to the individuals whose data Penn maintains.

- *A statement of authority* for the program, normally delegating institutional authority to a specific individual. For example, a statement of authority might read:

  > The Chief Privacy Officer (CPO) is responsible for coordinating and overseeing the privacy program. The CPO may designate other representatives of the organization to oversee and coordinate portions of the program.

- *Roles and responsibilities* for other stakeholders who have the responsibility to help carry out the activities of the privacy program. This may include:
  - Senior leaders
  - Privacy team members
  - Security and other information technologists
  - Internal and external auditors
  - Data owners, stewards, and custodians
  - Other employees and stakeholders

- *Governance structure and processes* that will continue to ensure that the organization's privacy program remains in alignment with the organization's business goals

- *Program documentation procedures* that formalize how the organization will establish, communicate, and maintain privacy standards, guidelines, procedures, and other documentation

- *Enforcement mechanisms* that establish how the organization will guide and enforce compliance with privacy policies and provide consequences for individuals and units that fail to comply with privacy program requirements

- *A review process* that will be conducted on a periodic basis to ensure that the privacy program continues to achieve its objectives, that those objectives continue to align with business objectives, and that the privacy program is functioning properly

- *An approval statement* that clearly describes the authority under which the program is enacted. This is normally done through the signature of the CEO or other senior leader. This approval statement gives force to the delegation of authority and other details outlined in the charter.

The specific contents of any organization's privacy program charter will depend on the organization's business and privacy objectives, operational culture, and other factors. Rather than being overly concerned about the specific section headings included in a charter, privacy managers should ensure that the charter provides the framework under which they may effectively implement the program.

Privacy Roles

Depending on the nature of an individual's or organization's involvement in the collection and processing of information, they may take on one or more data roles. The three primary roles are as follows:

- *Data subjects* are the individuals about whom personal information is collected. These may be the customers or employees of an organization or any other individuals about whom the organization collects personal information.

- *Data controllers* are the organizations that determine the purposes and means of collecting personal information from data subjects. If an organization collects and/or processes personal information for its own business needs, it is a data controller. It remains a data controller even if it outsources some of that collection or processing to service providers.

- *Data processors* are service providers that collect or process personal information on behalf of data controllers. For example, cloud service providers often serve in the role of data processor for their customers.

These terms take on particular importance when interpreting how laws and regulations apply to an organization. For example, some regulations allow data controllers to transfer some privacy and security responsibility to service providers, as long as the controller chooses a service provider that has gone through a certification process. Regulations, including the EU's GDPR, may also have very specific definitions of these terms, as you will discover later in this book as we explore those regulations in more detail.

After clearly defining roles in an organization, privacy leaders should ensure that each individual receives training appropriate to their role and has access to the policies and procedures relevant to their role.

Building Inventories

Once an organization has established accountable officials and privacy roles, the next step in developing a privacy program is to create a comprehensive *data inventory* of the personal information that the organization collects, processes, and maintains and the systems, storage locations, and processes involved in those activities. The inventory provides a crucial starting point for privacy professionals seeking to understand the organization's privacy needs.

This inventory may take many different forms, depending on the nature of the organization and the level of formality desired. The end goal is for the organization to have a clear picture of the types of personal information that it handles, the sources of that information, and the ways that information is stored and processed. This inventory should be maintained as a living repository of data updated when business activities or privacy practices change or when there are shifts in the regulatory landscape that require tracking new elements of information. It may then be used as the basis for conducting privacy assessments and implementing privacy controls.

Information security programs also depend on a similar inventory of all sensitive information maintained by the organization. The personally identifiable information included in a privacy-focused inventory is a subset of that sensitive information inventory. This offers an excellent opportunity for privacy and information security programs to partner and avoid redundant activity by simply including a personal information tag in the broader sensitive information inventory.

Conducting a Privacy Assessment

With a personal information inventory in hand, the organization may now turn to an assessment of the current state of its privacy program. This assessment should use a standard set of privacy practices, derived from either an industry standard framework or the regulatory requirements facing the organization. The remainder of this book will dive deeply into many of these frameworks and requirements.

For example, an organization might choose to adopt the privacy framework from the International Organization for Standardization titled "Security techniques—Extension to ISO/IEC 27001 and ISO/IEC 27002 for privacy information management—Requirements and guidelines" and documented in ISO 27701. An excerpt from this document appears in Figure 1.1.

FIGURE 1.1   Excerpt from ISO 27701

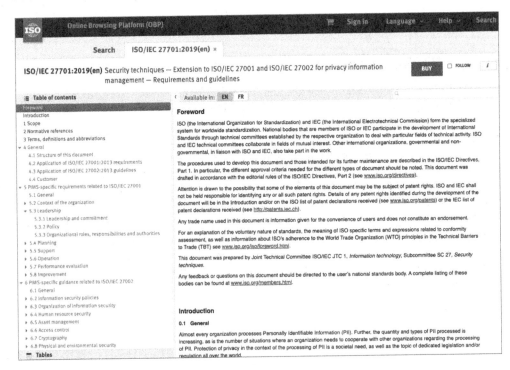

ISO 27701 is closely linked to ISO 27001 and 27002, the two ISO standards governing information security. This is another opportunity to align the interests of privacy and security programs. Annex F of ISO 27701 provides advice on applying the privacy standard in an organization that already uses the information security standards. These standards are also tightly linked to the National Institute for Standards and Technology's Cybersecurity Framework (CSF), allowing organizations to cleanly map controls between standards and frameworks that they adopt for both privacy and security.

The end result of the privacy assessment should be a *gap analysis* that identifies any places where the organization's current practices do not meet the level of control desired by the standard under which the assessment was performed. This gap analysis may then be used in remediation efforts to bring the organization up to the desired level of privacy performance.

Implementing Privacy Controls

The primary means that the organization uses to remediate privacy deficiencies is the implementation of *privacy controls* that are technical or administrative measures that improve privacy. For example, implementing mechanisms that fulfill the many GAPP criteria discussed earlier in this chapter qualify as privacy controls. Here are some examples of common privacy controls:

- Creation, review, or modification of privacy policies
- Use of encryption to protect personal information
- Purging of personal information when it is no longer needed to meet the purposes disclosed when it was collected
- Configuring access controls to limit the use of personal information to authorized individuals
- Implementing and maintaining a process to manage user privacy preferences
- Developing a standard process for investigating privacy complaints and following up on potential privacy incidents
- Conducting periodic testing and assessment of the organization's privacy program

Notice that some, but not all, of these controls are technical in nature, but all the controls advance the organization's privacy efforts.

Ongoing Operation and Monitoring

Once a privacy program is well established, the organization should continue to operate the program and monitor its effectiveness. This is normally done through a combination of periodic reviews, regular updates to the privacy assessment, and dashboard-style monitoring of the program's key metrics, such as compliance with data retention and disposal standards, turnaround time for processing privacy requests, and the number and severity of privacy incidents.

Organizations may also find themselves the subject of *privacy audits* based on legal or regulatory requirements. Audits are similar to assessments in nature, because they compare the current state of the privacy program to an external standard. However, unlike assessments, audits are always performed by an independent auditor who does not have a vested interest in the outcome. Audits may be performed at the request of internal management, a board of directors, or regulatory authorities.

Data Governance

Data governance is the set of policies, procedures, and controls that an organization develops to safeguard its information while making it useful for transactional and analytic purposes. As the name implies, data governance is primarily a business function. Governments have a method for creating, interpreting, and enforcing laws. Part of this process ensures that these laws are known to the citizenry. For organizations, data governance is an umbrella term covering the creation, interpretation, and enforcement of data use. Data governance efforts are crucial to privacy programs because they provide a framework for identifying and regulating the use of personal information throughout an organization.

Organizations develop numerous policies to govern their data. These policies promote data quality, specify the use of data attributes, and define access to different data domains. Additional governance policies identify how to secure data, comply with regulations, protect data privacy, and deal with data over time. Just as countries enforce laws, organizations implement procedural and technical controls to comply with data governance standards.

Strong executive support is vital to any data governance effort. An organization invests a significant amount of time and resources to define, develop, implement, and control access to data. For data governance to succeed, all levels of an organization must appreciate the importance of well-governed data. While technology is a critical component to facilitating adherence to policies, an information technology organization can't drive data governance efforts on its own. You need executive support across the organization for data governance efforts to succeed.

Data Governance Approaches

Data governance programs may operate using one of three different approaches:

- **Centralized** data governance programs have a core office that directs the data governance efforts of the entire organization.

- **Distributed** data governance programs may have organization-wide standards, but each business unit creates its own data governance program that achieves those shared objectives.

- **Hybrid** data governance programs combine the centralized and distributed approaches, with a centralized office providing oversight and guidance to distributed teams who focus on particular business units.

Data Governance Roles

It takes multiple people fulfilling a variety of roles for data governance to thrive. A crucial concept relating to data governance is data stewardship. Stewardship denotes looking after something, like an organization or property. *Data stewardship* is the act of developing the policies and procedures for looking after an organization's data quality, security, privacy, and regulatory compliance. The most vital role for effective data stewardship is that of the organizational data steward. An *organizational data steward*, or *data steward*, is the person responsible for data stewardship.

The data steward is responsible for leading an organization's data governance activities. As the link between the technical and nontechnical divisions within an organization, a data steward works with many people, from senior leaders to individual technologists. To establish policies, a data steward works with various data owners.

A *data owner* is a senior business leader with overall responsibility for a specific data domain. A *data domain*, or *data subject area*, comprises data about a particular operational division within an organization. Finance, human resources, and the physical plant are all examples of operational divisions. Data owners work with the data steward to establish policies and procedures for their data domain.

In large, complex organizations, data owners may choose to delegate day-to-day governance activities to subject area data stewards. A *subject area data steward* works in the data owner's organization and understands the nuances that apply within that organizational unit. A subject area data steward works on behalf of their data owner to handle daily tasks. For example, processing access requests as people rotate in and out of roles is a responsibility a data owner may delegate to their subject area data steward. The need for subject area data stewards arises from the intricacies of different data domains. To implement data governance policies, data stewards work with data custodians.

A *data custodian* is a role given to someone who implements technical controls that execute data governance policies. Data custodians are frequently information technology employees who configure applications, dashboards, and databases.

For example, unique laws govern an organization's finances, people, and physical plant. Figure 1.2 visualizes how an organizational data steward works both vertically and horizontally with the various data owners, subject area data stewards, and data custodians to actively steward, or take care of, the organization's data.

Access Requirements

One crucial component of data governance defines the access requirements for data. *Data access requirements* determine which people need access to what data. Access requirements differ by data subject area and can be as granular as a single field. For example, managers need access to details about their employees, including their names and contact information. Since managers are responsible for providing feedback, they also need access to performance data. However, no manager has a compelling need to view their employees' Social Security numbers (SSNs). Although SSNs are necessary for payroll and tax purposes, malicious actors can also use them for identity theft.

FIGURE 1.2   Organizational example

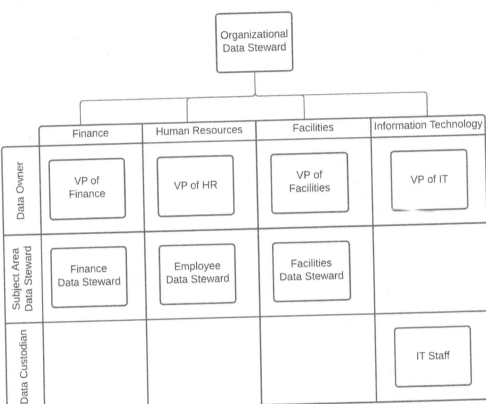

When determining access requirements, it is essential to develop a data classification matrix. A *data classification matrix* defines categories, descriptions, and disclosure implications for data. Table 1.4 is an example of a data classification matrix. It is vital to factor in data classification when considering access requirements to ensure proper data stewardship.

TABLE 1.4   Sample data classification matrix

Classification Term	Classification Description
Public	Data intended for public consumption—for example, anything on a public-facing website meets this classification. No disclosure implications.
Internal	Data intended for use within an organization—for example, a comprehensive organization chart including names. Disclosure compromises an organization's reputation or operations, but not its privacy or confidentiality obligations.

Classification Term	Classification Description
Sensitive	Data intended for limited use within an organization—for example, a list of employees and their compensation. Disclosure implies a violation of privacy or confidentiality.
Highly Sensitive	Data intended for restricted use, typically due to compliance obligations. Examples include Social Security numbers and bank account numbers. Disclosure implies a legal obligation in the event of a data breach.

A data steward works with a data owner to establish broad classifications, with subject area data stewards to develop procedures for granting access to information, and with data custodians to ensure the appropriate technical controls are in place to protect information.

Governing Information Processing

Data governance programs should provide oversight for all types of processing that the organization performs on personal information. This includes six core activities:

- **Collecting** personal information from individuals or other organizations
- **Using** personal information to achieve business objectives
- **Accessing** personal information by individual employees
- **Sharing** personal information internally and externally
- **Transferring** personal information internally and externally
- **Destroying** personal information when it is no longer necessary to meet business objectives

Managing the Privacy Budget

Privacy managers also have financial responsibility for their organization's privacy program. This means that they must participate in developing, implementing, and monitoring a budget.

Many privacy managers came up through the practitioner ranks and find themselves in their first management role, unfamiliar with many of the nontechnical skills required for the job. If that's your situation, you might find yourself unfamiliar with the skills and tools that can assist you with this task.

Organizational Budgeting

A *budget* is just a financial plan for the team. It outlines how much money is available to you over the course of the year and how you plan to spend that money.

Most organizations go through an annual budget planning cycle where the organization's leadership decides the following year's budget a few months before the year begins. This means that you'll have to work backward and will often find yourself preparing a budget at least six months in advance of it going into effect. Or, looking at it another way, depending on where you are in the budget cycle, it could be up to 18 months until the next time that you receive a budget adjustment. That's why planning in advance is so important.

 The budgeting process is *extremely* important for privacy managers. Successfully completing the budgeting process is how you obtain the funding that you need for your privacy program and privacy team.

As you go through the budget planning process, you'll need to follow the guidelines set by your organization. There are two major approaches to budgeting:

- *Incremental budgeting* approaches start with the prior year's budget and then make adjustments by either raising or lowering the budget. If your organization uses this approach, you'll frequently hear phrases like "We have a 3 percent budget increase this year" or "We're cutting the budget by 5 percent." It's up to the manager to advocate for additional budget and to make the new numbers work.

- *Zero-based budgeting* approaches begin from zero each year and managers are asked to justify their entire budget, rather than starting with the assumption that they will have the same amount of funding as they did the previous year.

Expense Types

There are two different types of expenses in the world of business budgeting: capital expenses and operational expenses. If you've ever heard anyone using the phrase "different flavors of money," this is what they're talking about. Money that falls into the capital expense budget typically can't be used for operational expenses, and vice versa. Therefore, it's important to understand each type of money and how it may be used.

Capital expenses (CapEx) are costs that an organization incurs as part of building out and maintaining its large assets. For example, if you buy or renovate a building, that's a fixed asset, and the costs associated with it are capital expenses.

Other examples of capital expenses are:

- Purchasing expensive computing equipment
- Buying vehicles
- Buying new multifunction printers

Operational expenses (OpEx) are the costs of running the business day to day that don't involve purchasing or maintaining an asset. The most common example of operational expenses is payroll costs. You're paying your employees to run your business, but you're not purchasing the employee, so your employees are not a financial asset. This makes payroll an operational expense.

Other examples of operational expenses are:

- Electricity costs
- Hardware maintenance agreements
- Office supplies

The line between capital and operational expenses can be a little fuzzy and will depend on your organization's financial practices. Some organizations use a dollar threshold to help differentiate between the two, whereas others have more complex guidelines. You should check with your financial accounting team for help sorting this out.

Both capital and operating expenses may be one-time or recurring. For example, your privacy team's payroll is a recurring operational expense, whereas the cost of hiring a privacy consultant to conduct an assessment is likely treated as a one-time operational expense. Similarly, the building of a new data center is a one-time capital expense whereas the replacement of your servers is a recurring capital expense. Privacy programs will likely have a focus on operational, rather than capital, expenses due to the nature of the costs that they incur.

Capital expenses and operating expenses are treated very differently by tax laws and financial reporting regulations. That's the reason that accountants are so concerned with differentiating between the two and why it's difficult to move money between capital and operating budgets in some organizations.

Budget Monitoring

Budget planning is typically an annual chore that follows a very well-defined life cycle. However, a privacy manager's budget responsibility doesn't end once the planning cycle concludes. In fact, the work has only just begun. During the course of the year, managers must monitor their budgets and track expenses to ensure that they finish the year within expectations.

Clearly, it's a bad idea to exceed your budget. You might be spending money that doesn't exist, and at the very least, you're going to wind up in hot water with your boss. Privacy managers should keep close tabs on their budgets and make sure that they don't finish the year in the red with a budget shortfall.

The longer you are in business, the more likely it is that you will experience unexpected expenses. You might not be able to predict what unexpected expenses will come up, but it is a fairly safe bet that something you didn't expect will surface. Managers can compensate for this by setting aside a contingency budget designed to cover unexpected expenses.

Although it's definitely a bad idea to exceed your budget, that also doesn't mean that it's a good idea to leave a lot of money on the table. Unless there were very unusual circumstances, a large surplus at the end of the year probably means that you didn't plan very well. You don't run the risk of spending money that isn't there, but you are preventing your company from using those funds elsewhere. In financial terms, you're creating an opportunity cost by holding funds that the organization could use to take advantage of some other opportunity.

You'll need to develop your own patterns for budget monitoring and reporting. For example, you might begin by reviewing your budget and spending on a weekly basis. Over time, as you get comfortable with financial planning, you might back off to a biweekly or monthly schedule.

Communicating about Privacy

Privacy managers find themselves communicating about privacy to others within their organization on a regular basis. This communication includes both broad awareness messages and tailored messages designed to achieve specific privacy objectives.

Creating Awareness

The success of a privacy program depends on the behavior (both actions and inaction) of many different people. Privacy training and awareness programs help ensure that employees and other stakeholders are aware of their privacy responsibilities and that those responsibilities remain top of mind. Privacy managers are responsible for establishing, promoting, and maintaining a privacy training and awareness program to foster an effective privacy culture in their organizations.

Employee Training

Employees within your organization should receive regular *privacy training* to ensure that they understand the risks associated with your uses of personally identifiable information and their role in minimizing those risks. Strong training programs take advantage of a diversity of training techniques, including the use of *computer-based training (CBT)*.

Not every user requires the same level of training. Organizations should use *role-based training* to make sure that individuals receive the appropriate level of training based on their job responsibilities. For example, a systems administrator should receive detailed and highly technical training, whereas a customer service representative requires less technical training with a greater focus on the front-line interactions that they may encounter in their work.

You'll also want to think about the frequency of your training efforts. You'll need to balance the time required to conduct training with the benefit from reminding users of their responsibilities. One approach used by many organizations is to conduct initial training whenever an employee joins the organization or assumes new job responsibilities and then use annual refresher training to cover the same material and update users on new privacy issues.

The team responsible for providing privacy training should review materials on a regular basis to ensure that the content remains relevant. Changes in the privacy landscape and the organization's business may require updating the material to remain fresh and relevant.

Role-Based Training

All users should receive some degree of privacy education, but organizations should also customize training to meet specific role-based requirements. For example, employees handling credit card information should receive training on Payment Card Industry Data Security Standard (PCI DSS) requirements. Human resources team members should be trained on handling employee information. IT staffers need specialized skills to implement privacy controls. Training should be custom-tailored to an individual's role in the organization.

Ongoing Awareness Efforts

In addition to formal training programs, a privacy program should include *privacy awareness* efforts. These are less formal efforts that are designed to remind employees about the privacy lessons they've already learned. Unlike privacy training, awareness efforts don't require a commitment of time to sit down and learn new material. Instead, they use posters, videos, email messages, and similar techniques to make privacy a top priority for those who've already learned the core lessons.

Building a Communications Plan

Training and awareness efforts should be part of a broader communications plan that privacy professionals develop to inform their communications with various stakeholders over the course of the year. This plan should coordinate all planned communications. In addition to the organization's awareness effort, the plan may include all legally required privacy notices and disclosures. The communications plan provides a single point of tracking and coordinating these messages to ensure that they are timed effectively and are not overlooked.

The communications plan should also ensure that employees have access to current privacy policies and procedures related to their roles and are notified when there are updates to those documents.

While many privacy programs emphasize transparency, companies should also be conscious of the risks of disclosing information. Prematurely sharing information about privacy risks may increase the opportunity for security incidents, create reputational damage, result in regulatory fines, or cause other harm to the organization. Communications plans should consider these risks and involve legal teams and other stakeholders when identifying appropriate timing of communications and levels of detail.

Privacy Program Operational Life Cycle

The privacy program operational life cycle describes the core activities of a privacy program and how the organization addresses each of its major privacy objectives. The four components of the privacy program operational life cycle are:

- **Assess** documents the baseline of the organization's privacy program, evaluates vendors and data processors, and conducts assessments of privacy-related matters. Chapter 3, "Privacy Operational Life Cycle: Assess," focuses on the Assess phase of the life cycle.

- **Protect** includes information security practices designed to safeguard information, the implementation of privacy by design (PbD) principles, the integration of privacy requirements into functional areas of the organization, and technical and organizational measures used to protect data. Chapter 4, "Privacy Operational Life Cycle: Protect," focuses on the Protect phase of the life cycle.

- **Sustain** includes monitoring the privacy program's effectiveness through internal monitoring practices and both internal and external audits. Chapter 5, "Privacy Operational Life Cycle: Sustain," focuses on the Sustain phase of the life cycle.

- **Respond** covers how the organization reacts to data subject information requests and privacy rights and how the organization responds to privacy incidents. Chapter 6, "Privacy Operational Life Cycle: Respond," focuses on the Respond phase of the life cycle.

The major benefit of the life cycle approach to privacy is that it helps maintain the flexibility that is so crucial to the privacy program's success. This life cycle allows the organization to adapt its privacy practices as business needs and regulatory requirements change. It also allows the organization to use the lessons learned from privacy incidents to improve its privacy controls and reduce the likelihood of a future incident.

 NOTE The focus of privacy programs has shifted over the years. While all four activities of the privacy program life cycle are crucial, early programs often found themselves in a reactive crisis management mode that focused on responding to privacy incidents. Today, most organizations spend much more time and energy in the earlier stages of the life cycle, as they hope to proactively manage risks to prevent incidents from occurring.

Summary

The privacy program serves as the umbrella organizational unit for all of an organization's efforts to protect personally identifiable information. The chief privacy officer (CPO), or other senior privacy leader, bears overall responsibility for ensuring that the privacy program is properly designed, implemented, and operated.

The CPO must ensure that the privacy program remains aligned with the objectives of the business overall as well as the operational objectives of other business functions, including procurement, accounting, human resources, information technology, and audit functions. In addition, the CPO should put monitoring procedures in place to evaluate the effectiveness of the program over time and detect opportunities for improvement.

Exam Essentials

Designate a senior individual accountable for the privacy program.   Placing responsibility for the design, implementation, maintenance, and monitoring of a privacy program in the hands of a senior official provides direct accountability for the program's goals and objectives. Organizations commonly designate a chief privacy officer (CPO) to hold these responsibilities, and that CPO may also serve as the organization's point of contact for privacy regulators.

Develop a privacy program designed to achieve the organization's privacy mission.   Privacy programs consist of the policies, procedures, tools, and practices used to achieve the desired level of privacy in an organization. Privacy programs should have a high-level strategic purpose/mission that is mapped to more tactical goals and even more specific objectives for achieving those goals. The purpose of a privacy program should change infrequently, whereas goals and objectives may change more frequently.

Describe the purpose of the privacy program.   The core of the charter is the scope statement, which defines the privacy objectives included in the program and the portion of the organization covered by the program. The charter should also address the business purpose of the program, a statement of authority, roles and responsibilities, governance structures, documentation, enforcement mechanisms, and processes for periodic program reviews.

Explain how privacy training and awareness ensure that individuals understand their responsibilities.   Privacy training programs impart new knowledge to employees and other stakeholders. They should be tailored to meet the specific requirements of an individual's role in the organization. Privacy awareness programs seek to remind users of the information they have already learned, keeping their privacy responsibilities top of mind.

Know that privacy managers are people managers.   Privacy managers lead a team of professionals and are responsible for the motivation, development, and management of those team members. This includes providing training that helps employees keep their skills current and certifications that help employees validate their skills.

Know that privacy managers are financial managers.   Privacy managers bear responsibility for managing a budget allocated to the privacy program. They must understand how to work within the budgeting and accounting processes used by their organization.

Review Questions

1. Which of the following types of information should be protected by a privacy program?

   A. Customer records

   B. Product plans

   C. Trade secrets

   D. All of the above

2. What data governance model operates by focusing all data governance resources in a single office that serves the entire organization?

   A. Centralized

   B. Distributed

   C. Hybrid

   D. Oppositional

3. Howard is assisting his firm in developing a new privacy program and wants to incorporate a privacy risk assessment process into the program. If Howard wishes to comply with industry best practices, at least how often should the firm conduct these risk assessments?

   A. Monthly

   B. Semi-annually

   C. Annually

   D. Bi-annually

4. Of the following fields, which fits into the "special categories of personal data" under GDPR?

   A. Banking records

   B. Union membership records

   C. Educational records

   D. Employment records

5. Katie is assessing her organization's privacy practices and determines that the organization previously collected customer addresses for the purpose of shipping goods and is now using those addresses to mail promotional materials. If this promotional use was not previously disclosed, what privacy principle is the organization most likely violating?

   A. Quality

   B. Management

   C. Notice

   D. Security

6. Kara is the chief privacy officer of an organization that maintains a database of customer information for marketing purposes. What term best describes the role of Kara's organization with respect to that database?

A. Data subject

B. Data custodian

C. Data controller

D. Data processor

7. Richard would like to use an industry standard reference for designing his organization's privacy controls. Which one of the following ISO standards is best suited for this purpose?

A. ISO 27001

B. ISO 27002

C. ISO 27701

D. ISO 27702

8. Which of the following organizations commonly requests a formal audit of a privacy program?

A. Management

B. Board of directors

C. Regulators

D. All of the above

9. Which element of a privacy program is likely to remain unchanged for long periods of time?

A. Mission

B. Goals

C. Objectives

D. Procedures

10. Which phase of the privacy program operational model includes the implementation of privacy by design (PbD) principles?

A. Respond

B. Sustain

C. Protect

D. Assess

11. Which one of the following statements is not correct about privacy best practices?

A. Organizations should maintain personal information that is accurate, complete, and relevant.

B. Organizations should inform data subjects of their privacy practices.

C. Organizations should retain a third-party dispute resolution service for handling privacy complaints.

D. Organizations should restrict physical and logical access to personal information.

12. Which one of the following is not a common responsibility for an organization's chief privacy officer?

    A. Managing privacy risks

    B. Encrypting personal information

    C. Developing privacy policy

    D. Advocating privacy strategies

13. When designing privacy controls, an organization should be informed by the results of what type of analysis?

    A. Impact analysis

    B. Gap analysis

    C. Business analysis

    D. Authorization analysis

14. Abe works for an organization that has several subsidiaries that operate independently. Those subsidiaries report to different leaders and have their own independent privacy programs. If the governance model does not change, what would be the appropriate way for Abe's privacy program to address this situation?

    A. Limit the objectives of his program.

    B. Limit the scope of his program.

    C. Include the subsidiaries in his program.

    D. Replace the subsidiary programs with his own.

15. Which element of the privacy program operational life cycle includes responding to data subject information requests?

    A. Protect

    B. Assess

    C. Sustain

    D. Respond

16. Leo is responsible for managing his organization's privacy budget. Which one of the following circumstances is the most preferred situation?

    A. Expenses greatly exceed budget.

    B. Expenses slightly exceed budget.

    C. Expenses are slightly under budget.

    D. Expenses are greatly under budget.

17. Which one of the following elements is *least* likely to be found in a privacy program charter?

    A. Scope statement

    B. Project schedule

    C. Roles and responsibilities

    D. Governance structure

18. Tanya is hiring a new incident analyst to help supplement the capabilities of her team. She is identifying the line item in her budget that will cover the salary and benefits for this new employee. What term best describes this expense?

  A. One-time

  B. Capital

  C. Unbudgeted

  D. Operational

19. In what Supreme Court case did the term "right to be let alone" first appear?

  A. *Olmstead v. United States*

  B. *Carpenter v. United States*

  C. *Roe v. Wade*

  D. *Katz v. United States*

20. Matt wants to share some information gathered from student records but is concerned about disclosing personal information. To protect privacy, he discloses only a table of summary statistics about overall student performance. What technique has he used?

  A. Anonymization

  B. Deidentification

  C. Aggregation

  D. Redaction

Chapter

2

Privacy Program Framework

THE CIPM EXAM OBJECTIVES COVERED IN THIS CHAPTER INCLUDE:

✓ **Domain II. Privacy Program Framework**

- II.A. Develop the privacy program framework

  - II.A.a Develop organizational privacy policies, procedures, standards, and/or guidelines

  - II.A.b Define privacy program activities

- II.B. Implement the privacy program framework

  - II.B.a Communicate the framework to internal and external stakeholders

  - II.B.b Ensure continuous alignment to applicable laws and regulations to support the development of an organizational privacy program framework

  - II.B.c Understanding data sharing agreements

- II.C. Develop appropriate metrics

  - II.C.a Identify intended audience for metrics

  - II.C.b Define reporting resources

  - II.C.c Define privacy metrics for oversight and governance per audience

  - II.C.d Identify systems/application collection points

Privacy frameworks are the key to developing a holistic privacy program that achieves organizational objectives, meets compliance obligations, and manages privacy risks. Privacy frameworks must be carefully designed to meet the specific needs of an organization and implemented with a deep awareness of the privacy-related requirements of all applicable laws and regulations. Finally, the privacy framework must be implemented with metrics for success defined at the outset so that program outcomes can be monitored and reported. This chapter covers defining, implementing, and establishing metrics for a privacy program framework.

Develop the Privacy Program Framework

Well-designed comprehensive privacy programs successfully implement the business-aligned privacy objectives. Chapter 1, "Developing a Privacy Program," described how to define the scope, objectives, and overall structures that create a strong program foundation. However, building a full privacy program based on these high-level concepts is a complex endeavor. Jumping right into building a privacy program on these foundations would be a bit like trying to build a house without a blueprint. Even on the strongest of foundations, just hammering things together would achieve, at best, a rather rickety result. Privacy frameworks provide the blueprint for constructing successful programs to meet organizational objectives.

Privacy frameworks serve as templates for designing comprehensive privacy programs. Frameworks usually break privacy programs down into discrete functional programmatic areas or activities. These categories may be based on the different functions of a privacy program or the different types of tasks and activities the program must perform, or they may even align with another business process, such as the stages of data life cycle management. Using a framework to help categorize the hundreds, or even thousands, of activities in a privacy program helps keep the program organized, ensures that nothing is left out, and provides a basis for tracking accountability and outcomes for different aspects of the program.

Examples of Privacy Frameworks

Some organizations may draw on an existing privacy framework, some may design their own, and others may use a hybrid approach. In selecting a privacy framework, there is no one-size-fits-all solution. Organizations must consider many factors when selecting a framework to ensure that it best fulfills their needs. Such factors include, for example:

- Does the framework account for the scope and scale of the organization's operations?
- Does the framework respond comprehensively to applicable regulations and other compliance concerns?
- Does the framework encompass the organization's sector or industry (private sector, governmental, not-for-profit)?
- Will the framework ensure comprehensive protection for private information across all the organization's systems and locations?
- Will the framework enable the privacy program to align with business strategy and objectives?

NIST

The National Institute of Standards and Technology (NIST) is well known for maintaining program frameworks related to data security and protection. The NIST Cybersecurity and NIST Risk Management frameworks are perhaps the most well known. NIST frameworks help organize complex programs by dividing program activities into separate functions. In the NIST cybersecurity framework, for example, the main functions are:

- Identify
- Protect
- Detect
- Respond
- Recover

Each of these functions describes a logical grouping of activities. The functional areas are further broken down into categories and subcategories. Once at the subcategory level, the framework describes concrete activities that must be performed as part of the program. Consider an example of a subcategory from the NIST Cybersecurity Framework. The Identify function begins with the "Asset Management" category. The first subcategory under asset management describes a specific program activity: "Physical devices and systems are inventoried and tracked." This type of framework allows program leaders to create well-defined policies and procedures and assign responsibility for each of these activities. Program managers can also then assess program performance in each area and roll up the results by category and function to maintain a big-picture view of program performance.

NIST has also developed a privacy framework that follows the same overall design as the Cybersecurity and Risk Management Framework. The NIST Privacy Framework has three main components:

Core The "Core" of the NIST framework describes the full set of functions and activities that should be included in the privacy program. The Core breaks down into five functional areas. Each of the five Core functions, in turn, breaks down into multiple categories. The five Core functions are:

Identify   Includes inventory and mapping, business environment, risk assessment, and data processing ecosystem risk management categories.

Govern   Includes governance policies, processes, and procedures; risk management strategy; awareness and training; monitoring; and review categories.

Control   Includes data processing policies, processes, and procedures; data processing management; and disassociated processing categories.

Communicate   Includes communication policies, processes, and procedures and data processing awareness categories.

Protect   Includes data protection policies, processes, and procedures; identity management authentication; and access control, data security, maintenance, and protective technology categories.

Each of the categories listed here breaks down even further into subcategories. The subcategories are specific enough to serve as useful standards of practice for privacy programs. Consider this example from the risk management category under the Identify function, subcategory ID.RA-P2, "Data analytic inputs and outputs are identified and evaluated for bias." This statement provides a clear instruction for privacy professionals to assess risk for a specific type of data.

Profiles   The NIST Privacy Framework profiles are a feature that allows organizations to select elements from the Core for prioritization. NIST identifies two types of profiles. A *current profile* describes the current state of privacy operations for an organization. A *target profile* describes the future state the organization aims to attain. This allows the organization to perform a gap analysis and set goals for the continuous improvement of the privacy program.

Implementation Tiers   The NIST Privacy Framework implementation tiers serve as sort of a framework for assessing the sophistication and maturity of privacy program capabilities. NIST uses four progressive tiers, where the first tier represents the lowest maturity level and the fourth tier represents the highest. The four tiers are:

- Tier 1: Partial
- Tier 2: Risk Informed
- Tier 3: Repeatable
- Tier 4: Adaptive

Implementation tiers complement NIST Privacy Framework profiles because they help organizations assess capabilities for selected profiles. Importantly, the NIST framework does not suggest that all privacy programs must reach Tier 4 in every area. Instead, the implementation tiers and profiles are tools that allow organizations to set different goals for different functions within their privacy programs. This flexibility helps align individual privacy programs with unique business strategies, goals, and risks.

NIST Framework

The NIST privacy framework is available online as a PDF at `https://nvlpubs.nist` `.gov/nistpubs/CSWP/NIST.CSWP.01162020.pdf`.

ISO 29100:2011

The International Organization for Standardization (ISO) also designs and publishes frameworks for cybersecurity and privacy. ISO's frameworks are based on developing minimum standards for program performance in a given area. ISO aims to create international standards so that frameworks can be broadly applied across jurisdictions. When it comes to privacy protection, ISO's Privacy Framework is known as ISO 29100:2011. ISO 29100 offers both a program framework and a set of privacy protection principles that are intended to help organizations develop quality programs while satisfying the legal requirements.

The ISO 29100:2011 is made up of six components:

- Actors and Roles
- Interactions
- Recognizing PII
- Privacy Safeguarding Requirements
- Privacy Policies
- Privacy Controls

While this framework is organized using different categories from NIST, each of these components addresses key functions for operating a privacy program. All six of these program components are intended to implement a set of privacy principles across an organization. The ISO Privacy Framework also outlines a set of 11 principles:

- Consent and choice
- Purpose and legitimacy specification
- Collection limitation
- Data minimization
- Use, retention, and disclosure limitation
- Accuracy and quality
- Openness, transparency, and notice

- Individual participation and access
- Accountability
- Information security
- Privacy compliance

These 11 principles are similar to the Fair Information Privacy Principles and those articulated privacy by design, discussed later.

PCI DSS

The Payment Card Industry (PCI) created a set of security standards for organizations that process credit card data in the United States. This framework is an example of a voluntary self-regulatory standard and is not enforced by the U.S. government. However, the system was created collaboratively by the major credit card issuers in the U.S. Compliance with the PCI standard is a contractual obligation for any organization that wants to accept major credit cards. One of the primary PCI security standards is the *PCI Data Security Standard (PCI DSS)*, which includes obligations to protect the privacy of customer data. While the PCI DSS standard itself is not law, the contractual obligations for compliance are legally binding. PCI DSS compliance is essentially mandatory for any organization that processes credit card data in the United States.

PCI DSS Framework

The PCI DSS framework is available online as a PDF at `https://docs-prv`
`.pcisecuritystandards.org/PCI%20DSS/Supporting%20Document/`
`PCI_DSS-QRG-v3_2_1.pdf`.

The PCI DSS standard is broken out into six goals. There are two or three specific compliance requirements associated with each goal. The PCI DSS framework goals include:

- Build and maintain a secure network and systems.
- Protect cardholder data.
- Maintain a vulnerability management program.
- Implement strong access control measures.
- Regularly monitor and test networks.
- Maintain an information security policy.

It is important to note that while the PCI DSS framework is comprehensive when it comes to protecting the security of credit card data, it doesn't cover everything an organization does. For example, the framework requirements refer principally to protecting "cardholder" data but do not address the many other categories of personal information that organizations commonly manage. The PCI DSS framework does not address vendor management, procurement, other forms of regulatory compliance, physical asset management, privacy notices, and many other important privacy protections that are not explicitly related to payment cards. For this reason, most organizations use PCI DSS as required alongside a broader privacy framework.

Fair Information Practice Principles (FIPPs)

Some multinational organizations may operate in dozens of countries and hundreds of distinct jurisdictions. It may be difficult to implement separate privacy policies for each law that requires them. Thankfully, the *Fair Information Practice Principles (FIPPs)* help organizations construct privacy policies that often satisfy a variety of privacy standards around the world. FIPPs first appeared in the U.S. Privacy Act in 1974 and have since spread to inform privacy practices around the world. FIPPs have been adopted to develop privacy policies by organizations as diverse as the University of California at Berkeley, the U.S. Department of Homeland Security, and the Asia-Pacific Economic Cooperative (APEC). Often, a FIPPs-based privacy policy will work in multiple jurisdictions with only minimal adjustments. There are eight core Fair Information Practice Principles:

- Transparency: Organizations should disclose the way they handle PII.

- Individual participation and choice: Organizations should involve individuals in decision-making about how their PII is collected, used, and shared. Ideally, this means obtaining consent.

- Purpose specification: Organizations should disclose the reasons for collecting, using, or sharing PII.

- Data minimization: Organizations should only collect the data they need for their disclosed purposes and no more.

- Use limitation: Organizations should only use PII for the reasons they have disclosed.

- Data quality and integrity: Organizations should ensure that the PII they use is accurate and up to date.

- Security: PII should be protected from criminal as well as inadvertent loss, misuse, or disclosure with security controls.

- Accountability: Organizations should take responsibility for protecting data privacy in all their dealings, including the actions of employees and vendors. An organization's privacy practices should be documented and auditable.

Privacy by Design (PbD)

As privacy frameworks are developed, privacy managers have opportunities to develop (or change) business processes so that compliance with privacy policies just happens by default. Compliance by default is less costly and less error-prone, and reduces risk far more effectively than conducting privacy compliance activities after the fact. Say, for example, that Brickabrack, Inc., has been collecting and storing huge data sets on individuals who visit its website by recording clicks, IP addresses, form responses, and more. These data sets often reveal the identities and geolocations of website visitors. Now Brickabrack has developed a new privacy policy that says they only store anonymous data about online traffic to help them optimize website performance. It would be incredibly costly for Brickabrack to employ people or software to comb through the millions of unstructured data points collected by the website every day to delete any inadvertently collected PII. Brickabrack is better off changing website tracking settings to avoid collecting things like IP addresses and locations in the first place. This approach is known as *privacy by design (PbD)*.

The PbD framework was first developed in Canada by Ontario's Privacy Commissioner in the mid-1990s. PbD adopts a "design thinking" perspective to help organizations integrate privacy protection into products, services, and operations as seamlessly as possible. Since the framework was developed, it has been broadly endorsed around the world by governments, some U.S. regulators such as the FTC, and many private-sector organizations. PbD is a requirement of the GPDR, as discussed later in this chapter. Organizations may even seek certification as PbD compliant through both private and governmental certification programs, depending on the jurisdiction. While there are now many versions of PbD frameworks, the original framework was based on seven core principles that largely align with FIPPs:

Proactive, Not Reactive; Preventive, Not Remedial   This principle is about creating a strong foundation of top-to-bottom organizational values around privacy that applies to all aspects of the organization. With such a strong commitment to privacy, organizations are better able to embed privacy into every decision.

Privacy as the Default Setting   This principle is about setting up business practices that implement Fair Information Practice Principles (discussed above) automatically. This PbD principle is particularly concerned with four FIPPS: purpose specification, collection limitation, data minimization, and use limitation. This principle is sometimes known as *privacy by default*.

Privacy Embedded into Design   This principle is about developing privacy practice as an integrated part of planning any activity in an organization, including products, services, operations, and technology. Specifically, this principle calls for completing privacy impact assessments (discussed later in this chapter) as a standard part of organizational decision-making. Privacy protections must also be embedded in the design and architecture of IT systems and business processes.

Full Functionality—Positive-Sum, Not Zero-Sum   This principle asserts that PbD should be implemented to enable, rather than inhibit, organizational strategy and objectives. This principle encourages organizations to view PbD as a value-add rather than as a regrettable cost. This means that privacy managers must fully understand and align with organizational strategies.

End-to-Security—Full Life Cycle Protection   PbD helps achieve information security goals because it calls for not incurring PII liability in the first place. Even where the collection of PII is reduced, it is still essential to protect the PII that is collected by following a well-developed data security program that protects and manages data throughout the data life cycle.

Visibility and Transparency—Keep It Open   This principle also encourages transparency around activities that ensure compliance.

Respect for User Privacy—Keep It User-Centric   PbD embeds the FIPP principles around individual participation and choice, as well as data quality and integrity. Some organizations may choose to do only the minimum required for compliance to offer individual choice and consent. However, PbD encourages organizations to center their values on respect for individual privacy and agency so that privacy becomes more than a mere compliance activity. Organizations may choose to adopt a user-centered approach to data privacy as a value so that their privacy programs may be reliable and trusted.

Develop Privacy Policies, Procedures, Standards, and Guidelines

Once an appropriate framework has been selected or developed for an organization, developing privacy policies, standards, and procedures will help shape the overall content of the privacy program. A *privacy policy* is typically an internal document that details how an organization manages private information and protects privacy. A privacy policy should identify the data that should be protected, the various controls that have been implemented to protect privacy, internal roles and responsibilities, the privacy standards that must be achieved, and the process for monitoring and improving the privacy program itself.

The privacy policy should describe the controls employed to protect private information. The controls may be technical, administrative, and physical. Technical controls may include firewalls, password protection, and encryption. Administrative controls may include employee training, defined roles and responsibilities, or other policies, such as those for data access, storage, classification, or retention. Physical controls may include secure locking storage for physical records or building access controls.

Privacy Notices

Privacy notices differ from privacy policies. Privacy notices are the public documents in which organizations disclose their privacy practices. Various regulations often include requirements detailing specific content that must be included in a privacy notice. Disclosing how an organization handles each of the eight FIPPs often provides a good basis for constructing privacy notices.

Define Privacy Program Activities

Once a privacy framework and foundational privacy policies have been developed, the rest of the privacy program may be defined in detail. Privacy program activities include all the operational functions and duties necessary to implement and follow the privacy policies across the organization. These activities include everything from data handling, to managing breaches, to employee training. A well-designed privacy framework helps by serving as a checklist to ensure that no area of the operation is neglected as privacy program activities are defined.

The importance of conducting a data inventory and developing a resulting data classification matrix was covered in Chapter 1. The data classification matrix enables the development of further policies and procedures that detail differential controls for different data classifications, role-based access for employees, appropriate employee training, and other privacy program activities that may vary depending on the level of data classification.

Education and Awareness

Appropriate employee training is a key pillar of success for any privacy program. Training needs vary by organization and by an employee's functional role. Employee education constitutes an important privacy control to help guard against inadvertent violations of the organization's privacy policy. Even with a solid framework and policy in place, untrained employees could disclose private information, collect information inappropriately, fail to adequately protect private information, neglect data retention requirements, and more. In general, privacy programs include two main categories of employee education:

- General privacy program awareness education
- Role-based training for specific functions

General privacy awareness education is most typically required for all employees. Privacy awareness education ensures that every employee is familiar with the contents of the organization's privacy policy and any prominent regulations affecting privacy. Privacy awareness education also usually covers what private information the organization processes, how that information is managed, and any privacy-related responsibilities that apply to all employees. These responsibilities could be as simple as requiring that all employees are up to date with their required information security training, or not letting anyone in the building who doesn't have an employee ID badge.

Role-based training usually targets employees with specific responsibilities for the privacy program. For example, employees responsible for company records may require training in the data retention policy and purging procedure. Compliance officers may need training on the aspects of privacy regulations that affect the organization. Role-based training may also apply to employees based on their level of access to private information. For example, a hospital may require HIPAA training for any employee with a role that requires access to medical records.

Monitoring and Responding to the Regulatory Environment

Privacy regulations are evolving rapidly around the world. Within the United States, every state has some sort of privacy or breach notification law on the books and each year more states are developing new privacy-related legislation. Globally, many countries are developing and updating national privacy regulations. Multinational alliances, such as the Asia-Pacific Economic Cooperation (APEC), also continually review their privacy standards and offer updated guidance. Even individual cities may enact privacy regulations. For example, New York City regulations restrict employers from asking job applicants about pending criminal proceedings.

Tracking all changes to global privacy regulations is daunting. Ideally, privacy programs track such changes both proactively and through periodic reviews. The regulatory tracking function of the program should continually monitor privacy regulations in all relevant jurisdictions in which the organization operates. Typically, information is available about pending privacy regulations months before they take effect. Even once new regulations are approved, there is usually a grace period before the new rules go into effect. Proactive monitoring of new regulations is essential to allow organizations time in advance to adapt their business process to comply with new regulations.

It is not realistic for a privacy program to proactively detect every regulatory change around the world. For this reason, the regulatory tracking function should also include a documented process for conducting periodic reviews for changes to the regulatory environment. Such periodic reviews should not only check for regulatory changes in relevant jurisdictions but also check for changes in jurisdictions themselves. For example, a federal agency may have been granted rule-making authority over a new industry. Or, conversely, a company may have expanded its products and services into a new sector that expands the scope of regulatory authority and compliance. A comprehensive review of this sort helps organizations manage compliance risk and helps to demonstrate due diligence.

Several tools are available to help privacy leaders monitor the regulatory environment. Online professional social networks, web forums, and email lists are all effective ways to get information about regulatory changes. In addition, several websites monitor privacy regulations in different jurisdictions. For example, the Electronic Frontier Foundation (www.eff.org) monitors U.S. privacy laws, the National Conference of State Legislatures (NCSL) maintains an updated list of U.S. state privacy laws (www.ncsl.org/research/telecommunications-and-information-technology/state-laws-related-to-internet-privacy.aspx), and the IAPP (https://iapp.org) itself provides useful news updates related to privacy regulations around the world. Finally, privacy leaders should collaborate with legal counsel as necessary. Legal counsel can be especially helpful in assessing the scope of various regulations and related compliance risks.

A privacy program must not only be designed to monitor the ever-evolving landscape of privacy regulations but must also have embedded mechanisms for the privacy program to change and adapt. To jump-start your privacy program, third-party consulting services that specialize in privacy compliance can help. A potential change in compliance obligations should trigger change management processes for the privacy program. Typically, this sort of change management is included in the privacy program's governance function.

Monitoring Internal Privacy Policy Compliance

Most established privacy frameworks include requirements for monitoring internal compliance with the privacy program. After all, a privacy program isn't very useful if an organization's employees don't carry out the program's activities. Both FIPPs and PbD emphasize the importance of accountability, meaning that an organization can demonstrate that it follows its own stated practices.

Ensuring internal compliance can be tricky in many organizations because a comprehensive privacy program imposes requirements on nearly every part of an organization. The employees responsible for complying with the program may all have different supervisors, and few, if any, report to the organization's privacy manager. Privacy managers, therefore, need to implement policies and procedures to ensure compliance.

For example, the NIST Privacy Framework has a specific category for developing internal compliance processes called "monitoring and review" under the "govern" function. NIST lists seven detailed subcategories of activities for internal monitoring that range from ensuring that privacy risk and governance are regularly evaluated to documenting procedures for responding to "lessons learned" that arise from resolving data privacy problems.

Finally, monitoring to ensure internal compliance should include *program assurance* or formal processes for evaluating compliance with the privacy program. Program assurance may include external audits where required. For example, the Gramm–Leach–Bliley Act (GLBA) requires regular external audits of financial services functions, which includes data privacy requirements. Many other statutes require internal audits or assessments of privacy practices. Privacy programs should include regular internal assessments or external third-party assessments that mirror formal audit processes. Such assessments help evaluate the program and, at the same time, help privacy managers prepare for external audits and remediate any issues before they occur.

Data Inventories, Data Flows, and Classification

To protect private information, an organization must know precisely what data it handles in the first place. This begins with performing a privacy assessment, completing a data inventory, and constructing data classification policies. The importance of conducting a data inventory and developing a resulting data classification matrix was covered in Chapter 1. The data classification policy enables the development of further policies and procedures that detail differential controls for different data classifications, role-based access for employees, appropriate employee training, and other privacy program activities that may vary depending on the level of data classification.

A data inventory and classification are a good starting point but are not sufficient for monitoring data as it moves around an organization. Data inventories tell an organization what data it holds, and data classification policies can tell an organization how it is to be protected, but an understanding of *data flows* is necessary to tell an organization where data is stored, how it is transmitted, and who needs to handle it at any given point. In the event of a breach or other privacy incident, well-documented data flows help track down exactly where in the workflow a lapse may have occurred. Data flows document how information identified in the data inventory is initially collected, where it is stored, how it is transmitted, any copies that are made, any sharing with third parties, and how it is ultimately purged.

Privacy Impact Assessments (PIAs)

Data privacy program activities are developed to protect privacy across all existing organizational activities and systems. But what about when something changes? What if a company expands into a new territory? Or adopts new and different technologies for data storage? Or adds new products and services? It is possible that organizations may make decisions that negatively affect data privacy. For example, expanding into a new territory may mean becoming subject to compliance obligations in a new jurisdiction. Offering a new product or service may mean collecting new PII. Without careful consideration, an organization may inadvertently create new privacy risks that are not adequately addressed by an existing data privacy program.

Privacy impact assessments (PIAs) are analyses conducted to assess data privacy protections to make sure they satisfy any compliance obligations and meet privacy program standards. They are used to analyze specific processes and technologies whenever an organization is considering a change that might affect privacy. PIAs are proactive tools and should be conducted as early as possible in any decision-making process that might affect data privacy. A PIA should describe the potential privacy impacts of any organizational change proposed, including the scale and scope of the change. Is the change to data privacy something negligible that is already covered by the existing privacy policy? Or is it a whole new type of data collection for which there are no privacy controls? PIAs also include an assessment of how the change might affect the organization's obligations to protect individual privacy under any relevant regulations or policies, including the organization's own privacy policy. Finally, a PIA should include recommendations for mitigating any privacy risks and, if necessary, amending the organizational privacy program to account for the proposed change.

Consider, for example, an organization that plans to implement a new online sales system. In conducting a PIA, the privacy manager may have the opportunity to ensure that appropriate privacy controls are in place, such as a policy for accessing customer data in the new system; that the new system can meet data minimization principles by limiting data collection; and that customer data isn't inadvertently shared with the sales system vendor.

PIAs aren't merely a good idea; sometimes they are required by regulators. Notably, Article 35 of Europe's GDPR requires organizations to perform PIAs when making changes to data processing that "is likely to result in a high risk to the rights and freedoms of natural persons." The GDPR also requires the supervisory authorities in each EU member state to develop approved lists of the types of data processing activities that do not require a PIA. This means that, unless listed as an exemption, organizations subject to GDPR should default to performing a PIA whenever an organizational change might impact data processing.

Exam Tip

In the text of the GDPR, privacy impact assessments are called *data protection impact assessments (DPIAs)*. Either or both terms may appear on the exam.

Incident Response and Process

Privacy programs must account for the likelihood that the organization will experience privacy incidents. A more serious incident may even be considered a privacy breach, depending on the jurisdiction. Privacy programs should include documented procedures for incident management, response, recovery, and notification. Often existing incident response plans from an organization's information security program can be referenced or reused. There are many frameworks for incident response that detail each step in the process. For example, the NIST Cybersecurity Framework includes detailed functions for detecting, responding to, and recovering from security incidents.

The NIST Privacy Framework explicitly references these functions from the Cybersecurity Framework to use in designing privacy incident response processes. While the NIST Privacy Framework references the Cybersecurity Framework as a blueprint for an incident response process, privacy incidents are not always the same as cybersecurity incidents. For example, if an organization discovers that the marketing department is collecting geolocation data on website visitors in a way that contradicts their public privacy notice, then a privacy incident may have occurred but not a cybersecurity incident.

When managing an incident, legal processes often come into play. Most often, a privacy incident triggers compliance obligations if it constitutes a data breach. In this context, *breach* is a legal term that may be defined differently in different jurisdictions. Typically, a breach occurs when there is an unauthorized disclosure of private information. Whether or not a disclosure is considered a breach depends on factors like the definition of PII in each jurisdiction, the definition of an unauthorized disclosure, whether and how the PII was encrypted, and other specific elements that define a breach in a given regulation. A breach in one state or country might not be considered a breach in another, so where the data is stored can impact when a breach is declared.

When a breach occurs, compliance obligations most often include requirements to notify affected individuals and/or government agencies. Regulations vary in terms of how quickly an organization must make the notification, the method of delivering the notification, and exactly what such a notification must contain. Privacy managers must have procedures in place to stay abreast of all applicable breach notification laws as well as capabilities to deliver required notifications. Privacy managers can employ legal counsel to determine jurisdictional requirements and to deliver notifications. Remember that communications between the privacy manager and legal counsel are considered privileged and are not subject to discovery requests.

It is critical to have all incident response processes, including legal and compliance steps, well established before an incident occurs. For this reason, incident response procedures should rely not only on documentation and training but also on regular practice drills. Tabletop exercises are popular methods of practice because they are relatively easy to conduct. Tabletop drills usually involve gathering all the relevant people and talking through a sample incident scenario. More intensive drills may simulate an incident by asking employees to role-play through a training incident in real time as if it was happening.

Remediation Oversight

Problems inevitably arise. Some incidents rise to the level of a breach, whereas others may only be internal compliance lapses that occur when employees fail to follow the procedures outlined by the privacy program. No matter the severity, the privacy program should include processes for evaluating incidents after they are resolved and implementing remediations to reduce the risk that such an incident might reoccur.

Remediations may range from simple steps to improve compliance with employee training requirements to an overhaul of network security technologies. The privacy program should assign clear responsibilities for handling remediations and establish a detailed procedure for documenting, implementing, and assessing such remediations over time. Privacy managers should collaborate with the proper functional leaders at an organization when designing and implementing remediations. A privacy manager cannot be everywhere at once, and functional leaders across the organization should share accountability for data privacy.

Handling Inquiries and Complaints

Well-designed privacy programs include a process for handling privacy complaints. This feature is identified in the NIST Privacy Framework as part of the Govern function. Specifically, the NIST framework suggests that "Policies, processes, and procedures for receiving, tracking, and responding to complaints, concerns, and questions from individuals about organizational privacy practices are established and in place."

For most organizations, the ability to receive privacy complaints involves establishing a confidential way for individuals, including employees, to report complaints without fear of retaliation. This often takes the form of a confidential complaint hotline or online complaint form. This function should report to an individual with a high degree of independence from any functions within the organization that may have a vested interest in outcomes arising from any complaints. Many organizations have some sort of office of ethics that reports directly to the board of directors to ensure autonomy and integrity.

Implement the Privacy Program Framework

Once the framework has been designed, the privacy manager may begin to implement the framework and the resulting privacy program activities. The process of implementing the framework requires robust communication, a deep understanding of applicable regulations, and the ability to manage data sharing with third parties.

Communicate the Framework

Once the privacy framework is designed, it is critical to communicate the framework clearly across the organization. The process of implementing a new privacy framework will impact every part of the operation and add privacy responsibilities to many job descriptions. As discussed in Chapter 1, executive sponsorship are critical at this phase, but executive sponsorship alone is not sufficient.

Even if employees are not in decision-making roles, they still need to know what will be expected and given time to prepare. Information technology is a good example because IT systems can take a long time to configure, test, and change. If, for example, a new privacy framework requires that all private information be encrypted in transit and at rest, major IT upgrades may be required before that functional area of the framework can be implemented.

Aligning with Applicable Laws and Regulations

Privacy programs must ensure compliance with all the laws and regulations that may apply to the organization's operations, as well as how those laws are enforced, including the scope and authority of oversight agencies. Organizations must consider regulations that apply in various territories as well as regulations that apply to various sectors or industries. Where the data resides can directly impact the cost of implementing privacy requirements and may also impact what vendors are used for storing and processing data.

Whether applicable laws and regulations are territorial or sectoral, privacy managers must understand where and when a regulation applies, how it is enforced, and the penalties for violations. Some laws specify fines for violations, and some allow an oversight agency to pursue civil penalties. Others, such as California's privacy law, include a *private right of action*, which allows individuals to sue an organization for damages when violations occur.

Territorial Regulations

Privacy programs must ensure compliance with all the laws and regulations that may apply in the various territories where an organization operates. In recent years, some jurisdictions, like the EU, have enacted comprehensive privacy regulations that apply broadly in their territory. Other jurisdictions, like the United States, continue to lack comprehensive national privacy legislation and instead rely on a patchwork of state and sector-specific laws. In general, federal statutes in the U.S. offer a mixed perspective on who owns and controls personal information held by third parties. Federal law generally allows businesses to control and use personal data while providing consumers with limited rights to know and control information collected about them.

While the EU's General Data Protection Regulation was among the first examples of comprehensive national privacy laws, many other countries have begun to follow suit. For example, Brazil has enacted the *Lei Geral de Proteção de Dados (LGPD)*, which translates as the General Data Protection Act. China has enacted the *Personal Information Protection Law (PIPL)*, and Canada has enacted the *Personal Information Protection and Electronic Documents Act (PIPEDA)*. These laws all have a lot in common with GDPR. While they vary in some specifics, these territorial regulations all serve as unified national data privacy regulations and confer greater rights on data subjects. This section explores both GDPR and California's Consumer Privacy Act in greater detail as examples of territorial regulations.

European Union's General Data Protection Regulation (GDPR)

The General Data Protection Regulation (GDPR) took legal effect in 2018 and set a new standard for privacy protection. The GDPR is a comprehensive EU-wide privacy regulation that applies to all EU member states and sectors. The GDPR unifies the privacy regulations of the member states and thus allows for the exchange of data across the EU. Even though the GDPR is an EU law, it has sweeping implications for any U.S.-based corporations that have operations in Europe or that transfer personal information to or from Europe. The GDPR is celebrated as a win by privacy advocates and a model for progressive privacy legislation in the United States.

Compared with existing U.S. law, the GDPR grants individuals far more rights to access and control how and by whom their data is accessed and used. In general, ensuring more rights for individuals means more restrictions for businesses that rely on customer data. For this reason, the GDPR may present challenges for some non-EU businesses. At a minimum, businesses may have to implement costly compliance programs and manage increased legal risks. GDPR may affect some U.S.-based corporations more than others. For example, some businesses in the United States, such as data brokers of large data sets for digital advertising, may generate revenue through the relatively unfettered use and disclosure of customer data from the EU.

GDPR SCOPE

The GDPR is notable for its breadth. The GDPR aims to protect all personal data for anyone located in the EU by regulating any entity that handles personal data. The GDPR defines several key concepts critical to understanding the full scope of the law:

Personal Data   Personal data includes any information that identifies an individual. Examples include name, geolocation information, and any characteristics of a person that might be used individually or in combination to identify someone. The GDPR refers to individuals protected by the law as *natural persons* or *data subjects*. Importantly, the GDPR does not restrict its scope to citizens of EU member states. GDPR rights and protections apply to anyone physically located within the EU at the time they are sharing their personal information.

U.S.-based privacy professionals should note that U.S. corporations may collect data that is not protected by U.S. law as personal information but that is considered personal information in the EU.

Data Controllers and Processors   The GDPR applies to both *controllers* and *processors* of data. A data controller is usually the entity that is ultimately in charge of data. The GDPR says that a controller "determines the purposes and means of the processing of personal data." A data processor is any other entity that handles personal data on behalf of a controller. For example, a retailer may hire a digital marketing firm to help it increase online sales with better website analytics. In this case, the retailer would be the controller and the marketing firm would be the processor. Under GDPR, both controllers and processors have obligations and liabilities. With this framework, the GDPR aims to protect data even as it changes hands.

Territorial Jurisdiction   As mentioned earlier, the GDPR confers rights on anyone in the EU, whether or not they are citizens of the EU. However, there is less certainty about whether non-EU organizations must comply with GDPR requirements. According to the text of the GDPR, it applies to all organizations established in the EU as well as any organizations that control or process data on EU data subjects for "the offering of goods or services" or for "the monitoring of their [EU data subjects'] behavior" within EU territory. This may be interpreted to mean that GDPR regulates any e-commerce website that a person in the EU happens to click on.

DATA SUBJECT RIGHTS

The GDPR provides comprehensive rights to data subjects. Not unlike many U.S. laws that apply to different industry sectors, the GDPR requires that all data processors and controllers provide transparent notice to customers explaining what data is collected, how data is used, and information about any third parties with whom data may be shared.

The GDPR imposes specific requirements that companies must satisfy to process personal data. Companies may collect personal data as needed to fulfill contracts with data subjects, to comply with legal obligations, to protect a data subject's "vital interests," to complete a task "in the public interest," and where the processing is necessary to interests of the business. Businesses must obtain consent from data subjects before collecting personal data in almost all other circumstances.

Consent must be meaningful and controllers must be able to show that they have obtained consent. GDPR requires that written consent must be "clearly distinguishable from other matters," easy to understand, and accessible. This means that a consent clause may not be buried in some long and obtuse end-user agreement. Data subjects may also retract their consent whenever they like. Most U.S. privacy laws, in contrast, require (at most) that data subjects be given the chance to opt out of data collection and use, whereas GDPR generally requires an opt-in by default.

The GDPR provides a notable list of additional *data subject rights*. These are contained in Articles 15–22 of the GDPR and include the well-known *right to erasure*, also known as the *right to be forgotten*. The right to be forgotten means, quite simply, that EU data subjects have the right to ask data controllers to erase all of their personal data. A request for erasure may be made in several circumstances, including when a data subject withdraws consent. In such cases, controllers are required to erase the personal data in question "without undue delay." After receiving a request to be forgotten, a data controller or processor may only retain personal data as required to meet other legal compliance obligations. Other data subject rights include the following:

- *Right of access*: Data subjects have the right to know what data is collected and why, to know how their data will be processed and with whom their data may be shared, and to obtain a copy of their personal data as well as information about how to request erasure under GDPR.

- *Right to rectification*: Data subjects have the right to request corrections to the information collected about them.

- *Right to restriction of processing*: Data subjects have the right to request that controllers halt processing activities, without requesting full erasure, in some circumstances.

- *Notification obligations*: Controllers have to notify data subjects when they fulfill requests for erasure, rectification, or restriction of processing.

- *Right to data portability*: Data subjects have the right to get a copy of their data in "machine-readable format" so that it can be ingested by other information systems. This right, for example, helps prevent companies from locking customers into their products by keeping their data in a proprietary format that can't be moved to a competitor.

- *Right to object*: Data subjects have the right to object to any processing of their personal data they believe to be out of compliance with GDPR or to opt out of certain processing activities, such as direct marketing. The burden is on the data controller to demonstrate that data processing activities are authorized under GDPR in order to resume.

- *Automated individual decision-making, including profiling*: This right means that AI, or any "automated processing" alone, can't make any decisions that have a significant or legal impact on a person.

The GDPR also includes requirements for data controllers and processers. Chapter 4 of the GDPR lists each of these obligations in detail. For example, Article 25 of the GDPR requires data protection by design and by default. Under this article, controllers must implement practices to protect data subjects' privacy when they first design their data processing procedures and throughout all data processing activities. Article 25 requires the use of techniques, such as pseudonymization and the implementation of oversight procedures principles such as data minimization and purpose specification, to be followed by default when data are collected in the first place. Article 25 of the GPDR is an example of a requirement for privacy by design (PbD), as discussed earlier in this chapter.

The GDPR contains many more important requirements for data controllers and processors. It also enables EU member states to develop and monitor codes of conduct and certification programs for data controllers and processors in their jurisdictions. Among the many provisions of GDPR, some prominent requirements for data controllers and processors are as follows:

- Controllers must implement controls to ensure that data processors comply with GDPR.

- Data processors may only process data (or allow third parties to process data) as specified by the data controller.

- Data controllers and processors must maintain detailed records of data processing activities and comply with any requests from EU supervisory authorities.

- Data controllers and processors must have appropriate information security controls.

- Data processors must notify the relevant data controller of any privacy breach "without undue delay." Data controllers must notify the appropriate member state supervisory authority of any breach within 72 hours. Controllers must also notify affected individuals of data breaches "without undue delay" if the breach is likely to pose a "high risk to the rights and freedoms" of the individual as described by the GDPR.

- As described earlier in this chapter, the GDPR requires DPIAs when considering a change to data processing operations, as well as consultation with the appropriate member state supervisory authority whenever a DPIA suggests elevated risk.

- Data controllers must appoint a *data projection officer (DPO)* inside the organization with responsibility for data privacy.

Penalties for violating the GDPR can be steep. Depending on which provision of the GDPR is violated and whether the violation was intentional or negligent, administrative penalties for infringements may reach up to €20,000,000, or 4 percent of a company's annual revenue, whichever is greater. Data subjects may also pursue damages for any harm caused by a violation of the GDPR. Some compliance functions of the GDPR, like the DPO function, can be outsourced to a third party.

California Consumer Privacy Act (CCPA) (2018)

The United States has no comprehensive federal regulation. To address the lack of federal privacy protection in the U.S., California enacted the California Consumer Privacy Act (CCPA). CCPA goes further than U.S. federal law in granting consumers more rights to control their personal information.

 The CCPA shares many features common to progressive privacy regulations that give individuals greater control over their data. Such laws often include a more expansive definition of personal information and confer individual rights to ensure that people know what information is collected, get copies of their information, restrict the use of their information, or request that their information be deleted. These features may appear in newer state laws, industry privacy frameworks, international safe harbor programs (discussed later in this chapter), or international laws such as the GDPR.

The CCPA includes an expansive definition of the personal information it protects. The definition of personal information includes common identifiers that one may expect, such as name, Social Security number, and street address. But the law also includes IP addresses, email addresses, biometric information, web browsing history, geolocation data, retail transaction records, and more in the definition of protected personal information. CCPA even considers "inferences drawn from any of the information" to be personal information and subject to the CCPA's requirements. While the definition is expansive, the CCPA does contain exceptions. For example, CCPA does not apply to consumer data regulated by other state or federal laws that preempt CCPA, such as the Health Insurance Portability and Accountability Act (HIPAA) or the Gramm–Leach–Bliley Act (GLBA).

The CCPA provides Californians with a set of consumer rights, including:

Right to Know   Businesses are required to notify customers about what information they collect and how that information is used "at the point of collection" and may not collect or use information in any other ways.

Upon request by a consumer, businesses must disclose what categories of information they've collected about them. If requested, businesses must provide consumers with a copy of their personal information in a "portable" format. Consumers may not be charged a fee for these disclosures.

Right to Delete   Upon request, businesses must delete any personal information that has been collected about a consumer. Some exceptions to deletion include, for example, information needed to complete transactions, detect cyberattacks or fraud, comply with legal requirements, and a handful of other limited circumstances.

Right to Opt Out   Consumers have the right to restrict businesses from selling their personal information to third parties. If businesses intend to sell personal information, they must notify consumers and inform them of their right to opt out.

Nondiscrimination   Businesses may not treat anyone differently because they exercise their consumer rights under the CCPA. Businesses must charge the same prices and provide the same quality of products and services.

Notably, the CCPA is enforced, in part, by providing a limited *private right of action* that permits California citizens to pursue civil penalties directly for violations. To pursue a private civil action, the consumer must claim that their "unencrypted or nonredacted personal information" has been disclosed in a way not authorized by the law. Such unauthorized disclosures could occur as the result of a security breach, accidental disclosure, or even by a company that shares data with advertisers in violation of the CCPA. In addition, the unauthorized disclosure must include a combination of a person's name and some other indicator of identity, such as a Social Security number or driver's license number. Consumers may pursue damages that range from $100 up to $750 per incident. Consumers may also pursue actual damages if they are greater than $750.

The CCPA requires businesses to encrypt, redact, or otherwise store data so that personal information may not be read or tied to an individual if accessed by a third party. If the data in question is properly deidentified and encrypted, then the incident is not considered an unauthorized disclosure under CCPA. The CCPA requires businesses to implement safeguards to deidentify information and "prohibit reidentification." If the business is using encryption to ensure deidentification, encryption practices must meet the standard of preventing reidentification.

Sectoral and Industry Regulations

Privacy programs must also comply with many sectoral, or industry-specific, regulations in addition to territorial laws. The United States is especially reliant on sectoral statutes because it lacks a comprehensive federal privacy law. In the U.S., various sectoral regulations govern privacy for financial services, education, telecom, medical services, governmental access to private information, and more. This section explores two sectoral regulations that govern medical and financial privacy as examples.

The Health Insurance Portability and Accountability Act (HIPAA)

In 1996, Congress passed the *Health Insurance Portability and Accountability Act (HIPAA)*. HIPAA was enacted to improve several aspects of the healthcare system, including the sharing of data among providers and insurers, the process of switching health plans, and more. HIPAA also set important standards for maintaining the privacy and security of medical information.

HIPAA privacy and security rules apply to *protected health information (PHI)*. PHI includes medical information about patient health that is collected by healthcare providers for medical records, during conversations with healthcare providers, individual medical information stored by health insurance companies, and information used in healthcare billing or payment. HIPAA also protects electronic personal health information (ePHI). ePHI includes any PHI stored or transmitted electronically.

HIPAA SCOPE

HIPAA is a complex piece of legislation that regulates privacy across a wide range of healthcare-related activities. As mentioned earlier, not all medical information is protected by HIPAA under all circumstances. HIPAA applies to certain *covered entities* and to certain healthcare *transactions*. When a covered entity conducts a covered transaction, that entity and the transaction itself are both regulated under HIPAA. HIPAA-covered entities fall into three broad categories:

Health Insurance Plans   This category includes health insurance companies, health maintenance organizations (HMOs), employer health plans, and government health programs, such as Medicare, that cover healthcare costs.

Healthcare Clearinghouses   These organizations help manage the sharing of healthcare information by converting healthcare data into formats that can be read by differing health information systems.

Healthcare Providers   Providers include doctors, hospitals, mental health professionals, dentists, long-term care facilities, pharmacies, and more.

HIPAA also extends to third-party *business associates* of covered entities if they meet certain conditions. A business associate is any third-party individual or organization that works with a covered entity to fulfill healthcare-related functions and that has access to PHI or ePHI. HIPAA requires covered entities to have written agreements with any third parties, called *business associate agreements (BAAs)*, that require the business associate to conform with HIPAA.

The HIPAA Privacy Rule (described in the next section) also designates specific organizational types to illustrate which parts of an entity are subject to the Privacy Rule. For example, organizations may be "hybrid entities," where only part of the business is a covered entity. The rule clarifies organizational obligations for the Privacy Rule for affiliated entities, shared healthcare arrangements, and HMOs.

HIPAA covers quite a broad set of healthcare-related transactions that include everything from health insurance claims to medical referrals. HIPAA does more than regulate the privacy of data used in these transactions. Under the law, the U.S. Department of Health and Human Services (HHS) administers specific standards for conducting these transactions electronically. In addition to protecting patient privacy, these standards attempt to add some uniformity and definition that all covered entities must use in common. These standards help reduce medical errors, increase oversight and accountability, enable medical research, and increase the speed of transactions. Any organization that falls into any of the covered entity categories listed *and* that engages in any of these common healthcare-related transactions is subject to the provisions of HIPAA.

There are some specific exceptions under HIPAA. Some records are not covered under HIPAA, even for covered entities. These include personnel records for employees, academic records covered by the Family Education Rights and Privacy Act (FERPA), and information that has been properly anonymized so that it could not be used to identify a patient.

HIPAA-Covered Transactions

According to the federal government's guidance for HIPAA, the following transactions are covered by HIPAA: "payment and remittance advice, claims status, eligibility, coordination of benefits, claims and encounter information, enrollment and unenrollment, referrals and authorizations, and premium payments." You can read more about HIPAA at www.cms.gov/Regulations-and-Guidance/Administrative-Simplification/Transactions/TransactionsOverview.

HIPAA PRIVACY REQUIREMENTS

The HHS Centers for Medicare & Medicaid Services (CMS) provides the rules and standards for organizations subject to HIPAA. In the year 2000, HHS established the HIPAA *Privacy Rule* that lays out guidelines for protecting the privacy of PHI. The Privacy Rule does the following:

- Requires the implementation of information privacy practices
- Limits use and disclosure of PHI without patient authorization
- Gives patients additional rights concerning their medical information, including the right to view and correct their medical records

All HIPAA-covered entities and business associates are subject to the Privacy Rule. The HHS Office of Civil Rights (OCR) is responsible for implementing and enforcing the Privacy Rule and may impose monetary penalties for violations. Let's take a closer look at the specific provisions of the rule and its enforcement.

INFORMATION PRIVACY PRACTICES

The Privacy Rule requires covered entities to implement standards and practices to safeguard PHI. These standards and practices must be contained in the covered entity's written *privacy policy and procedures* documentation. These must be consistent with the Privacy Rule. Covered entities are required to retain any records related to their privacy policies and related activities, such as complaints or public notices, for six years.

 A privacy *policy* differs from a privacy *notice*. A privacy policy generally refers to an organization's internal practices for protecting information privacy. A privacy notice is published by an organization to inform consumers about how it collects, uses, retains, and shares personal data.

Other privacy safeguards include:

- The requirement to designate a privacy official responsible for the privacy policy
- Implementing a process for addressing privacy complaints
- Training employees on privacy practices
- Implementing reasonable privacy safeguards

Safeguards may be physical, administrative, or technical. For example, safeguards may include ensuring all filing cabinets are appropriately locked (physical), only allowing need-to-know personnel to possess a key to the filing cabinets (administrative), or providing an electronic checkout system for accessing files (technical). Covered entities cannot retaliate against anyone for filing a privacy complaint or ask patients to waive any rights under the Privacy Rule as a condition of care or coverage.

USE AND DISCLOSURE

The Privacy Rule aims to protect patient privacy to the greatest extent possible while allowing for information sharing as necessary for the provision of healthcare services and to maintain public health and safety. The Privacy Rule is therefore intended to block covered entities from selling PHI to advertisers or sharing PHI with prospective employers.

The Privacy Rule regulates both the *use* and *disclosure* of PHI. According to HIPAA, *use* of PHI regulates how PHI is handled within an organization. Regulations relating to use help ensure that PHI is only used for intended purposes and that access to PHI is not intentionally or inadvertently abused. HIPAA defines the use of PHI as

> . . . the sharing, employment, application, utilization, examination, or analysis of such information within an entity that maintains such information.

Rules that regulate *disclosure* of PHI are intended to prevent organizations from sharing PHI with third parties. If PHI is shared with third parties by any means, it is considered a disclosure. It is important to remember that not all disclosures are illegal under HIPAA. The Privacy Rule, rather, regulates when and how disclosures may be made. HIPAA defines disclosure as follows:

> . . . the release, transfer, provision of access to, or divulging in any manner of information outside the entity holding the information.

The Privacy Rule has specific requirements detailing how covered entities may use and disclose PHI. These requirements are intended to ensure that patients know how their PHI is used and shared, that PHI is only used to provide healthcare services (with limited exceptions), and that patients must provide authorization before their PHI can be used for anything else.

Without a patient's explicit authorization, covered entities may only disclose PHI to designated parties for a few specific purposes, including the following:

- To the patients themselves

- As necessary to deliver healthcare services (treatment, billing, running a clinic, etc.)

- By informal permission of the patient—for example, a patient allowing another person to pick up prescriptions

- If, in the process of sharing PHI in an authorized way, other PHI is disclosed incidentally

- For activities in the public interest (the rule defines 12 specific activities that qualify, including, for example, disclosures required by law, essential government functions, and serious threats to health and safety)

- Limited sharing for research and public health purposes

For any other use or disclosure of PHI, the covered entity must obtain written authorization from the patient. Covered entities may not require patients to waive this right in exchange for services. Authorizations can't be written too broadly. For example, a provider can't ask an individual to grant blanket permission to share data for any purpose. Authorizations must be written so that they are easily understood and must specify the PHI to be disclosed, to whom, and for what purpose.

As mentioned at the beginning of this section, the goal of the Privacy Rule is to keep PHI as private as possible while allowing for necessary sharing. Even when PHI is shared in a permitted way or with patient authorization, the Privacy Rule includes an important principle to further improve privacy across all uses and disclosures. This is the principle of *minimum necessary* usage and sharing. This means that covered entities should limit access to patient data to need-to-know personnel, redact unnecessary information when disclosing data for permitted purposes, keep track of where all PHI is stored and make sure extra copies aren't floating around, and generally default to keeping data private and restricted unless explicitly permitted. As part of their privacy policies and procedures, covered entities must document their practices for managing and disclosing PHI.

Generally speaking, any use or disclosure of PHI not explicitly allowed by the law under the conditions described here is considered a breach. Breaches may be caused intentionally, such as when a healthcare organization is the victim of a cyberattack. Unauthorized uses and disclosures may also be accidental, such as when healthcare information is inadvertently disclosed to the wrong party. In the case of an accidental use or disclosure of PHI, the law may not define the event as a breach in some limited circumstances, such as accidental disclosures made to other authorized employees at same entity.

Naturally, breaches put patients at risk, but breaches also create risks and obligations for healthcare organizations. Breaches usually trigger further requirements for healthcare organizations to notify patients and the HHS department. A breach in itself may not constitute a

HIPAA violation, but breaches may certainly bring increased regulatory scrutiny and, potentially, investigations by government oversight agencies.

INDIVIDUAL RIGHTS

The Privacy Rule offers individuals certain rights related to their PHI. As a foundation for these rights, individuals first have the right to know how a covered entity manages their data. Covered entities are therefore required to publish a *Privacy Notice* that explains how PHI is used and shared, the covered entities' obligations to protect patient privacy, the privacy practices in place, and patient privacy rights. These Privacy Notices provide an important vehicle for OCR enforcement because they allow investigators to determine whether an organization's behavior differs from its published Privacy Notice. These Privacy Notices must be conveyed directly to an individual if an organization has a direct treatment relationship with that person. Privacy Notices must also be posted wherever healthcare services are delivered and available by request. Organizations need to make a good-faith effort to obtain a written acknowledgment from patients that they've received the Privacy Notice.

Patients have the general right to access and review their medical records. This includes any health information used for medical care, paying for healthcare, complaints, and other elements of the medical record. There are a few important exceptions to this right:

- Psychotherapy notes
- Information gathered for legal actions
- Lab results specifically restricted by the Clinical Laboratory Improvement Amendments (CLIA)
- Circumstances in which a covered entity believes allowing the patient access to medical records may cause that person to harm themselves or others

Additional patient rights include the right to request corrections to medical records, to get a list of any entities to whom their PHI has been disclosed, and to request restrictions on the disclosure of PHI.

ADDITIONAL CONSIDERATIONS

The Privacy Rule allows patients to designate *personal representatives* who are treated the same as the patient with respect to privacy rights. Parents are considered personal representatives for their minor children unless parental rights have been legally revoked.

The Privacy Rule also addresses *preemption*. States may enact additional privacy protections for PHI that are more stringent than HIPAA, and many states have done so. However, state laws may not preempt HIPAA by creating exceptions or less stringent regulations. HIPAA recognizes that states need to make use of health information in some cases, however, and makes some allowances for states to use PHI without patient consent. For example:

- State requirements to report health information for record-keeping (such as births and deaths)
- States' use of PHI for certain public health purposes, such as reporting vital statistics or enforcing public health regulations
- State requirements to report information about health plans for oversight purposes

HIPAA PRIVACY ENFORCEMENT

The OCR works with covered entities to encourage voluntary HIPAA compliance whenever possible. For example, if an organization is made aware of a violation, it is typically allowed 30 days to make a correction. In this situation, the OCR does not impose a fine as long as the violation wasn't due to willful neglect. If the violations are not corrected through voluntary compliance, the OCR may impose fines. OCR penalties may range from $100 to $50,000 per violation. For repeated violations of the same HIPAA provision, fines may accrue up to a maximum of $1.5 million per year. If an organization violates multiple provisions, fines could be even higher. These penalties may vary based on the seriousness of the violations, the level of negligence of the offender, and any record of previous violations.

An individual who intentionally violates the Privacy Rule by stealing or sharing PHI may also be subject to criminal prosecution by the U.S. Department of Justice (DOJ). Criminal penalties also vary, beginning at a fine of up to $50,000 and up to one year in prison and topping out at fines of up to $250,000 and up to 10 years in prison. The penalties increase if the offense was intended for personal gain or malicious harm. Note that enforcement for a specific violation is handled through either civil penalty or criminal prosecution, not both. If the DOJ handles enforcement via criminal prosecution, the OCR does not impose civil penalties. Some incidents involve multiple violations. For example, the DOJ may prosecute an employee for a criminal violation, whereas the OCR imposes penalties on the covered organization for compliance lapses.

Gramm–Leach–Bliley Act (GLBA)

The Financial Services Modernization Act of 1999 is more commonly known as the Gramm–Leach–Bliley Act (GLBA) after the names of the lead lawmakers who sponsored the legislation. GLBA establishes broad federal regulation to improve information privacy and security within the financial services industry.

Exam Tip

This act may appear on the exam under the name GLBA *or* its official name, the Financial Services Modernization Act of 1999.

GLBA SCOPE

GLBA regulates businesses that offer financial services. Financial services and products may include obvious products like credit cards and bank loans. Less obvious activities include collecting debts, loan servicing, check cashing services, tax services, and higher education institutions that offer student loans. Firms that manage investments for others are also included.

If a business is *significantly engaged* in offering financial services, then it is considered a *financial institution* and is regulated under GLBA. The standard of significant engagement hinges principally on two factors: the formality of offering financial services and the frequency of offering financial services. For example, if a barber occasionally allows a good customer to come back and pay later, then the barber probably does not meet the standard. However, if the barber starts a formal credit program as a regular service, then the barber would be significantly engaged in offering financial services.

GLBA has three sections that have implications for privacy compliance. These are known as the GLBA Privacy Rule, Safeguards Rule, and Red Flags Rule. These rules are enforced by the FTC.

GLBA PRIVACY REQUIREMENTS

The GLBA *Privacy Rule* is intended to protect consumer privacy, both by better informing consumers about how their financial information is used and by regulating the use of consumer information by financial institutions. Financial institutions must share their privacy notices with customers when they first begin a business relationship and provide updated privacy notices every year after.

As with privacy notice requirements under other laws, the GLBA-required notice must describe a financial institution's privacy practices and disclose how customer information is collected, used, and shared. The notice must also inform customers about any third parties who may access their data. The privacy notice must also reference the information security practices in place to protect customer data as described in the GLBA Safeguards Rule (see the next section).

GLBA also recognizes a legal difference between *customers* and *consumers*. Customers have an ongoing regular relationship with a financial institution. For example, an account holder at a bank would be a customer. Consumers, however, may only conduct isolated transactions with a financial institution, such as cashing a check at a bank or visiting a bank's website. For *customers*, financial institutions must provide their full privacy notices with all the details listed in GLBA when the customer relationship begins and then annually thereafter. For *consumers,* the financial institution only needs to provide a summary privacy notice that includes instructions for finding the full notice.

GLBA SAFEGUARDS REQUIREMENTS

The GBLA *Safeguards Rule* provides a framework for financial institutions' obligations for protecting information security. In 2022, the Safeguards Rule was revised to add requirements that account for the increasing impact of technology on business. The rule requires financial institutions to implement written information security programs that are continually updated with the goals of safeguarding customer information security and confidentiality. The requirements for safeguards echo those of other similar laws discussed in this chapter. Financial institutions are required to attempt to anticipate threats as well as risks of any unauthorized information access or disclosure. These organizations must implement appropriate measures to protect against these threats and risks. When considering the risk of unauthorized access, the Safeguards Rule emphasizes protecting against scenarios where the consumer may be harmed as a result.

Under GLBA, information security programs must designate a qualified individual to manage information security, conduct written information security risk assessments, assess and monitor third-party partners to make sure those partners can meet the standards of the financial institution's information security program, and implement staff training. The revised rule also adds additional requirements for implementing information security safeguards, including:

- Conduct a periodic review of access controls.

- Conduct a periodic inventory of data, systems, and personnel.

- Encrypt data in transit and at rest if possible, otherwise implement effective alternatives.

- Assess information systems and applications for information security.

- Implement multifactor authentication (MFA) for systems that house customer data.

- Dispose of customer information within two years unless there's a legitimate business purpose for retention.

- Assess planned changes to information systems and networks for information security.

- Implement logging and monitoring of the activities of authorized users.

All of these safeguards must also be monitored and regularly tested for effectiveness and compliance. Finally, the qualified person in charge of the information security program provides annual written reports to the organization's board of directors.

GLBA also offers guidance on the types of controls financial institutions should consider for lowering their risk. GLBA emphasizes three categories of information security controls: workforce training, securing of information systems, and ongoing monitoring of information systems for problems. As companies consider information risk, GLBA is concerned not only with safeguards that reduce the risk of cyberattacks but also with the risk of data loss or exposure due to failures in information systems or procedures, or human mistakes.

RED FLAGS RULE

The Red Flags Rule adds obligations for financial institutions or any creditor to proactively monitor consumer data for indications of identity theft by watching for "red flags." The rule requires covered institutions to have a written plan for monitoring for these red flags. The rule doesn't specify exactly which factors should be monitored as red flags but does provide guidance to help organizations detect them. The Rule creates five categories of red flags to help organizations develop monitoring procedures. As stated in the Red Flags Rule, these include:

- Alerts, notifications, or other warnings received from consumer reporting agencies or service providers, such as fraud detection services

- The presentation of suspicious documents

- The presentation of suspicious personal identifying information, such as a suspicious address change

- The unusual use of, or other suspicious activity related to, a covered account

- Notice from customers, victims of identity theft, law enforcement authorities, or other persons regarding possible identity theft in connection with covered accounts held by the financial institution or creditor

The Rule also provides a few examples to help businesses understand the sort of suspicious activities in question. For instance, some of these examples include watching for sudden major changes or discrepancies on a consumer's credit report.

In addition to identifying red flags, the rule requires a written plan for protecting consumers from identity theft and must include procedures to "detect, prevent and mitigate identity theft." The rule also requires that these procedures include a process for validating the legitimacy of any consumer changes of home address and to notify consumers if an address in any credit report information is significantly different from the consumer's real address. This helps detect identity fraud.

Scope and Authority of Oversight Agencies

Privacy managers must understand the agencies that regulate their organizations. In the United States, regulatory agencies are typically part of the executive branch of state or federal governments. Other countries employ similar systems for enforcing privacy laws. In the EU, for example, supervisory authority (as mentioned earlier in the section on GDPR) is shared by the European Commission and data protection authorities in each member state. Regulators may also be nongovernmental. For example, voluntary industry self-regulatory systems may employ a regulatory function to ensure member compliance. For example, accreditation processes for private colleges and universities are handled by a system of nongovernmental accreditation authorities.

All regulatory agencies are charged with implementing and enforcing regulations. They often have the authority to conduct investigations and impose penalties for violations. Governmental agencies may also have law enforcement powers that grant them the authority to request search warrants or even make arrests.

Privacy managers must understand which of these agencies have the authority to regulate their organizations' operations. This means understanding the concept of *jurisdiction*. These three types of jurisdictional authority are especially relevant for privacy managers:

- *Territorial jurisdiction* refers to a regulator's authority over operations in a certain geographic area. For example, the Nevada Department of Transportation has territorial jurisdiction within Nevada's state borders.

- *Subject matter jurisdiction* refers to the authority of an agency to regulate a type of activity. For example, the U.S. Securities and Exchange Commission (SEC) has the authority to regulate all investment banks in the United States.

- *Personal jurisdiction* refers to the authority of an agency over individuals or entities. For example, the EU may assert the right to regulate any organization that conducts business in the EU, even if those businesses are not based in EU territory.

With a firm understanding of regulatory agencies and jurisdiction, privacy managers should know which agencies have authority to regulate their organizations, which activities those agencies regulate, and the enforcement powers of each agency. Some key regulatory agencies that affect many U.S. and multinational organizations include the following:

U.S. Federal Trade Commission (FTC)   The FTC broadly regulates private sector businesses in the United States. There are some exceptions; some industries, such as the financial sector and telecom, are regulated by other agencies with subject-matter jurisdiction. The FTC has broad authority to enforce privacy rules under the Federal Trade Commission Act as well as degrees of shared authority with other agencies for rulemaking and enforcement established in additional legislative acts. The FTC can regulate privacy because the FTC Act prohibits *unfair and deceptive acts and practices (UDAP).* *Unfair practices* occur when a business does something unethical or violates regulations or policies in a way that causes harm to consumers. For example, if a company fails to implement required data security and privacy controls and suffers a breach, it may be guilty of unfair practices. *Deceptive practices* occur when an organization misleads consumers about their real business practices in a way that harms the consumer. For example, if a company sells customer PII for profit even though its privacy notice says it would never do such a thing, the company may be guilty of deceptive practices. The FTC has the power to investigate violations and to seek civil penalties against violators.

U.S. Federal Communications Commission (FCC)   The FCC regulates the telecom industry and enforces several federal statutes in the United States related to telecommunications. Most prominently, the FCC enforces the Telecommunications Act of 1996, which includes privacy-focused provisions that impose requirements on telecom carriers for the handling of customer proprietary network information (CPNI). Like the FTC, the FCC has the power to investigate possible violations and seek civil penalties for noncompliance. Notably, the FCC and FTC share enforcement responsibility for some regulations and use the same framework for guarding against unfair and deceptive practices.

EU Data Protection Authorities (DPAs)   In the EU, regulatory authority for GDPR is largely delegated to EU member states. Each EU member state appoints its own *data protection authority* that has territorial jurisdiction under GPDR within that state. DPAs have the authority to investigate suspected violations, order organizations into compliance, suspend data control and/or processing activities, and even levy steep administrative fines as described earlier in the GDPR section of this chapter.

Office of the Privacy Commissioner of Canada (OPC)   Canada's *Office of the Privacy Commissioner* has the regulatory oversight authority for two key privacy laws in Canada. First, the OPC has oversight authority for *Canada's Privacy Act*, which regulates the Canadian federal government's handling of personal information. Second, the OPC has oversight authority for Canada's *Personal Information Protection and Electronic Documents Act (PIPEDA)*, which regulates privacy across the private industry sector in Canada. The OPC has the authority to investigate suspected violations, including the power to call witnesses and order the production of evidence. The OPC does not, however, have the direct power to impose fines or penalties. If the OPC is not able to rectify compliance issues using voluntary means, then it seeks remedies through Canada's federal court system.

Understand Privacy Implications of Doing Business with or Basing Operations in Countries with Inadequate or No Privacy Laws

It can be incredibly tricky for global businesses to offer products and services, especially services that rely on the exchange of personal data, across international boundaries. Countries with robust consumer privacy protections may not allow businesses from countries with less robust privacy protections to operate. In many cases, it may be illegal for a company from one country to process data in another.

In some cases, governments have entered into agreements to make *safe harbor* programs available to organizations in member countries. Safe harbor programs related to international data transfer protect companies from legal penalties for doing business in countries with inadequate data privacy laws, provided that certain standards are met. Safe harbor programs usually specify standards for data protection at a level that satisfies the strictest legal standard of any member country. Organizations often have to seek third-party certification to verify that their privacy programs meet the standard in order to participate in an international safe harbor program.

In the EU, the GDPR represents one of the most robust data privacy regulations in the world. This presents complications for multinational organizations exchanging data to and from the European Union. There are several mechanisms to allow multinational organizations to transfer data in and out of the EU, including:

- **Adequacy decisions.** If another country has data privacy regulations in place on par with the GDPR, then the European Commission may make an *adequacy decision* to allow a business to transfer data between the EU and that country.

- **Binding corporate rules (BCRs).** If a non-EU country does not have adequate data privacy laws, organizations may adopt a set of internal rules and standards that guarantee that personal data will be managed based on the standards set by the GDPR. If approved by the EU, these *binding corporate rules* become contractual obligations for the company and allow data transfers to take place to and from the EU within the conditions set forth by the BCRs. Importantly, all parties to such data transfers must be included in the same BCRs.

- **Standard contractual clauses (SCCs).** For smaller organizations, the EU offers predefined contract language that, if adopted and approved, allows data transfers to and from the EU. These *standard contractual clauses* limit the scope and flexibility of international data transfers and are therefore best suited for smaller business relationships. If an EU company wants to exchange data with a single U.S. subsidiary, for example, they may opt to use SCCs rather than engage in the lengthy and expensive process of setting up customized BCRs.

 As of this writing, the EU has not made an adequacy decision in favor of the United States. In the past, the EU did allow data transfers with the U.S. via the U.S.-EU Privacy Shield program. This program allowed U.S. organizations to seek a certification verifying that they employ privacy protections at a level acceptable to the EU. However, this program was struck down in a 2020 ruling by the Court of Justice of the European Union (CJEU). This ruling, known as *Schrems II*, came in the wake of the revelations by Edward Snowden that revealed the extent of U.S. government surveillance of private individuals. Since the Schrems II ruling, the U.S. and the EU have been working on designing a new framework to facilitate data transfer between the U.S. and the EU. As of March 2022, the U.S. and the EU had reached an "agreement in principle" on the new Transatlantic Data Privacy Framework. This framework would obligate the U.S. to implement regulatory reforms and safeguards to satisfy the privacy standards of the EU. At the moment, this framework is still in development, but it could go into effect in the near future.

APEC Privacy Framework

The Asia-Pacific Economic Cooperation (APEC) was founded in 1989 to help accelerate economic growth among member nations. As of 2021, APEC has 21 member nations, including the United States, Australia, Canada, Indonesia, Japan, South Korea, Mexico, and Russia, among others (see `https://www.apec.org/about-us/about-apec`). APEC aims to promote international trade by reducing barriers and streamlining international cooperation. APEC develops frameworks to help reconcile differing regulatory requirements among member nations so that conflicting regulations do not unintentionally restrict trade.

It may be surprising to note that India is not a current member of APEC, even though India shares a geographic affinity with many APEC members and was the world's fifth-largest economy by GDP in 2020.

Among its many initiatives, APEC manages a privacy framework to allow for data transfer among member nations. The privacy framework was adopted by APEC in 2005 to facilitate collaboration among member nations for digital trade. The framework is not a specific regulation, nor is it a binding agreement of any sort. The framework provides an agreed starting point for bilateral or multilateral trade agreements among APEC members. The APEC privacy framework details nine core principles:

- *Preventing Harm*
- *Notice*
- *Collection Limitation*
- *Uses of Personal Information*
- *Choice*
- *Integrity of Personal Information*
- *Security Safeguards*
- *Access and Correction*
- *Accountability*

The APEC privacy framework shares some features with GDPR. It offers a minimum standard for data privacy protection among its members, defines personal information in a similarly broad fashion, and provides for some similar individual rights, such as the right to expect that personal data will be held securely and to be notified of data collection, usage, and disclosures. But keep in mind that GDPR is a legal statute across all EU member states and enforceable within EU jurisdiction. The APEC privacy framework is not a law, and even when members or companies choose to use the framework, the APEC privacy framework does not overrule domestic legislation in member nations.

To implement the APEC privacy framework consistently and with regulatory oversight, APEC also created a safe harbor program based on the framework. The APEC program is known as the *Cross-Border Privacy Rules (CBPR)* system. Joining the CBPR system is also voluntary for APEC member nations. Member nations must identify a government agency to provide regulatory oversight and enforcement. Member nations must also designate at least one third-party organization to verify compliance for participating businesses.

In the United States, the FTC provides regulatory oversight and TrustArc provides third-party verification of compliance with CBPR. Once a U.S. company earns certification through TrustArc and is approved to participate in the CBPR system, the company is free to conduct digital trade with other APEC members, including transfers of personal data, following the standards outlined by the APEC privacy framework.

The CBPR should at least match the strictest data protection standards of member nations. Nations with stricter privacy standards may choose not to join safe harbor programs that would force them to adopt lower standards. However, nothing in the CBPR explicitly prohibits disclosures of personal data as required by domestic laws in member nations. For example, the CBPR system does not provide legal grounds for a U.S. company to refuse to comply with a duly authorized government order for disclosure.

For nations with strict data privacy laws, safe harbor programs may present potential weaknesses. First, the safe harbor program may hold participants to a lower privacy standard. Second, stricter privacy standards may not be enforceable in all member nations, no matter what the safe harbor program requires. Concerns of this sort played into the EU's decision to strike down the U.S.-EU Privacy Shield program.

Managing a Global Privacy Function

For multinational organizations, it is critical to maintain a privacy program that fulfills the requirements of different privacy regulations around the world. It may not be feasible for a company to maintain unique privacy policies and programs for every jurisdiction in which it operates. Organizations can address this challenge in several ways.

First, basing a privacy program on a commonly recognized global framework, such as the Fair Information Practice Principles, helps to satisfy many privacy requirements around the world. Importantly, many frameworks are not mutually exclusive and may be combined in a single privacy program that is even more universally applicable. Designing aspects of a privacy program framework to satisfy multiple redundant compliance requirements at the same time is also known as *rationalizing* compliance requirements.

Second, organizations may consider seeking certifications or approval to participate in broad international data sharing programs that allow them to do business broadly with member countries and organizations. Examples of such programs include APEC's CBPR framework or a BCR agreement for doing business in the EU under GDPR.

Finally, organizations may want to consider designing privacy programs that comply with the strictest compliance standards to which the organization may be subject. In most cases, a privacy program that meets a strict compliance standard also is satisfactory in jurisdictions with less stringent requirements. For example, a business that wants the ability to operate across the United States may design a privacy program that complies with California's CCPA. A program that meets CCPA requirements is likely to meet the privacy requirements of most U.S. states as well. A company that operates globally may opt to design a program that complies with GDPR for the same reason.

It isn't possible to design a single privacy program that works across all jurisdictions in every case. For example, privacy laws in Europe, the United States, and other nations restrict the disclosure of private information to law enforcement without due legal processes, such as the issuance of an authorized search warrant. In other countries, the law may require the unfettered disclosure of personal information to law enforcement. These conflicts are difficult to resolve because an organization may not be able to comply with the laws of one country without violating the laws of another. In these cases, companies may opt to develop different privacy programs, or even separate divisions of the organization, to respond to the nuances present in different jurisdictions.

Data Sharing Agreements

When conducting business across various jurisdictions, organizations must be mindful of risks related to sharing data with third parties. When that third party operates in another sector or territorial jurisdiction, it may not be subject to the same data privacy requirements. Organizations may be held responsible for privacy violations committed by third parties in such cases.

First and foremost, privacy programs must include activities related to evaluating the privacy practices of any vendor or other third parties prior to agreeing to sharing any private information. This is also referred to as *vetting vendors* or performing *vendor due diligence*. There are several ways to evaluate vendor privacy practices:

- Review the vendor's public privacy notices and any available data management policies. If these aren't online, then they can be requested from the vendor.

- Create a checklist of privacy expectations and ask vendors to describe how they comply with each of the expectations.

- Ask vendors for references from other customers and ask specific privacy-related questions of those references.

- Search public records of enforcement actions as well as news feeds to make sure that a vendor hasn't been party to any high-profile privacy breaches.

- Consider employing a third-party privacy and/or data security consultant that offers vendor evaluation as a service.

Even after an exhaustive *vendor evaluation*, high risk may remain. At best, a vendor evaluation can only describe a vendor's history and current practices. A vendor evaluation can't tell you what a vendor may do in the future. What's to prevent a vendor from immediately abandoning costly privacy practices as soon as they land a big contract?

One primary way to mitigate this risk is by creating *data sharing agreements* before allowing any third parties to access an organization's data. A few examples of data sharing agreements have already been discussed in this chapter. For example, HIPAA-required BAAs are formal data sharing agreements. BCRs and SSCs could also be considered a form of data sharing agreement that allows organizations to engage in data transfers from EU data sharing agreements, however, can and should be employed with any third party regardless of jurisdiction. Even if the third party operates in the same jurisdictional context, that third party may employ a different privacy framework or a lesser set of privacy standards.

Any organization may ask third parties to enter into data sharing agreements that commit the third party to protect data privacy at a specified level. Data sharing agreements typically specify what data may be shared and for what purpose, require the third party to commit to the data privacy standards of the originating organization, and transfer financial and legal liability for any violations to the third party. Many organizations develop standard contractual language that may be appended to any other contract.

Develop Appropriate Metrics

Privacy programs are expansive operations that cover every aspect of an organization and include a huge range of activities. Privacy managers and other executive leaders need to ensure that their programs are achieving the intended outcomes for their organizations. Indeed, most common privacy program frameworks include requirements for assessment program outcomes with clearly defined metrics.

Metrics are used to measure whether a privacy program is achieving expected results. Good metrics are specific, measurable, and well defined. For this reason, metrics are usually numbers. A metric is a standard of performance that allows an organization to set targets. For example, a business may use market share as a metric and set a target to own some specific percentage of market share for some product in five years. Privacy program metrics may look different in different organizations. Privacy program metrics must be selected to respond to the goals of the organization, compliance obligations, specific risks, the chosen privacy framework, and other operational realities.

Finally, it is important to develop a targeted set of baseline metrics while developing and implementing the privacy program framework. If metrics are properly aligned with program goals, then the metrics will help those responsible keep the program on track. Importantly, metrics should not become goals in themselves. Instead, metrics should help to assess progress toward program goals. Metrics should be carefully selected to make sure they are indicators of progress toward the specific goals of the organization. Measuring performance against predefined metrics also brings more objectivity to the process of assessing the program. If metrics are not predetermined, then it becomes all too easy to cherry-pick privacy program data down the road.

Reporting Resources and Collection Points

As metrics are developed, the privacy program should also identify how the data for evaluation metrics will be reported and from what source. For example, if an organization chooses to use the number of privacy incidents per year as a metric, it is important to define what constitutes a privacy incident, where those incidents are recorded, and how the total number of incidents will be reported each year. It is important to define these *reporting resources* for metrics in advance.

Collection points are defined processes for collecting the data that will be used for metrics. For example, the privacy manager may produce an incident report after each incident and file those reports in a document management system. That document management system serves as a collection point for information on the number of incidents reported each year. Similarly, an HR training system may help to record compliance with a metric related to employee privacy program awareness education. Defining the reporting resources and collection points in advance helps ensure that data about the privacy program is collected in the first place and speeds the collection of the data when the time comes to report on privacy program performance.

Identify Intended Audience for Metrics

A good place to start in the development of metrics is by identifying appropriate audiences. For example, the chief information officer (CIO) may need to monitor the performance of technical security controls, whereas the chief financial officer may be concerned with monitoring for audit performance. Relevant audiences often include:

- Board of directors
- Executive leadership (C-suite, department heads)
- Employees
- Regulatory authorities and/or auditors
- Investors

Each of these audiences may need access to different metrics to make decisions related to the organization's privacy program. For example, employees may use metrics to ensure that they fulfill privacy program requirements that apply to them, such as a metric related to responding to privacy-related customer requests. Auditors may need to look at metrics in general to confirm that the privacy program is adequately assessed.

A given metric may be more applicable for some audiences than others. For example, the CIO may require detailed analyses of all privacy incidents and breaches, whereas the CEO may only need to know how many incidents occurred at a high level. It is important to identify which audiences are primary audiences for a given metric, which are secondary, and which are tertiary. In general, *primary audiences* have direct responsibility for relevant activities in the privacy program and/or for achieving privacy performance targets. Secondary audiences may be more concerned with broader strategy and use privacy metrics to inform other aspects of the business. *Tertiary audiences* may not have any direct operational involvement, but the organization benefits by keeping them informed. Communication and reporting may then be adjusted accordingly for each metric by audience.

Define Privacy Metrics for Oversight and Governance per Audience

Once audiences for reporting metrics have been defined, the privacy program should identify metrics that respond to the needs of each audience. Some metrics address compliance with the privacy program itself and/or specific regulations. Compliance metrics are likely to appeal to privacy managers, functional managers with privacy responsibilities, and those involved in program assessment and assurance, like auditors and regulators. Business oriented metrics, such as measuring the program's return on investment or resource utilization, may be more useful to the organization's executives and/or board of directors.

Compliance Metrics

Metrics that help an organization evaluate compliance typically draw on functional areas detailed in the privacy framework. Compliance metrics measure the outcomes that the privacy program is designed to address. Examples of metrics will vary depending on an organization's needs. Organizations often identify a metric and then set specific performance standards, or targets, for each metric (Table 2.1).

TABLE 2.1   Metric examples

Metric category	Performance standard examples
Collection (notice)	Make privacy notices disclosing data collection practices publicly available on 100% of customer-accessible web pages.
Responses to data subject inquiries	Respond to 100% of data subject inquiries within X days.
Data management	100% of data purged as required by the data retention schedule by the end of every fiscal year.
Data privacy incidents	The total number of data privacy incidents reduces by X percent per year.
Training and awareness	100% of employees complete introductory data privacy awareness program each year.
PIA/DPIA	DPIAs are completed in advance of implementing new technologies for data processing 100% of the time.
Privacy risk	Achieve an annual internal data privacy audit score of X.

Some privacy program frameworks provide additional guidance on developing metrics. NIST, for example, provides the Performance Measurement Guide for Information Security. While this document refers to the NIST Cybersecurity Framework (not the Privacy Framework), it still may serve as a useful guide for the development of metrics. The document is available here:

```
https://csrc.nist.gov/publications/detail/sp/800-55/
rev-2/draft
```

Trend Analysis

Trend analysis is useful in demonstrating the relationship between two or more variables to understand whether a given area is improving, holding steady, or worsening. Trend analysis commonly includes tracking some outcomes over time. For example, tracking the number of privacy incidents over time is a quick and easily visualized way to assess the efficacy of a privacy program at a glance. Trend analysis also allows organizations to set metrics as ratios or rates of improvement, rather than only as absolute numbers.

For example, an absolute measurement related to data privacy incidents may reveal that the organization had 413 privacy breaches last year. It is difficult to tell if that is good or bad without some standard of comparison. For example, a trend analysis might instead show that the organization had 413 breaches, which represents an average reduction of 22 percent per year in the five years since the privacy program was implemented.

Trend analysis can also do more than track outcomes over time. It can track an outcome for a business relative to an industry standard, privacy costs versus the average costs of breaches, and privacy incidents by division of the company or per IT system. While it is possible to get quite creative and sophisticated in trend analysis, it is often advisable to stick with simpler metrics that are used consistently year after year to improve outcomes.

Privacy Program Return on Investment (ROI)

Well-managed privacy programs add immense business value. Some of this value is difficult to quantify. An organization that develops a strong reputation for protecting privacy is likely to earn long-term trust and loyalty from customers, vendors, partners, and employees. By design, privacy programs also organize and manage an organization's critical data. In today's digital world, defining business processes for managing an organization's data often creates opportunities to manage core business processes more effectively and helps reduce costs across the enterprise. *Return on investment (ROI)* is a metric that looks at the costs of implementing privacy protections as an investment to avoid the costs of potential privacy incidents. There are a few different methods for calculating the potential costs of incidents. Common calculations categorize privacy risks and calculate a value for each risk. Such calculations typically factor in the prevalence of incidents related to a specific risk, the likelihood that such an incident will occur at an organization, and the cost of incidents when they occur. Once risks are assigned a value, that value may be weighed against the cost of lowering those risks.

The costs of *not* having a robust privacy program in place, however, are often far more visible than the benefits. Privacy breaches can be very costly. When breaches occur, companies must consider the cost of disrupted operations, lost sales, recovery of data and systems, possible penalties for noncompliance, cost of identity protection for the victims of privacy breaches, legal costs, and lawsuits. Privacy managers can help bring these costs into focus by reviewing reports from the regulators that oversee privacy regulations for their organization's operations. For example, U.S. regulators typically publish annual reports detailing breaches reported in that year as well as any penalties imposed.

Finally, information has value. Sometimes, personal information even has identifiable market value. For example, many prominent social media companies earn revenue by selling user information to data brokers and advertisers. In this case, the market value of personal information can be explicitly quantified. In other cases, businesses may have a defined amount of revenue associated with every customer in their database. This may be true of a subscription-based business, where every customer represents a regular revenue stream. If monetary value can be assigned to the information an organization holds, then it is easier to weigh that value against the cost of protecting it.

Business Resiliency Metrics

Business resiliency, also referred to as business continuity, refers to the capabilities of an organization to continue operations throughout adverse events. In many cases, business resiliency includes disaster recovery capabilities as well. When it comes to privacy, resiliency metrics help measure an organization's ability to continue operations in spite of privacy incidents. Resiliency relies on the organization's readiness to respond to disasters and continue operations, so appropriate metrics in this area may include the following:

- Incident response drills conducted
- Documented data recovery procedures
- Penetration testing
- Drills conducted to test data recovery capabilities
- Reviews of preplanned disaster-related communication strategies

Privacy Program Maturity Level

Organizations may also measure the capabilities of the privacy program itself. A capability maturity model is a framework for assigning levels of maturity to functional areas within a program. Maturity levels are not meant to grade a program's performance on a scale that goes from bad to good. Instead, maturity models measure the development of a program functional area on a scale more akin to "beginner to expert." Maturity models don't assume that every function has to operate at the highest level, but rather give an organization the ability to determine which functions need to operate at which level to meet program objectives. Like most useful metrics, maturity models tend to assign a number to each level of maturity, ascending from low (level 1) up to the highest level of maturity in the model. Most models have only four or five levels of maturity.

As discussed earlier in this chapter, the NIST Privacy Framework implementation tiers serve as a four-level model. While NIST does not identify these tiers as a capability maturity model, the tiers align with many maturity models and may certainly be used by organizations to set maturity level targets.

The American Institute of Certified Public Accountants (AICPA) has also developed a privacy maturity model to align with a privacy program that implements GAPP principles (discussed in Chapter 1). The AICPA maturity model includes five levels:

Ad Hoc   Procedures and processes are generally informal, incomplete, and inconsistently applied.

Repeatable   Procedures or processes exist; however, they are not fully documented and do not cover all relevant aspects.

Defined   Procedures and processes are fully documented and implemented and cover all relevant aspects.

Managed   Reviews are conducted to assess the effectiveness of the controls in place.

Optimized   Regular review and feedback are used to ensure continuous improvement toward optimization of the given process.

There are many other examples of capability maturity models that may be employed as metrics for measuring data privacy programs. In selecting a maturity model, privacy managers should ensure that the model they select supports organizational alignment, the chosen privacy framework, and any specific compliance requirements. For example, a company may already use an established capability maturity model in other parts of the business, so it may be advisable to use the same model to establish metrics for the privacy program. If the organization has adopted a set of standards, such as NIST or GAPP, then it may be better to adopt the NIST implementation tiers or the AICPA maturity model.

Resource Utilization

Resource utilization metrics may be of greatest interest to CFOs and CIOs. To measure ROI, it is important to also understand the resources the privacy program consumes. These include human resources, such as privacy professionals, and hours devoted across the organization to privacy protection. Resources may also include technology systems that implement privacy controls, training time and expense, space and equipment for employees, and third-party services, such as legal counsel.

Summary

Privacy program frameworks are a key blueprint for developing a comprehensive privacy program. For this reason, an organization must select and/or design a privacy framework that meets its needs. Privacy frameworks account for all aspects of an organization's operations, align with organizational strategy and objectives, and cover compliance needs for all applicable laws and regulations.

Once the privacy framework is selected, privacy managers can use the framework to develop and implement a privacy program that meets all the organization's needs. No matter what privacy framework is implemented, the resulting privacy program should include capabilities for employee education and training, compliance with ever-evolving regulations, ensuring internal compliance, assessing privacy risks, responding to incidents, implementing remediations, and handling complaints.

In implementing a framework and the resulting privacy program, privacy managers must communicate the framework and its requirements clearly across their organizations. Privacy professionals must also take care to be sure the framework monitors and adapts to applicable regulations across all relevant jurisdictions, even as those regulations continue to change after the framework is implemented.

Finally, the privacy framework must include the development of appropriate metrics to measure outcomes. Metrics should be tailored for the needs of specific audiences, such as executives, employees, auditors, and regulators. Metrics may take the form of records of compliance activities, such as tracking privacy incidents, or measure business outcomes, such as return on investment.

Exam Essentials

Know the elements of prominent privacy frameworks.   Aspiring privacy managers do not need to memorize the details of the various privacy frameworks. However, it will be helpful to be familiar with the prominent privacy frameworks identified in this chapter. It is important to understand the differences between the privacy frameworks and to be able to identify the key principles of each framework.

Understand why a privacy framework is important.   Understand the reasons organizations should invest in designing a privacy framework before implementing privacy program activities. For example, privacy frameworks serve as a blueprint to ensure that the resulting privacy program responds comprehensively to the needs of the organization. A well-designed privacy framework will address an organization's strategic goals and compliance needs and mitigate privacy risks.

Understand the applicable regulations.   Privacy managers need to know which prominent regulations may impose compliance obligations on their organizations as they implement privacy frameworks. Regulations such as HIPAA, GLBA, GDPR, and the CCPA are important to understand because they apply to a great number of global enterprises.

Explain regulatory authority and jurisdiction.   Privacy managers need to know how laws and regulations are enforced, by which agencies, and the penalties that may be applied for noncompliance. Understanding regulatory authority and scope also requires an understanding of the various forms and limitations of jurisdiction.

Identify appropriate metrics.   To successfully implement and manage privacy program frameworks, it is important to identify metrics for success in advance. By embedding metrics in the privacy program from the outset, privacy managers can ensure that employees know what is expected of a successful program, support decision-making about the privacy program, and manage the collection of the data needed to report on program metrics.

Review Questions

1. The EU's GDPR is most equivalent to which U.S. federal law?

    A. The FTC Act

    B. HIPAA

    C. None

    D. GLBA

2. Which of the following is *not* one of the nine principles of the APEC framework?

    A. Notice

    B. Integrity of personal information

    C. Security safeguards

    D. Right to rectification

3. Marcia is the privacy program manager at a large company. She implemented a new privacy program one year ago and now, a year in, she is concerned that the program is not going well because not all employees have completed the required training. Marcia attends a meeting of company executives to ask for more funding for the program to support the training program. The CFO objects, reasoning that the privacy program is going just fine because the company did well on its last audit. The CEO isn't sure, so she sends Marcia back to develop a report on how many privacy-related customer complaints they've had before she decides to allocate new funding. What most likely went wrong here?

    A. Marcia failed to secure proper executive sponsorship for her program in the first place.

    B. Marcia neglected to define specific metrics for the program at the beginning.

    C. The privacy program was not properly aligned with business strategy and objectives.

    D. Marcia does not have adequate procedures in place for monitoring internal compliance.

4. Marcia is the privacy program manager at a large company. She implemented a new privacy program one year ago and now, a year in, she is concerned that the program is not going well because not all employees have completed the required training. Marcia attends a meeting of company executives to ask for more funding for the program to support the training program. The CFO objects, reasoning that the privacy program is going just fine because the company did well on its last audit. The CEO isn't sure, so she sends Marcia back to develop a report on how many privacy-related customer complaints they've had before she decides to allocate new funding. A week later, Marcia returns with the report that the CEO requested, but the CFO still isn't convinced that training is worth the cost. "I know not everyone has been through the training," reasons the CFO, "but adding more training programs is prohibitively expensive. I just don't think it's worth it." What metric might Marcia use to address the CFO's concern?

    A. ROI

    B. Business resiliency

    C. Trend analysis

    D. Resource utilization

5. Geoff is helping a small data analytics startup company based in the United States expand their business by offering analytics services for companies in the EU. Which of the following routes is Geoff most likely to recommend to allow data transfers from EU companies to the startup?

   A. U.S. Privacy Shield

   B. Standard contractual clauses

   C. Binding corporate rules

   D. APEC

6. When defining a privacy program framework, it is important to map out how information moves around internally so that data can be tracked. Which term best describes this activity?

   A. Data classification

   B. Data flow mapping

   C. Data inventory

   D. Access control

7. Aidan is a new privacy manager struggling to implement a privacy program at a beloved small-town retail shop called Middleburg Threads. Aidan has implemented an initial privacy program framework and completed the initial risk assessment. He found that privacy policies weren't written down anywhere, the computers in the back office aren't password protected, and perhaps most concerning of all, the company has outsourced online sales, including credit card processing, to another small local business. There doesn't seem to be any sort of formal contract in place. Which of the following might be the best place for Aidan to start?

   A. Implement information security controls.

   B. Immediately implement privacy awareness education for employees at the store.

   C. Develop a formal contract that includes the PCI DSS framework.

   D. Develop an incident response procedure because of the high risk.

8. Annie is a CEO at a rapidly growing company. Currently, the company only does business in the United States, but Annie dreams of expanding across North America. Annie also wants customer privacy to be the hallmark of her company's reputation, so she wants to do more to protect privacy than the minimum required for compliance. Annie is considering privacy program frameworks, and she is trying to choose between adopting a FIPPs-based approach and a PbD approach. How would you advise Annie and why?

   A. Select FIPPs because it is required by the U.S. Privacy Act.

   B. Select PbD because it emphasizes respect for personal privacy beyond compliance.

   C. Select FIPPs because it offers the most robust personal privacy protections.

   D. Select PbD because it is required in Canada.

9. Ahmad had just been hired to run the information privacy program at Accounting Unlimited, a large corporate bookkeeping and accounting firm. Ahmad starts by assessing the current privacy program. He is pleased to note that Accounting Unlimited employs robust privacy practices. Employees follow good processes and maintain privacy controls in most (but not all) areas. However, when he asks for the documentation on all the privacy procedures, he gets a patchwork of documents from different departments. Some of the documents are out of date and some are missing. How might Ahmad classify this privacy program's maturity level?

   A. Ad hoc

   B. Repeatable

   C. Adequate

   D. Defined

10. Jorge has finished implementing a NIST-based privacy framework for his employer. The executive team at Jorge's company realize they cannot focus on every single activity in the large privacy program, so they want to pick out a few important privacy activities to monitor closely and improve. Which part of the NIST framework might help with this?

   A. NIST Core

   B. Privacy Maturity Model (PMM)

   C. Profiles

   D. Implementation tiers

11. Melinda is an experienced pediatrician, and she has finally taken the leap to open her own clinic. She prides herself on her commitment to focusing only on her patients, so she wants to outsource some of her administrative functions, such as billing and scheduling. What does Melinda need to include in the contract when she hires a vendor for these functions?

   A. A data sharing agreement

   B. BCRs

   C. BAA

   D. Vendor evaluation

12. Pierre is working on implementing a privacy program based on the NIST privacy framework. He is concerned with making sure that the program includes robust identity management. On which function of the NIST framework should Pierre focus?

   A. Protect

   B. Control

   C. Govern

   D. Identify

13. Eduardo is a privacy program manager for Surfside Rentals, a small chain of stores in California that rent out surfing equipment. While Surfside Rentals has been in business for years, the company has recently decided to start offering a credit card program. Customers who sign up for the new credit card earn "juice points" that count toward free rentals for every dollar spent. Eduardo carefully monitors for any changes in privacy compliance requirements for the company. Given Surfside Rental's recent business moves, which new type of jurisdictional category should Eduardo worry about?

    A. Personal jurisdiction

    B. Territorial jurisdiction

    C. Subject-matter jurisdiction

    D. Federal jurisdiction

14. Dimitri cashed a paycheck at County Bank three months ago, but he doesn't have an account there and hasn't been back since. Under GLBA, County Bank should consider Dimitri as which of the following?

    A. Customer

    B. Consumer

    C. Visitor

    D. No relationship with the bank

15. Jennifer is an IT manager and has spent the last five years implementing privacy controls on IT systems that she hopes will reduce privacy incidents over time. Which type of metric will be most helpful to Jennifer?

    A. ROI

    B. Business resiliency

    C. Resource utilization

    D. Trend analysis

16. Which of the following would be the least useful as a privacy program metric?

    A. Number of PIAs completed

    B. Overall privacy program expenditures

    C. Quality of the incident response program

    D. Tabletop drills completed

17. BlindDateDublin.com, an Irish dating website, was found responsible for repeatedly and purposely violating multiple provisions of the GDPR. The resulting privacy violations caused some people in the EU to lose their jobs and exposed others to social stigmas and other harms. What is the largest penalty BlindDateDublin.com might face?

    A. €30,000,000

    B. €20,000,000 or 4% of annual revenue, whatever is greater

    C. 8% of annual revenue

    D. €10,000,000

18. Which of the following is not a benefit of performing privacy impact assessments?

   A. Make risk-informed business decisions.

   B. Fulfill GDPR requirements.

   C. Calculate potential compliance costs.

   D. Evaluate the impact of privacy breaches after they occur.

19. Nadya runs a small local bakery in Trenton, New Jersey. Her peanut butter cookies are so popular that she has received hundreds of requests to ship boxes of her cookies nationwide. Since Nadya does not have time to run her bakery and an online ordering process, she plans to contract with eSales, Inc., to manage a website, online orders, payments, and shipping. Nadya values the trust and loyalty of her customers and wants to be sure their privacy is protected. She has looked into eSales, Inc.'s privacy notices and asked them about their privacy practices in detail. From all she can tell, Nadya is satisfied with eSales, Inc.'s commitment to privacy, but she knows that eSales is growing rapidly and might be spreading itself pretty thin. What else could Nadya do to protect the privacy of her online customers?

   A. Ask eSales, Inc. to sign a data privacy agreement.

   B. Switch to a more stable vendor that will have time to pay adequate attention to the needs of small business.

   C. Hire a privacy program manager for the bakery charged with monitoring vendors, such as eSales, Inc.

   D. Nadya has already performed adequate due diligence and should be assured that eSales, Inc. will protect her customers' privacy well.

20. BizCorp has defined GLBA audit performance as a privacy program metric. Which of the following is most likely a secondary audience for this metric?

   A. CIO

   B. CFO

   C. Privacy program manager

   D. Investors

Chapter

3

Privacy Operational Life Cycle: Assess

THE CIPM EXAM OBJECTIVES COVERED IN THIS CHAPTER INCLUDE:

✓ **Domain III. Privacy Operational Life Cycle: Assess**

- III.A. Document current baseline of your privacy program

    - III.A.a Education and awareness

    - III.A.b Monitoring and responding to the regulatory environment

    - III.A.c Assess policy compliance against internal and external requirements

    - III.A.d Data, systems, and process assessment

    - III.A.e Risk assessment methods

    - III.A.f Incident management, response, and remediation

    - III.A.g Determine desired state and perform gap analysis against an accepted standard or law (including GDPR)

    - III.A.h Program assurance, including audits

- III.B. Processors and third-party vendor assessment

    - III.B.a Evaluate processors and third-party vendors, insourcing and outsourcing privacy risks, including rules of international data transfer

    - III.B.b Understand and leverage the different types of relationships

    - III.B.c Risk assessment

    - III.B.d Contractual requirements and review process

    - III.B.e Ongoing monitoring and auditing

- III.C. Physical assessments

    - III.C.a Identify operational risk

A common feature of most privacy program frameworks is that they seek to enable continual improvement. Privacy programs must be dynamic to respond to changing organizational structures, employees, business strategies, technologies, regulations, and privacy threats. Of course, privacy managers must measure how well their programs do in achieving the stated goals. But they must also measure the effectiveness and relevance of the goals themselves. The metrics set as a part of the program framework (discussed in Chapter 2, "Privacy Program Framework") tell the privacy manager what to measure. Assessment is the act of measuring. In conducting a program assessment, it is important to consider all the activities of an organization that might have an impact on data privacy. This includes the core management of data privacy within the organization, data sharing with any third parties, physical privacy, mergers, acquisitions, and divestitures, as well as documented methods for performing privacy risk assessments.

Document Your Privacy Program Baseline

Assessments are about comparing reality with some desired state. Sometimes, the desired state is to maintain the current level of achievement. Sometimes the aim is to improve in a certain area. Sometimes the desire is merely to monitor how much some outcome varies over time. In the world of marathons, runners sometimes assess their races by trying to achieve a personal best time, or "PB." In attempting to achieve a PB, runners must have some sort of time to beat, which is usually their previous PB. This is their baseline.

Privacy managers must also establish baselines across their programs in order to determine the success of their programs. For example, if a program metric measures a reduction in privacy-related incidents in a year, the privacy manager must know how many incidents occurred last year to do the math. It is important to start with a well-defined baseline of privacy program activities to have something to set performance targets and measure progress. The baseline assessment should respond to the established metrics and cover all important areas of the privacy program. These include education and awareness, monitoring the regulatory environment, policy compliance, data management, risk assessment methods, incident management, compliance risk, and program assurance.

Education and Awareness

Education, awareness, and training programs for employees are a key pillar of all comprehensive privacy program frameworks. Mature privacy programs usually offer many different levels of employee training. At the most basic level, all employees with any exposure to protected information should be expected to regularly complete a basic *privacy awareness education* program. Awareness education ensures that employees are familiar with privacy concepts, risks, policies, and procedures in place at the organization.

More advanced employee education options often involve *role-based training.* Role-based training is designed to equip employees to perform specific functions within the privacy program. For example, there may be specific role-based training for managers to teach them how to assess privacy program compliance in their departments, for IT staff responsible for maintaining technical privacy and security controls, for HR staff responsible for maintaining and tracking employee privacy training programs, and more. Privacy programs should document the key roles and responsibilities required to run the program, and each role should have adequate and up-to-date training.

Monitoring and Responding to the Regulatory Environment

Chapter 2, "Privacy Program Framework," discussed several ways in which privacy programs may design activities to monitor and respond to the regulatory environment. These processes enable an organization to respond to changes in regulation as well as changes in the organization that might be in the scope of new regulations. When developing a privacy program baseline, organizations should have documented procedures for monitoring the regulatory environment and records that such monitoring has taken place as expected.

Assess Policy Compliance against Internal and External Requirements

A privacy program may be well documented in every way, but the program only protects private information if employees actually comply with program requirements. For this reason, it is often helpful to talk to employees, look for records of program activities, and assess changes and improvements made in response to metrics, assessments, and program assurance. For example, do all employees complete the required privacy awareness education program each year? Where are those records? How is compliance verified?

It is also helpful to inspect systems that store and process data where possible. Such systems may be physical or digital. In a retail business, for example, are credit card receipts left out in plain view of other customers? Do all the point-of-sale computers have strong, unique passwords? Do company databases that store private information have the appropriate data protection controls in place, such as encryption?

It is also important to verify compliance with external regulations. If the organization is subject to GDPR or any similar regulation, then it is important to check for controls that ensure data subject rights are protected, DPIAs have been performed as required, and the other requirements of GDPR are met and monitored.

Data, Systems, and Process Assessment

Any baseline assessment of a privacy program must include a close-up analysis of how data is managed at the organization. Before analyzing data, systems, and data life cycles in detail, it is important to understand key requirements for data management that are detailed in the privacy program framework for the organization. For example, many frameworks include procedures for data minimization, to ensure that data are only collected, processed, shared, and stored as needed. Records management policies are another key control that should outline how long data should be stored and when data must be purged. With this understanding, it is possible to assess how well an organization's data management processes meet the requirements.

Map Data Inventories, Flows, Life Cycle, and System Integrations

Data Lifecycle Management (DLM) is a framework for managing data as it moves throughout an organization. A DLM strategy has three primary goals: data security and confidentiality, data integrity, and data availability. DLM divides the data life cycle into five stages. The names of these five stages vary a bit between organizations, but generally include the following:

Data Collection, Acquisition, or Creation   Data may be collected from customers, manually entered, acquired through automation (such as website tracking data), acquired in large data sets, or created within the organization itself. It is far easier to track all data from the point of origination than to track down rogue data sets after the fact. Tracking data from the point of collection also allows the organization to monitor compliance with its own policies and any regulations related to data collection.

Data Storage, Organization, and Backup/Recovery   Almost by definition, data is stored someplace as soon as it is collected. During the data storage stage of DLM, data should be stored so that it is appropriately protected to meet the security and confidentiality goal of DLM. This means that data is usually organized for storage based on the organization's data classification policy so that relevant controls may be applied based on the data classification. Backup and recovery methods must be implemented to ensure data availability as well.

Data Usage, Sharing, and Processing   Once stored, the data may be used by the organization to conduct business. Data must be used in compliance with policies and laws, which usually means that a series of controls are in place to manage access, ensure that data is used only for authorized purposes, privacy training and awareness are in place, and data usage is documented for program assurance and audit. Any exceptions to how data is allowed to be used or shared must also be documented.

Data Archiving   When data is no longer in active use, it must be stored securely in accordance with the organization's records management policy. It is a good idea to store inactive data in specialized archival systems so that out-of-date or inactive data doesn't show up alongside data in active usage and cause confusion. Archival storage solutions also may be made more secure because fewer people need access, and they save costs because the data doesn't often require processing. Of course, archived data may need to be restored to active storage if necessary.

Data Destruction   Data should be purged when it is no longer needed and there is no requirement to save it. All data held by an organization represents a potential privacy risk. Minimizing the data a company holds is one of the surest ways to reduce this risk. Sometimes, data can be destroyed at the point of collection. For example, tools that automatically collect website data can strip out any identifying information, such as customer IP addresses, before relaying the data for storage. Sometimes, data must be retained in archival form for a set amount of time before it can be destroyed.

Importantly, DLM frameworks are not rigid or sequential. Data may exist in multiple phases simultaneously and/or move back and forth among phases. A DLM approach is useful for privacy managers to document existing practices and procedures that are specific to each stage in the data life cycle. These baselines will enable the privacy manager to identify and remediate risks for each stage, design metrics, and set appropriate performance targets.

Risk Assessment Methods

There are various methods for conducting privacy risk assessments. Some of the most common and formalized methods for conducting privacy risk assessments are discussed later in this chapter. These include:

- Privacy threshold analysis (PTA)
- Privacy impact analysis (PIA)
- Data protection impact analysis (DPIA)
- Legitimate interest analysis (LIA)
- Transfer impact analysis (TIA)

In addition to these tools for conducting focused risk assessments, organizations should conduct their own comprehensive data privacy risk assessments across their operations. Such assessments analyze the categories and quantity of data managed by the organization, measure the effectiveness of the data privacy protections in place, and identify specific risks. Based on those risks, an assessment can quantify the likelihood of an incident, the possible severity of an incident, and the potential costs of any incidents. There are several methods organizations may use to assess the likelihood and severity of an incident related to a given area of risk. For example, it is possible to assign a simple 1, 2, or 3 to score the likelihood and severity.

Incident Management, Response, and Remediation

Incident response procedures should be in place as required by the privacy program framework and satisfy any applicable compliance obligations. For example, many regulations include requirements to notify individuals if their private information is exposed as part of an incident. Incident management procedures should be fully documented and include roles and responsibilities, training and drills, and ongoing assessment of the incident response function itself.

Perform Gap Analysis against an Accepted Standard or Law

After conducting a baseline privacy program assessment, the organization has solid foundational knowledge of its privacy program. This baseline may then be compared against a desired state. The desired state for the privacy program must include, at a minimum, compliance with applicable regulations, such as GDPR. The desired state may also include reaching higher levels of program maturity, improved performance against predetermined metrics, or any combination of objectives. The key is that a well-understood baseline is the starting place for any improvement plan.

A gap analysis determines the difference between the baseline and the desired state for any given area of privacy protection. Capability maturity models, described in Chapter 2, help identify standards for improvement over time.

Program Assurance

Program reviews are tools that help ensure that the privacy program is functioning as it should. When assessing a privacy program, it is important to check for records of regular program reviews. Reviews may be conducted in several ways. They may be formal or informal, internal or external; involve part or all of the privacy program; and be conducted proactively or in response to an incident.

Program assurance reviews usually involve examining policies and procedures to ensure they are complete, updated, and respond to compliance obligations. Reviews also look for evidence that policies and procedures are followed appropriately and completely. For example, a person conducting a review may want to see documentation tracking how many employees have completed privacy awareness education, how often privacy awareness education is offered, and procedures for training new employees during onboarding.

An organization should have evidence that program reviews are conducted as part of the privacy program's standard operating procedures. Informal privacy program reviews should be conducted by privacy and functional managers on an ongoing basis. Informal reviews may take many forms, but they should be documented for program assurance, often by including a review date on the policy or program documentation.

Organizations should also use program *audits* to conduct more formal reviews. Audits are reviews conducted by designated individuals or teams that more formally measure a privacy program's performance. Audits compare program activities with an established framework for compliance, such as a set of legal requirements or an organization's internal standards. Audits should be conducted on a regular schedule as well as in response to privacy or security incidents. Remember that audits will require evidence that program activities are being conducted per the policy and procedures.

Many organizations have an *internal audit* function established as part of their compliance operations. An internal audit team is usually not part of the functional area being reviewed and can provide more objective assessments. Internal audits are used to measure how effectively employees implement and adhere to policies, procedures, and controls for privacy. Internal audits are a management tool to help an organization monitor internal compliance and improve privacy protection.

External audits are usually conducted by third-party companies and provide the highest level of objectivity. Some regulations, such as GLBA, require regular external compliance audits. External audits are typically used to provide program assurance to external share holders, such as legal regulators, shareholders, or industry self-regulatory entities. Often, external audits are used to certify compliance with a given standard, such as the requirements for a safe harbor program.

Organizations should maintain updated policies and procedures for conducting audits and other informal program assurance reviews. There should be evidence that audits and reviews have been conducted, as required, in the form of audit or review final reports, recommendations, or documented findings. Finally, there should be evidence that an organization considers findings from program assurance activities and implements changes to address any identified gaps.

Processors and Third-Party Vendor Assessment

No organization should ever trust a third party with its data before a thorough vetting process. Before trusting a third party with an organization's data, it is critical to perform a detailed evaluation of the third party's privacy program and identify any risks. Third parties are often vendors that provide data processing services, so this evaluation process is often referred to as vendor vetting, vendor evaluation, vendor risk assessment, vendor due diligence, or some similar variation. It is important to note that data sharing may also occur with third parties who are not explicitly vendors. In fact, there is even risk associated with a vendor who uses other vendors for data processing. This is known as fourth-party vendor risk.

Organizations may share data with nonprofit professional organizations. Healthcare providers may share data with medical researchers; schools may compare academic outcomes. In many of these examples, there may not be an explicit contractual relationship with a vendor, so any assessment must also look for evidence of privacy risk evaluation with non-vendor third parties.

Evaluate Processors and Third-Party Vendors

Third-party privacy risk assessments often take the form of questionnaires that ask vendors to describe aspects of their privacy programs. As mentioned in Chapter 2, these assessments may also include checking business references and public records to assess a third party's privacy track record. All such evaluations should be well documented, so an assessment of a privacy program should be able to find evidence of such an evaluation for any active third-party data sharing arrangement. If a vendor is unwilling to share the information required for vetting, then it may be helpful to offer to sign a mutual nondisclosure agreement (NDA). If a vendor is still unwilling or unable to share the information, then data sharing with that vendor is much riskier. The following are common aspects of a privacy program you need to evaluate:

Privacy and Information Security Policies In addition to reviewing any public privacy notices, privacy managers often ask vendors for copies of their internal privacy and information security policies to review. At a bare minimum, a vendor documentation should document the presence or lack of a privacy policy and whether it was made available for review. A vendor may not be subject to the same regulations or privacy risks, so it is important to perform a gap analysis to ensure that a vendor privacy policy responds to all the regulatory obligations of the primary organization.

Access Controls A vendor evaluation should document the access control procedures of the third party, by asking the third party to either describe their access controls or supply a copy of their documented access control procedures. There should also be evidence that the access control procedures are reviewed or audited regularly and in compliance with applicable regulations.

Where Personal Information Is Being Held An organization must understand precisely how and where any potential third-party partner stores private information. If, for example, a vendor stores information on servers in another country, then engaging that vendor may trigger additional compliance obligations or present new privacy risks.

Based on the vendor evaluation, an organization may review any identified risks and impose requirements on the vendor to help mitigate those risks. It is critical to set limits that restrict how vendors use, store, process, and share private information to minimize risk. These requirements may be included in the agreements or contracts as discussed later in this chapter. An organization may also opt to minimize and/or deidentify the data it shares in the first place if possible.

Understand Sources of Information

In evaluating potential third-party data sharing partners, information may come from a variety of sources. These sources may be individuals, programs, or organizations that may be able to furnish valuable information for assessing vendor risk.

Internal Audit   Many organizations have an internal audit function as discussed in the "Program Assurance" section earlier in this chapter. Internal audits typically produce reports that identify strengths and weaknesses and offer recommendations for improvement.

Information and Physical Security   An organization's information and physical security programs should complement the privacy program and include a program framework, education, incident response, compliance, controls, program assurance, and other activities that function similarly to those described in a privacy program. Just as with privacy, information security programs should be assessed regularly and the resulting reports should be available.

Data Protection Authority   If the organization operates within the scope of GDPR, then it may also help to consult the appropriate DPA. Data privacy incidents should be reported to the DPA, and the DPA should have any publicly available records of privacy violations or sanctions that may have been imposed on the organization in question.

Risk Assessment

Assessing the level of privacy and compliance risk managed by a third party should ideally include all the elements of performing an internal risk assessment. Privacy risk can be much more difficult to assess with a third party, however. It is much more difficult to have visibility into all the processes, procedures, and records held by a third party. In addition, much of the information that would help assess privacy and compliance risk may not be shareable because of regulations that restrict disclosure or because the third party considers the information confidential.

However, it is still important to start by understanding what categories and quantities of data an organization is interested in sharing with a third party. This includes a detailed understanding of the processing activities the third party would perform, where and how the data is stored, and how the data is managed. A third party must be able to manage records retention for any data your organization shares, including the ability to store, archive, retrieve, and purge data as required. The organization and the third party must agree on minimum standards for data privacy protections to ensure compliance and prevent privacy incidents.

Technologies and Processing Methods

When assessing a vendor, it's critical to understand the technologies, methods, and other third parties that the vendor may use to deliver services. A common example is the use of cloud computing services for data storage and processing. When performing a vendor assessment, you should understand and evaluate these factors. For instance, a data processor running operations using public cloud computing may be using servers and computing physically located all over the world. If a data controller is subject to a requirement to conduct all data processing in a certain country, then they may not be able to use this processor.

When a third-party partner is using cloud computing services, it's also critical to vet the vendor and their cloud computing services for information security and privacy practices, as described earlier in this chapter. Cloud computing services can be easily overlooked in vetting a vendor because they are not often managed directly by the vendor.

Legal Compliance

Third-party data sharing partners may not operate in the same jurisdictions as your organization. This means that your organization may impose new compliance obligations on the third party. Likewise, sharing data with a third party may bring your organization into the scope of new regulations. For example, third parties may use cloud computing services located in countries with different privacy regulations.

Contractual Requirements (Incident Response, etc.)

When assessing vendor risk, it is critical to review the terms and conditions of all contracts and other agreements with third parties that involve any access to private information. Contracts are powerful tools that may be used to create legal obligations for third parties to protect private data. Contractual terms often transfer risk to third parties for data they manage. This reduces financial risk, but also provides an organization with added assurance that it is in the best interest of the third party to ensure data privacy and compliance.

Contractual requirements related to privacy are intended to help the originating organization retain control of its data, transfer risks to a third party, and require data privacy protections and legal compliance. Common contractual terms include:

- Restricting the third party from using, processing, storing, or disclosing data in any way other than as specified in the contract without specific authorization.

- Requiring the third party to maintain records retention practices and to return or purge any data upon request and/or at the end of the contract.

- Requiring the third party to maintain a privacy program that includes key activities such as training and awareness, incident management, privacy risk assessments, program assurance and audit, data management, an information security program, and any other requirements consistent with an organization's own privacy program.

- Requiring the third party to notify the organization of any breaches or incidents within a set time. Note that GDPR requires data processors to notify data controllers of personal data breaches "without undue delay." It would be better to have specific time frames, like 24 or 48 hours, rather than general time frames.

- Requiring the third party to accept financial risk for any privacy or compliance incidents, penalties, or other costs where the third party is at fault.

- Requiring a copy of the third party's Certificate of Insurance (COI) to verify insurance coverage for privacy and compliance risks and requiring the third party to name the organization as a certificate holder.

- Enumerating specific laws and regulations to which the organization is subject and requiring that the third party certify compliance with all applicable laws and regulations.

- Other contract terms may address specific types of data, processing activities, technologies, dispute resolution, or other terms and conditions that respond to specific risks identified by an organization.

Cross-Border Transfers

Engaging a third party for data processing can trigger the need to engage in special arrangements for cross-border data transfers. The need to be aware of differing regulations in different countries has already been addressed, but there also may be a need to securely transmit data across international boundaries. Sometimes, the need for cross-border transfer arrangements may be obvious, such as when engaging a third party physically located in another country. Other times, however, the need for cross-border transfer arraignments may be less apparent. For example, the third party may not be based in another country itself but may employ subcontractors or services that are.

Once a need to transfer data internationally has been identified, transfer impact assessments (TIAs) are a useful tool for analyzing the impact, risks, and requirements for such transfers. TIAs are discussed later in this chapter in the section called "Privacy Assessments and Documentation."

Contractual Requirements and Ongoing Monitoring

Many of the risks identified while assessing a third party can be addressed in the contract for data sharing. Contracts have the force of law and can include a provision that requires third-party processors to manage the identified risks. For example, a contract can require compliance with GDPR, impose a records retention schedule, detail minimum standards for safeguarding data security and privacy, and more. Contracts can also transfer financial liability for any violations or incidents to the third party.

Many data sharing partnerships are intended to last for multiple years. For this reason, it is important to create controls that ensure that all the contractual requirements continue to be monitored and upheld, year after year. Contracts are also useful tools for setting forward-looking requirements for program assurance. Contractual provisions can require the third party to perform ongoing assessments or audits to ensure compliance with the contract itself. In addition, contracts include a provision that entitles the original organization to audit the third party for privacy practices. Finally, contracts should anticipate regulatory change and include language to require third parties to adapt to regulatory change in the future.

Physical Assessments

With so much focus on data privacy in the virtual world, it can sometimes become all too easy to neglect the operational risk stemming from the physical side of privacy protection.

Physical risks address anything tangible that uses, processes, stores, or transmits data. These operational risks must be identified and assessed.

Data Centers and Offices   Create an inventory of physical locations where data may be stored and accessed. Such an inventory identifies possible risks and areas for implementing appropriate controls. Such controls may include access controls (discussed next) as well as surveillance systems, alarm systems, security personnel, and regular security inspections.

Physical Access Controls   Document access controls for the physical spaces identified above. This may include physical locks and keys or keycards, procedures for granting and/or rescinding access, ID badge requirements, training on physical access, and any other controls that secure access to physical spaces.

Document Retention and Destruction   Records retention has already been discussed with respect to data, but physical records must also be managed according to records retention policies. This may involve identifying secure facilities for archiving physical records and services for incinerating or shredding documents as required.

Device Security   Safeguards for digital information must also be applied to the physical devices that store that information. USB drives, computers, mobile phones, and servers may all house private information. Policies and procedures should ensure that devices are secured and detail how and when devices may be moved, who can access devices, and how devices are procured, transferred, and retired. Remember also that devices like scanners, copiers, and fax machines may produce paper records that need to be secured.

Media Sanitization and Disposal   Procedures should be in place to ensure the physical secure deletion of data from all media when a device is repurposed or retired from service. This often involves the physical destruction of the data storage technology. For example, a computer hard drive may be removed and destroyed before the computer is reassigned to a new employee.

Mergers, Acquisitions, and Divestitures

An organization's privacy program must also be responsive to changes in the organization itself. When an organization goes through a merger, purchases another business, or sells parts of itself (called a divestiture), there may be profound impacts on data privacy protection. New acquisitions may bring new types of data, new compliance and legal obligations, risks, technologies, and more. Organizations must have processes in place to integrate new acquisitions with existing data privacy programs, update the data privacy program to respond to new requirements, and adequately protect privacy and legacy data before divestitures. There are several processes that can be used to evaluate mergers, acquisitions, and divestitures:

Due Diligence   Performing due diligence related to a merger or acquisition is not unlike performing due diligence before engaging a new vendor. A due diligence check should examine the new organization to understand the data it controlled or processed, the systems and software involved in data processing, the applicable jurisdictions and regulations, its privacy program framework, and its information security program. A pre-merger due diligence check also includes documenting all third-party data sharing agreements, vendors, or other data processors, including cloud computing. For divestitures, due diligence would focus on ensuring that all data privacy protection obligations are understood before the transfer. For example, data may need to be purged prior to the transfer, obligations may need to be passed on to new owners as part of any transfer agreement, or legacy data may need to be retained securely by the original organization.

Contractual and Data Sharing Obligations   Long-term obligations to data privacy protections do not suddenly become null and void when ownership of an organization is transferred via a merger, acquisition, or divestiture. For example, if an IT firm that manages healthcare data has a BAA in place with a client, then the Business Associate Agreement (BAA) should become the responsibility of any organization that acquires the IT firm. Organizations may inherit data privacy protection obligations via contracts as well as through interjurisdictional data sharing arrangements. Organizations that transfer data to or from the EU may have binding corporate rules (BCRs) or standard contractual clauses (SCCs) in place, for example, that will impose requirements on any new parent company. When divesting, the original organization must ensure that all such obligations are inventoried, disclosed, and transferred as part of any agreement.

Risk Assessment and Alignment   As discussed in Chapters 1 and 2, organizations should approach all risks strategically with an understanding of how much risk an organization is willing to tolerate. This way, data privacy protections may be adjusted to fit the organization's risk tolerance level. Some organizations want to keep risk as low as possible and err on the side of maximizing data privacy protections, while other organizations may allow somewhat greater risk for a variety of reasons. For example, an organization may want to allow its employees to have broader access to private data in order to make better decisions. When transferring ownership of an organization, it is critical to perform a data privacy risk assessment to determine the new organization's level of risk. Once a risk assessment is completed, the next step is to complete an analysis to determine how well the new organization's level of risk aligns with the risk tolerance of the potential new owner.

Post-Integration Planning and Risk Mitigation   After integrating a new business unit via a merger or acquisition, the privacy program framework must be extended to cover the new operation. This means ensuring that all data privacy protections in place at the parent company are implemented for the new operations. In addition, the overall privacy program framework may have to change to account for the new operation. If the preacquisition evaluation steps described earlier have been followed, much of the information needed for post-integration should already be available.

Privacy Assessments and Documentation

As mentioned earlier, there are several specific methods for performing targeted privacy risk assessments. Each of these addresses different risks and compliance requirements. It is important to note that, in almost every case, privacy risk assessments should be performed in advance of making changes that might adversely affect an organization's privacy risk. These assessments are meant to help organizations make better decisions and plan appropriate safeguards. These assessments are not effective if performed after the fact.

Privacy Threshold Analyses (PTAs)

Privacy threshold analyses (PTAs) often serve as good starting points for evaluating an organization's practices for assessing systems and for privacy protection impacts. A PTA is an analysis, often in the form of a questionnaire, that identifies whether information systems contain PII or other private information that might require further analysis, controls, or inclusion in privacy notices. A PTA may be used to determine whether further assessments, such as PIAs or DPIAs, should be conducted.

PTAs are useful because they help initially identify the types of data held by different systems. For this reason, PTAs align well with the process of conducting data inventories, as described in Chapter 1. PTAs should be conducted whenever a new information system is considered, but they may also be conducted when a system contains unknown data or when a system is repurposed. If a PTA identifies data stored in each system that constitutes PII or other forms of legally protected information, then the organization may trigger further risk analyses.

PIAs, DPIAs, and other risk analyses are often more involved and costly than PTAs. PIAs and DPIAs may also include resource-intensive recommendations for risk mitigation or trigger requirements to notify legal authorities of data privacy risks. There's no point in performing such intense privacy risk assessments unless the system contains private data that requires specific protections. For this reason, PTAs are useful starting points for identifying systems that should be prioritized for deeper risk assessments.

Define a Process for Conducting Privacy Assessments

Based on the outcomes of PTAs, an organization may decide to complete one or more additional privacy risk assessments. Common examples assess risk related to new business operations or technologies, data privacy rights under GDPR, international data transfers, and more.

Privacy Impact Assessment (PIA)

As mentioned in Chapter 2, a PIA is a key tool for analyzing privacy risks proactively to inform key organizational decisions. In the United States, PIAs have been required for federal agencies since 2002, when the E-Government Act was passed. The PIA process should be triggered by changes in an organization that may impact data privacy protections. As an example, the U.S. Department of Homeland Security (DHS) requires a PIA when adopting new technologies or systems, creating new programs or data collections, updating systems, or issuing new rules that impact data privacy. According to DHS, a PIA has three goals:

- Ensure conformance with applicable legal, regulatory, and policy requirements for privacy.
- Determine the risks and effects.
- Evaluate protections and alternative processes to mitigate potential privacy risks.

While not always explicitly required in the United States (unless your organization is a government entity), PIAs enable organizations to consider the implications of changing vendors, technologies, subsidiaries, products and services, markets, customers, policies, and more. When an organization makes a change that might impact data protections, a PIA analyzes the potential privacy risks and recommends ways to manage those risks. When assessing privacy protections, it is important to look for documentation of policies for PIAs, procedures for creating PIAs, and evidence that PIAs have been produced in accordance with those policies and guidelines.

Data Protection Impact Assessment (DPIA)

A DPIA is a type of PIA that is required by the GDPR. If an organization has operations in the EU, then any assessment of data privacy protection should include checking for processes to ensure DPIAs are completed as required. Unlike in the United States, in the EU DPIAs are mandatory for all organizations covered by the GDPR. DPIAs under the GDPR have specific requirements. As mentioned in Chapter 2, DPIAs are triggered whenever a change to data processing is likely to impact privacy protections. DPIAs must include, at a minimum:

- Description of the proposed changes to data processing activities and the purpose(s) of the change
- Assessment of how much data processing is necessary in proportion to accomplish the purpose
- Assessment of data privacy risks
- Plans to mitigate any increased data privacy risks

For multinational organizations that maintain some level of operations in the EU, it may be most efficient to standardize internal PIA practices on the GDPR DPIA template. The DPIA accomplishes the goals of the PIA, even in jurisdictions where it isn't required, and establishes a practice for compliance in Europe.

Legitimate Interest Assessment (LIA)

An LIA is often conducted by organizations subject to GDPR before initiating new data processing activities. GDPR requires that an organization must have a "legitimate interest" to conduct data processing activities lawfully. Specifically, the GDPR's article 6(f) tells us that data processing is lawful when it "is necessary for the purposes of the legitimate interests pursued by the controller or by a third party, except where such interests are overridden by the interests or fundamental rights and freedoms of the data subject. . . ." An LIA establishes a legal basis for data processing by documenting the purpose of the proposed processing, establishes the necessity of data processing to achieve the stated purpose, and analyzes the potential impact on the individual data privacy rights conferred by GDPR.

Transfer Impact Assessment (TIA)

A transfer impact assessment (TIA) is performed when engaging in international data transfers. Ideally, some form of a PIA or DPIA has already been performed when initiating data sharing with a third party. The PIA process should already include an analysis of privacy risks and protections, which would include any contractual requirements for data protection. The TIA adds an important requirement: to analyze the laws of the country or countries in which data will be transferred.

A nation's laws may trump contractual terms in many instances. For example, if a country has a law authorizing governmental agencies to access private data at any time, as in the United States and China, then a third party in that country may be required to disclose private data no matter what an underlying contract says. In addition to laws that may undermine privacy protections, there may be other risks associated with transferring data to other countries. Some countries may have unstable governments with legal systems vulnerable to sudden change. Private companies may be subject to sudden governmental takeover or nationalization. Countries may suffer from corruption in the private and public sectors. Other countries may have unstable infrastructure that may create risks to the availability or security of private information.

TIAs have become increasingly important since the European Court of Justice issued the Schrems II decision (discussed in Chapter 2) because the European Court of Justice found that the laws of the United States did not guarantee adequate data protection, even for organizations certified via safe harbor programs or other contractual agreements.

Regularizing Privacy Assessment Activities

Each of these privacy risk assessments should be incorporated into an organization's standard operating procedures. The processes for conducting these assessments should be reviewed along with the rest of the privacy program and evaluated as part of any program assurance activities.

Summary

The assessment phase of the Privacy Operational Life Cycle is about examining everything an organization does that might have privacy implications. Assessment begins with a review of an organization's internal privacy program, but that alone is not sufficient. Assessment must also examine data sharing with third parties, physical privacy controls, mergers, acquisitions, and divestitures, as well as documented procedures for conducting ongoing privacy assessments.

Assessing relationships with third-party vendors and data processors is key to managing privacy risk. Processes should be in place for evaluating third-party data privacy risks, including understanding the data shared with third parties, how that third party safeguards privacy, where the data is stored, and how the third party is allowed to process the shared data. In addition, arrangements for third-party data sharing should consider information from audits, examinations of physical and information security, and information from regulators. Finally, the process for sharing data with any third party must involve a compressive assessment of compliance and privacy risks.

Physical measures to safeguard privacy are critical and yet are often overlooked. Physical privacy protection assessment requires a detailed understanding of all the physical locations where data are stored or accessed. Each of those locations must be appropriately secured through access controls, like locked doors, as well as other controls, such as employee training in physical security. Devices that store and access data must be carefully managed, protected, and tracked. Media, such as hard drives, that store private data must be sanitized of any trace of private information when no longer needed.

Mergers, acquisitions, and divestitures change the operational scope of an organization. Newly acquired business units or subsidiaries bring new data into the scope of an organization's privacy program, new technologies, and potentially new jurisdictions and compliance obligations. An organization's privacy program must be updated to safeguard privacy related to new operations and fully integrated into any new operations.

Privacy assessments are important tools that help an organization assess and respond to privacy risks related to operational changes. These assessments help privacy programs to adapt to changes in the business as they happen. Some privacy assessments, such as DPIAs, are legal requirements in some jurisdictions.

Exam Essentials

Be able to develop data life cycle management (DLM) practices. DLM is essential for assessing the baseline for a privacy program. DLM identifies data, categorizes data, and tracks data as it moves through systems and business processes. DLM usually tracks data across five life cycle phases, from acquisition to destruction. These phases may also occur simultaneously.

Know that compressive vetting processes should be in place for third-party data sharing.   Organizations are often under pressure to engage vendors to launch new products and services or to enter new markets. However, it is important to vet all vendors to ensure that they employ adequate data privacy safeguards. You must understand how and where vendors store and process data, assess the risk of sharing data with vendors, and ensure that contracts are in place to manage risk.

Be able to describe the importance of the physical side of data privacy.   Physical locations that house private information must be properly secured and managed. By the same token, devices that store digital information must also be physically secured and appropriately purged of all data that is no longer needed. Finally, remember to assess privacy practices for physical records, such as customer receipts or older legacy filing systems.

Be able to respond and adapt to new business areas.   Mergers, acquisitions, and divestitures change the makeup and operational scope of an organization. Mergers and acquisitions bring new data, systems, and regulatory obligations that must be assessed for risk and integrated into the privacy program. Divestitures may also reshape the privacy program by reducing scope or creating the need to safeguard legacy data in archive form.

Be familiar with privacy assessment methods.   Targeted proactive privacy assessments help analyze potential operational changes for their impact on privacy protection. PTAs, PIAs, DPIAs, TIAs, and LIAs are triggered when organizations consider making changes to systems or processes that might impact data privacy. Remember that DPIAs, in particular, are a requirement of GDPR.

Review Questions

1. Nathan's company has completed due diligence processes and a risk assessment, and is about to sign an agreement with a new vendor to manage his customer database. The vendor has agreed to uphold Nathan's standards for data privacy, but Nathan is concerned that any privacy incidents with his customer database could be incredibly costly for his company. How should Nathan protect his company from financial risk?

   A. Require the vendor to certify that all employees have completed appropriate data privacy training.

   B. Work with the appropriate data protection authority to determine if the vendor has a history of privacy incidents.

   C. Add language to the contract allowing Nathan's company to order the vendor to undergo external audits.

   D. Include a contractual clause obligating the vendor to assume financial liability for privacy incidents.

2. Julian has just started as a new manager for a small independent auto parts distributor. When Julian arrived, the team was just finishing up a long-term project to upgrade all the computers in the building. Since the team is small and doesn't have any dedicated IT people, they had to complete the upgrades however they could while still doing their regular jobs. Thankfully, all the computers are now upgraded. The old hardware has been shut down and stored in the back until the business decides what to do with them. The assistant manager, Bella, thinks the old computers are too outdated to sell, so she suggests donating them to a local school. After all, Bella points out, their small company has been a beloved community partner for decades. Julian, however, is concerned about donating the old computers. Why should Julian worry?

   A. A GLBA audit might consider the donation to be an improper allocation of company assets.

   B. The new computers might be using the same passwords as the old computers.

   C. The company might be liable for damages if the equipment fails after being donated.

   D. The hard drives might need to be fully sanitized to remove all company data before donating.

3. Meghan is the CEO of a growing data processing company. Her company is expanding internationally, and Meghan's company is joining a safe harbor program to facilitate cross-border data sharing. Which of the following processes should Meghan expect to certify her company's compliance with the safe harbor program?

   A. Internal audit

   B. Program assurance

   C. Transfer impact assessment

   D. External audit

4. ShoeStop is a large chain of retail shoe stores that has just purchased another retail foot-wear business called Footbarn. The new acquisition will add six more stores to the ShoeStop family. Hassan is the ShoeStop privacy program manager, and he has been assigned to train staff who are transitioning from Footbarn into the ShoeStop privacy program. While training the IT staff from Footbarn on the procedures for physically securing company server rooms, the Footbarn staff look confused and alarmed. One of the Footbarn IT staff members points out that Footbarn doesn't have any server rooms, since they outsourced all data storage to a cloud provider three years ago. This is alarming to Hassan because ShoeStop does not currently use cloud computing services. What might have gone wrong during the acquisition process in this case?

   A. Failure to upgrade ShoeStop's data centers to secure modern cloud computing solutions

   B. Failure to implement a contract between ShoeStop and the cloud computing provider to manage risk and transfer liability

   C. Failure to check for existing third-party data processors during preacquisition due diligence

   D. Failure to ensure compliance with the requirement for data processors to provide data controllers with timely notification of privacy incidents

5. Jan is a privacy manager and is reviewing her company's performance after a recent tabletop drill simulating a privacy incident. During the exercise, the team realized the company still held private data on employees who had long ago retired, which was in violation of the company's records retention policy. When confronted, the HR staff seemed surprised by the records retention policy. Which of the following should Jan consider to help her company improve in this area?

   A. Implement Data Lifecycle Management (DLM).

   B. Perform a privacy threshold analysis (PTA) on HR systems.

   C. Hold role-based training for HR staff.

   D. Request an internal audit of HR records retention compliance.

6. Which of the following is not required to be included as part of a DPIA?

   A. Description of the purpose of the processing

   B. Data protection incident response plans

   C. Assessment of the necessity of the processing activity

   D. Plans to mitigate any risks to data subject rights

7. Marcel is the IT manager for a company that operates traffic surveillance cameras around the world. He plans to move his extensive database of images and video to the cloud. What is he required to do first?

   A. Perform a due diligence check on his preferred cloud provider.

   B. Complete a DPIA.

   C. Ensure that records retention policies are in place for all image and video files.

   D. Baseline his company's privacy program.

8. Molly is a privacy manager at a large advertising company. Her company is in the process of selling off its least profitable subsidiary. The company is only selling the brand name and not the underlying assets. The assets will remain with Molly's company. Molly's CFO invites her to a meeting to discuss any privacy concerns related to the sale. What should Molly recommend?

   A. Develop contract language with the new owner of the subsidiary to ensure that all compliance risk is transferred to the new owner.

   B. Document how any legacy data is managed and integrate it into the company's DLM plan.

   C. Ensure that all legacy data is securely deleted, including the destruction of storage media (e.g., hard drives) if necessary.

   D. Perform a thorough due diligence check on the proposed new owner before completing the sale of the subsidiary.

9. Which of the following is not an important part of evaluating a potential data processing partnership?

   A. Assessing risk

   B. Evaluating the vendor's technology and systems

   C. Analyzing legal compliance issues

   D. Implementing privacy safeguards on partner systems

10. Javier is charged with responding to privacy-related customer requests for a small company. Most commonly, these are requests to disclose data processing activities or for erasure. He is falling behind in his work because it is such a struggle to locate the data, figure out which employees manage that data, and determine how many copies of the data exist. Which of the following processes should the company implement to help with this?

    A. DLM

    B. PIA

    C. Internal audit

    D. Access policies

11. ShoeStop is a large chain of retail shoe stores that has just purchased another retail footwear business called Footbarn. The new acquisition will add six more stores to the ShoeStop family. Hassan is the ShoeStop Privacy Program Manager, and he has been assigned to train staff who are transitioning from Footbarn to the ShoeStop privacy program. While training the IT staff from Footbarn on the procedures for physically securing company server rooms, the Footbarn staff look confused and alarmed. One of the Footbarn IT staff members points out that Footbarn doesn't have any server rooms, since they outsourced all data storage to a cloud provider three years ago. This is alarming to Hassan because ShoeStop does not currently use cloud computing services. Which of the following is *not* a risk area that should concern Hassan?

    A. The third-party cloud service may store data in a country with insufficient data privacy protection regulations.

    B. The third-party cloud service may operate in another jurisdiction and be subject to unknown legal requirements.

C. The contract with the cloud provider may not adequately protect ShoeStop from risk.

D. The third-party cloud service may be a low-cost and low-quality provider that might not meet ShoeStop's standards for information security.

12. Marla has just inherited her grandmother's accounting practice. During her first week, Marla discovers that the office space is crammed full of historical paper records packed into file boxes. The boxes are neatly stacked but occupy almost every square foot of unused floor space, even in the reception area. Some of the boxes are so old that they are falling apart. Marla immediately decides she needs to digitize all the firm's records and clean the place up. In the meantime, she knows she still needs to manage all those paper files. What should Marla do first to ensure privacy?

A. Move all the records out of the reception area and store them behind locked doors.

B. Implement a records retention policy and destroy the old records to reduce risk.

C. Inventory the records to implement Data Lifecycle Management practices.

D. Develop a privacy policy for the office and make sure the staff are trained on the policy.

13. Janice is a privacy manager at Adverts, Inc., a marketing company that places ads for businesses. Adverts is way behind schedule in launching its new website, so the IT manager has decided to bring in a contractor he knows from his previous employer to help accelerate the work. The IT manager wants the contract to start immediately so that the team can meet the deadline. Why should Janice be concerned?

A. The vendor has not been evaluated.

B. Janice is unsure if contracture has been through privacy education and awareness training.

C. Contract terms have not been established to transfer risk to the vendor.

D. Janice is unsure of the vendor's physical location.

14. An Italian company is considering outsourcing their database services to a company located in Boston. Which of the following should they complete first?

A. DPIA

B. TIA

C. PTA

D. PIA

15. You are concerned that your organization may not be properly prepared to deliver required notifications to individuals in case of privacy breaches. Which of the following privacy program areas should you assess?

A. Education and awareness

B. Incident management

C. Monitoring the regulatory environment

D. Risk assessment

16. Which of the following would be the least applicable as part of a physical assessment?

   A. Ensuring that all data centers are open only to those with approved keycard access

   B. Procedures for purging paper files according to the records retention policy

   C. Ensuring computing devices are password protected

   D. Implementing digital surveillance systems at secure facilities

17. Which of the following is a reason to be concerned about the geographic location where vendors store their data?

   A. GDPR prohibits companies from storing private information in non-EU countries.

   B. Data stored in another country may trigger cross-border transfer requirements.

   C. Data controllers must have physical access to all data centers used to store their private data.

   D. It is not possible to include cloud computing services in vendor evaluation if the cloud services are not owned by that vendor.

18. Which of the following is a reason for performing a baseline assessment of your organization's privacy program?

   A. A baseline is necessary for measuring improvement.

   B. To prepare for and respond to audits.

   C. To conduct and document privacy risk assessments.

   D. A baseline helps discover and mitigate gaps in the program.

19. Aiofe's Dublin-based company is planning to move to a new online platform to manage the company's website and online sales. They have already selected a vendor and are in the process of planning for the new platform. During a presentation by the vendor, Aiofe learns that the new online platform will be capable of capturing much more information about visitors to the website, including the ability to track geolocation data and identify unique visitors to the website. Aiofe is intrigued because this sort of information could really help her business improve its website. What would be a good idea for Aiofe to do before adopting this new online platform?

   A. Complete an LIA.

   B. Complete a comprehensive vendor evaluation.

   C. Ensure that BCRs or SCCs are in place before collecting any personal information from outside the EU.

   D. Conduct a PTA on the new platform.

20. Which of the following should a third-party data processor be required to do when they discover a data privacy incident?

   A. Notify the data controller.

   B. Report it to the DPA.

   C. Initiate an internal audit to improve safeguards.

   D. Perform a DPIA.

Chapter

4

Privacy Operational Life Cycle: Protect

THE CIPM EXAM OBJECTIVES COVERED IN THIS CHAPTER INCLUDE:

- IV.D.d. Define roles and responsibilities for managing the sharing and disclosure of data for internal and external use

- IV.D.e. Determine and implement guidelines for secondary uses (ex: research, etc.)

- IV.D.f. Define policies related to the processing (including collection, use, retention, disclosure, and disposal) of the organization's data holdings, taking into account both legal and ethical requirements

- IV.D.g. Implement appropriate administrative safeguards, such as policies, procedures, and contracts

The third phase of the privacy operational life cycle, Protect, ensures that the personal information handled by an organization is protected against a variety of risks, including unauthorized disclosure, tampering, or destruction. When working in the Protect phase of a privacy program, privacy professionals share many goals with cybersecurity professionals, who also have a strong interest in protecting systems and data. In this chapter, we explore the relationship between privacy and cybersecurity as we cover the Protect phase of the privacy operational life cycle.

Privacy and Cybersecurity

The fields of privacy and cybersecurity are closely related and interdependent. This occurs to such an extent that many people who do not work in either field consider them the same. However, though these fields are related to each other, they remain separate and distinct.

As you've already read, the purpose of a privacy program is to safeguard the privacy rights that individuals have for their personal information. The purpose of a cybersecurity program is to protect the confidentiality, integrity, and availability of data maintained by an organization. Before we describe the relationship between the two, let's take a deeper look at the goals of a cybersecurity program.

Cybersecurity Goals

When most people think of cybersecurity, they imagine hackers trying to break into an organization's system and steal sensitive information, ranging from Social Security numbers and credit cards to top-secret military information. Although protecting sensitive information from unauthorized disclosure is certainly one element of a cybersecurity program, it is important to understand that cybersecurity actually has three complementary objectives, as shown in Figure 4.1.

Confidentiality ensures that unauthorized individuals are not able to gain access to sensitive information. Cybersecurity professionals develop and implement security controls, including firewalls, access control lists, and encryption, to prevent unauthorized access to information. Attackers may seek to undermine confidentiality controls to achieve one of their goals: the unauthorized disclosure of sensitive information.

FIGURE 4.1   The three key objectives of cybersecurity programs are confidentiality, integrity, and availability.

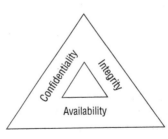

Integrity ensures that there are no unauthorized modifications to information or systems, either intentionally or unintentionally. Integrity controls, such as hashing and integrity monitoring solutions, seek to enforce this requirement. Integrity threats may come from attackers seeking the alteration of information without authorization or nonmalicious sources, such as end-user error or a power spike causing the corruption of information.

Availability ensures that information and systems are ready to meet the needs of legitimate users when those users request them. Availability controls, such as fault tolerance, clustering, and backups, seek to ensure that legitimate users may gain access as needed. Similar to integrity threats, availability threats may come either from attackers seeking the disruption of access or from nonmalicious sources, such as a fire destroying a data center that contains valuable information or services.

Cybersecurity analysts often refer to these three goals as the CIA Triad when performing their work. They often characterize risks, attacks, and security controls as meeting one or more of the three CIA Triad goals.

Relationship between Privacy and Cybersecurity

Now that you have a good understanding of the nature of privacy and security programs, you may already be developing a sense of the relationship between the two. Privacy depends on cybersecurity. In fact, you've already read that Security for Privacy is one of the 10 GAPP principles. The bottom line is that you can't protect the privacy of information unless you can guarantee the security of that information.

The relationship is more complex than that, however, as shown in Figure 4.2.

Cybersecurity and privacy programs share a common goal: the protection of electronic personal information. They each also have their own independent goals.

Privacy programs must also concern themselves with the protection of nonelectronic personal information, such as paper records. They also must be concerned about all 10 GAPP principles, not just security. Principles such as notice, choice, and consent generally fall outside the scope of security programs.

Cybersecurity programs concern themselves with the confidentiality, integrity, and availability of *all* sensitive electronic information. This includes sensitive, but nonpersonal, information, including business plans, trade secrets, and product designs.

FIGURE 4.2   The relationship between privacy and cybersecurity

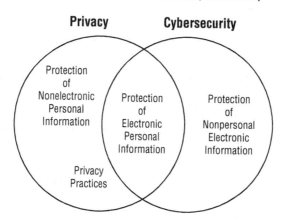

All differences aside, privacy and cybersecurity are close cousins in the business world. Privacy and security professionals often share a common ethos and understanding of each other's work, but it is also important that they understand the fundamental differences between their goals.

Cybersecurity Controls

As an organization analyzes its risk environment, technical and business leaders determine the level of protection required to preserve the confidentiality, integrity, and availability of their information and systems. They express these requirements by writing the *control objectives* that the organization wishes to achieve. These control objectives are statements of a desired security state, but they do not, by themselves, actually carry out security activities. *Security controls* are specific measures that fulfill the security objectives of an organization.

Exam Tip

Privacy laws often contain language requiring that organizations implement appropriate safeguards to protect the security of PII, but they typically stop short of prescribing specific security controls. Privacy and security professionals must work together to design a set of controls that meets the intent of the legislation and protects the interests of the organization and its stakeholders.

Security Control Categories

Security controls are categorized based on their mechanism of action—the way that they achieve their objectives. There are three different categories of security control:

- *Technical controls* enforce confidentiality, integrity, and availability in the digital space. Examples of technical security controls include firewall rules, access control lists, intrusion prevention systems, encryption, and others.

- *Operational controls* include the processes that we put in place to manage technology securely. These include user access reviews, log monitoring, vulnerability management, and others.

- *Managerial controls* are procedural mechanisms that focus on the mechanics of the risk management process. Examples of administrative controls include periodic risk assessments, security planning exercises, and the incorporation of security into the organization's change management, service acquisition, and project management practices.

Organizations should select a set of security controls that meets their control objectives based on the criteria and parameters that they either select for their environment or have imposed on them by outside regulators. For example, an organization that handles sensitive information might decide that confidentiality concerns surrounding that information require the highest level of control. At the same time, they might conclude that the availability of their website is not of critical importance. Given these considerations, they would dedicate significant resources to the confidentiality of sensitive information while perhaps investing little, if any, time and money protecting their website against a denial-of-service attack.

Many control objectives require a combination of technical, operational, and management controls. For example, an organization might have the control objective of preventing unauthorized access to a data center. They might achieve this goal by implementing biometric access control (technical control), performing regular reviews of authorized access (operational control), and conducting routine risk assessments (managerial control).

Security Control Types

We can also divide security controls into types, based on their desired effect. The types of security control include the following:

- *Preventive controls* intend to stop a security issue before it occurs. Firewalls, passwords, lighting, and encryption are examples of preventive controls.

- *Detective controls* identify security events that have already occurred. Intrusion detection systems, alarm systems, and cameras. are detective controls.

- *Corrective controls* remediate security issues that have already occurred. Restoring backups after a ransomware attack is an example of a corrective control.

- *Deterrent controls* seek to prevent an attacker from attempting to violate security policies. Trained guard dogs, security guards, and barbed wire fences are examples of deterrent controls.

- *Physical controls* are security controls that impact the physical world. Examples of physical security controls include fences, perimeter lighting, locks, fire suppression systems, and burglar alarms.

- *Compensating controls* are controls designed to mitigate the risk associated with exceptions made to a security policy.

Data Protection

Cybersecurity professionals spend significant amounts of their time focusing on the protection of sensitive data. We serve as stewards and guardians, protecting the confidentiality, integrity, and availability of the sensitive data created by our organizations and entrusted to us by our customers and other stakeholders.

As we think through data protection techniques, it's helpful to consider the three states where data might exist:

- *Data at rest* is stored data that resides on hard drives, on tapes, in the cloud, or on other storage media. This data is prone to pilfering by insiders or external attackers who gain access to systems and can browse through their contents.

- *Data in motion* is data that is in transit over a network. When data travels on an untrusted network, it is open to eavesdropping attacks by anyone with access to those networks.

- *Data in Process* is data that is actively in use by a computer system. This includes the data stored in memory while processing takes place. An attacker with control of the system may be able to read the contents of memory and steal sensitive information.

We can use different security controls to safeguard data in all of these states, building a robust set of defenses that protects our organizations' vital interests.

Data Encryption

Encryption technology typically uses mathematical algorithms to protect information from prying eyes, both while it is in transit over a network and while it resides on systems. Encrypted data is unintelligible to anyone who does not have access to the appropriate decryption key, making it safe to store and transmit encrypted data over otherwise insecure means.

Different encryption technologies may be used to protect data in transit over a network and data at rest on a storage device. Data in transit is commonly protected by the use of the *Transport Layer Security (TLS)* protocol. Data at rest may be protected by the encryption of individual files and/or the use of *full-disk encryption (FDE)* technology.

Exam Tip

Full-disk encryption is an extremely important security control for laptops, mobile devices, portable storage media, and other devices that may be easily lost or stolen. If these devices contain PII, the FDE technology protects that PII from unauthorized disclosure even when the physical device falls into the wrong hands.

Data Loss Prevention

Data loss prevention (DLP) systems help organizations enforce information handling policies and procedures to prevent data loss and theft. They search systems for stores of sensitive information that might be unsecured and monitor network traffic for potential attempts to remove sensitive information from the organization. They can act quickly to block the transmission before damage is done and alert administrators to the attempted breach.

DLP systems work in two different environments:

- Host-based DLP
- Network-based DLP

Host-based DLP uses software agents installed on systems that search those systems for the presence of sensitive information. These searches often turn up Social Security numbers, credit card numbers, and other sensitive information in the most unlikely of places!

Detecting the presence of stored sensitive information allows security professionals to take prompt action to either remove it or secure it with encryption. Taking the time to secure or remove information now may pay handsome rewards down the road if the device is lost, stolen, or compromised.

Host-based DLP can also monitor system configuration and user actions, blocking undesirable actions. For example, some organizations use host-based DLP to block users from accessing USB-based removable media devices that they might use to carry information out of the organization's secure environment.

Network-based DLP systems are dedicated devices that sit on the network and monitor outbound network traffic, watching for any transmissions that contain unencrypted sensitive information. They can then block those transmissions, preventing the unsecured loss of sensitive information.

DLP systems may simply block traffic that violates the organization's policy, or in some cases, they may automatically apply encryption to the content. This automatic encryption is commonly used with DLP systems that focus on email.

DLP systems also have two mechanisms of action:

- *Pattern matching*, where they watch for the telltale signs of sensitive information. For example, if they see a number that is formatted like a credit card or Social Security number, they can automatically sound an alert. Similarly, they may contain a database of sensitive terms, such as "Top Secret" or "Business Confidential," and alert when they see those terms in a transmission.

- *Watermarking*, where systems or administrators apply electronic tags to sensitive documents and then the DLP system can monitor systems and networks for unencrypted content containing those tags.

Watermarking technology is also commonly used in *digital rights management (DRM)* solutions that enforce copyright and data ownership restrictions.

Data Minimization

Data minimization techniques seek to reduce risk by reducing the amount of sensitive information that organizations maintain on a regular basis. The best way to achieve data minimization is to simply destroy data when it is no longer necessary to meet the original business purpose.

If an organization can't completely remove data from a data set, they can often transform it into a format where the original sensitive information is deidentified. The *deidentification* process removes the ability to link data back to an individual, reducing its sensitivity.

An alternative to deidentifying data is transforming it into a format where the original information can't be retrieved. This is a process called *data obfuscation*, and several tools are available to assist in this process:

- *Hashing* uses a hash function to transform a value in the data set into a corresponding hash value. If a strong hash function is applied to a data element, we may replace the value in our file with the hashed value.

- *Tokenization* replaces sensitive values with a unique identifier using a lookup table. For example, we might replace a widely known value, such as a student ID, with a randomly generated 10-digit number. We'd then maintain a lookup table that allows us to convert those back to student IDs if we need to determine someone's identity. Of course, if you use this approach, you need to keep the lookup table secure!

- *Masking* partially redacts sensitive information by replacing some or all sensitive fields with blank characters. For example, we might replace all but the last four digits of a credit card number with Xs or asterisks to render the card number unreadable.

Although it isn't possible to retrieve the original value directly from the hashed value, there is one major flaw in this approach. If someone has a list of possible values for a field, they can conduct something called a *rainbow table attack*. In this attack, the attacker computes the hashes of those candidate values and then checks to see if those hashes exist in our data file.

For example, imagine that we have a file listing all the students at our college who have failed courses but we hash their student IDs. If an attacker has a list of all students, they can compute the hash values of all student IDs and then check to see which hash values are on the list. For this reason, hashing should only be used with caution.

Backups

Backups play an important role in data protection. They are copies of data stored on tape, disk, the cloud, or other media as a last-ditch recovery option. If a natural or human-made disaster causes data loss, administrators may turn to backups to recover lost data.

Your *disaster recovery plan (DRP)* should fully address the backup strategy pursued by your organization. Indeed, this is one of the most important elements of any business continuity plan and disaster recovery plan.

Many system administrators are already familiar with various types of backups, so you'll benefit by bringing one or more individuals with specific technical expertise in this area onto the DRP team to provide expert guidance. There are three main types of backups:

Full Backups   As the name implies, *full backups* store a complete copy of the data contained on the protected device. Full backups duplicate every file on the system regardless of the setting of the archive bit. Once a full backup is complete, the archive bit on every file is reset, turned off, or set to 0.

Incremental Backups   *Incremental backups* store only those files that have been modified since the time of the most recent full or incremental backup. They use an archive bit attached to each file to track that file's backup status. Only files that have the archive bit turned on, enabled, or set to 1 are duplicated. Once an incremental backup is complete, the archive bit on all duplicated files is reset, turned off, or set to 0.

Differential Backups   *Differential backups* store all files that have been modified since the time of the most recent full backup. Only files that have the archive bit turned on, enabled, or set to 1 are duplicated. However, unlike full and incremental backups, the differential backup process does not change the archive bit.

 Some operating systems do not actually use an archive bit to achieve this goal and instead analyze filesystem time stamps. This difference in implementation doesn't affect the types of data stored by each backup type.

The most important difference between incremental and differential backups is the time needed to restore data in the event of an emergency. If you use a combination of full and differential backups, you will need to restore only two backups—the most recent full backup and the most recent differential backup. On the other hand, if your strategy combines full backups with incremental backups, you will need to restore the most recent full backup as well as all incremental backups performed since that full backup. The trade-off is the time required to *create* the backups—differential backups don't take as long to restore, but they take longer to create than incremental ones.

The storage of the backup media is equally critical. It may be convenient to store backup media in or near the primary operations center to easily fulfill user requests for backup data, but you'll definitely need to keep copies of the media in at least one offsite location to provide redundancy should your primary operating location be suddenly destroyed. One common strategy used by many organizations is to store backups in a cloud service that is itself geographically redundant. This allows the organization to retrieve the backups from any location after a disaster. Note that using geographically diverse sites may introduce new regulatory requirements when the information resides in different jurisdictions.

Using Backups

In case of system failure, many companies use one of two common methods to restore data from backups. In the first situation, they run a full backup on Monday night and then run differential backups every other night of the week. If a failure occurs Saturday morning, they restore Monday's full backup and then restore only Friday's differential backup. In the second situation, they run a full backup on Monday night and run incremental backups every other night of the week. If a failure occurs Saturday morning, they restore Monday's full backup and then restore each incremental backup in original chronological order (that is, Wednesday's, then Friday's, and so on).

Most organizations adopt a backup strategy that utilizes more than one of the three backup types along with a media rotation scheme. Both allow backup administrators access to a sufficiently large range of backups to complete user requests and provide fault tolerance while minimizing the amount of money that must be spent on backup media. A common strategy is to perform full backups over the weekend and incremental or differential backups on a nightly basis. The specific method of backup and all of the particulars of the backup procedure are dependent on your organization's fault-tolerance requirements. If you are unable to survive minor amounts of data loss, your ability to tolerate faults is low. However, if hours or days of data can be lost without serious consequence, your tolerance of faults is high. You should design your backup solution accordingly.

Policy Framework

An organization's *policy framework* contains a series of documents designed to describe the organization's cybersecurity program. The scope and complexity of these documents vary widely, depending on the nature of the organization and its information resources. These frameworks generally include four different types of documents:

- Policies
- Standards

- Procedures
- Guidelines

In the remainder of this section, you'll learn the differences between each of these document types. However, keep in mind that the definitions of these categories vary significantly from organization to organization and that it is very common to find the lines between them blurred. Though at first glance that may seem incorrect, it's a natural occurrence as security theory meets the real world. As long as the documents are achieving their desired purpose, there's no harm in using whatever naming system is preferred in your organization.

Cybersecurity Policies

Policies are broad statements of management intent. Compliance with policies is mandatory. An information security policy will generally contain generalized statements about cybersecurity objectives, including the following:

- A statement of the importance of cybersecurity to the organization
- Requirements that all staff and contracts take measures to protect the confidentiality, integrity, and availability of information and information systems
- Statement on the ownership of information created and/or possessed by the organization
- Designation of the chief information security officer (CISO) or other individual as the executive responsible for cybersecurity issues
- Delegation of authority granting the CISO the ability to create standards, procedures, and guidelines that implement the policy

In many organizations, the process to create a policy is laborious and requires senior management approval, often from the CEO. Keeping policy statements broadly worded provides the CISO with the flexibility to adapt and change specific security requirements with changes in the business and technology environments. For example, the five-page information security policy at the University of Notre Dame simply states:

> The Information Governance Committee will create handling standards for each Highly Sensitive data element. Data stewards may create standards for other data elements under their stewardship. These information handling standards will specify controls to manage risks to University information and related assets based on their classification. All individuals at the University are responsible for complying with these controls.

This type of policy allows an organization to maintain a high-level document and use it to guide the development of standards, procedures, and guidelines that remain in alignment with enterprise goals and objectives.

By way of contrast, the federal government's Centers for Medicare & Medicaid Services (CMS) has a 95-page information security policy. This mammoth document contains incredibly detailed requirements, such as:

A record of all requests for monitoring must be maintained by the CMS CIO along with any other summary results or documentation produced during the period of monitoring. The record must also reflect the scope of the monitoring by documenting search terms and techniques. All information collected from monitoring must be controlled and protected with distribution limited to the individuals identified in the request for monitoring and other individuals specifically designated by the CMS Administrator or CMS CIO as having a specific need to know such information.

The CMS document even goes so far as to include a complex chart describing the many cybersecurity roles held by individuals throughout the agency. An excerpt from that chart appears in Figure 4.3.

FIGURE 4.3   Excerpt from CMS roles and responsibilities chart

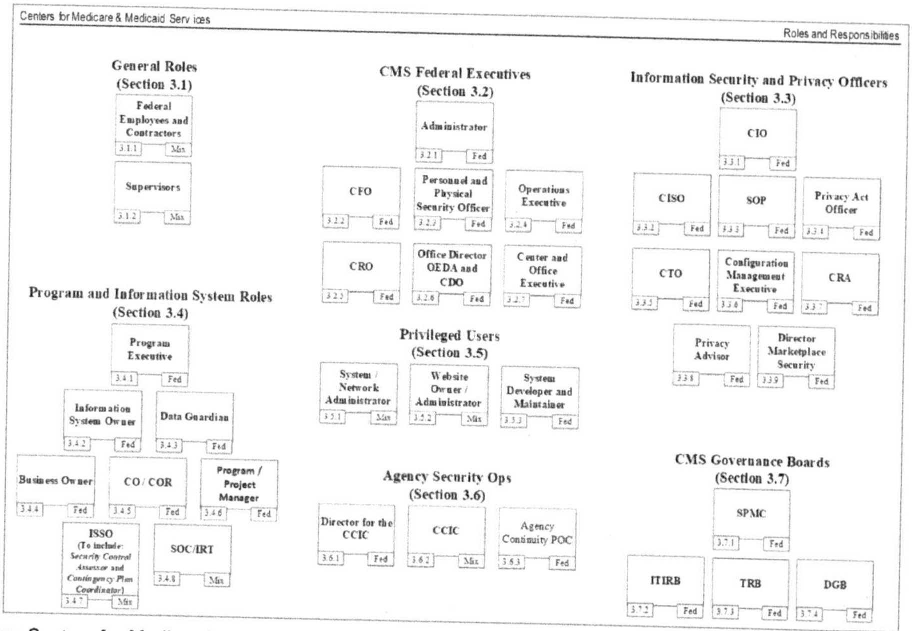

Source: Centers for Medicare and Medicaid Services Information Systems Security and Privacy Policy. (www.cms.gov/Research-Statistics-Data-and-Systems/CMS-Information-Technology/InformationSecurity/Downloads/CMS-IS2P2.pdf)

This approach may meet the needs of CMS, but it is hard to imagine the long-term maintenance of that document. Lengthy security policies often quickly become outdated as necessary changes to individual requirements accumulate and become neglected because staff are weary of continually publishing new versions of the policy.

Cybersecurity Standards

Standards provide mandatory requirements describing how an organization will carry out its information security policies. These may include the specific configuration settings used for a common operating system, the controls that must be put in place for highly sensitive information, or any other security objective. Standards are typically approved at a lower organizational level than policies and, therefore, may change more regularly. Organizations may choose to develop their own standards, adopt standards created by external groups, or use a hybrid approach where they modify existing standards to meet their needs.

For example, the University of California (UC) at Berkeley maintains a detailed document titled *Minimum Security Standards for Electronic Information,* available at `https://security.berkeley.edu/minimum-security-standards-electronic-information`. This document divides information into four different data protection levels (DPLs) and then describes what controls are required, optional, and not required for data at different levels, using a detailed matrix. An excerpt from this matrix appears in Figure 4.4.

FIGURE 4.4   Excerpt from UC Berkeley Minimum Security Standards for Electronic Information

MSSEI Controls	DPL 0 (TBD)	DPL 1 Individual	DPL 1 Privileged	DPL 1 Institutional	DPL 2 Individual	DPL 2 Privileged	DPL 2 Institutional	DPL 3 (TBD)	Guidelines
1.1 Removal of non-required covered data		o	√	√	√	√	√		see secure deletion guideline and UCOP disposition schedules database
1.2 Covered system inventory			√	√		√	√		1.2 guideline
1.3 Covered system registration			+	√		√	√		1.3 guideline
1.4 Annual registration renewal			√	√		√	√		1.4 guideline
2.1 Managed software inventory			+	√	o	√	√		2.1 guideline
3.1 Secure configurations		o	+	√	√	√	√		3.1 guideline
4.1 Continuous vulnerability assessment & remediation			+	√		√	√		4.1 guideline

Berkeley UNIVERSITY OF CALIFORNIA

The standard then provides detailed descriptions for each of these requirements with definitions of the terms used in the requirements. For example, requirement 3.1 in Figure 4.4 simply reads "Secure configurations." Later in the document, UC Berkeley expands this to read "Resource Custodians must utilize well-managed security configurations for hardware, software, and operating systems based on industry standards." It goes on to define "well-managed" as including the following:

- Devices must have secure configurations in place prior to deployment.

- Any deviations from defined security configurations must be approved through a change management process and documented. A process must exist to annually review deviations from the defined security configurations for continued relevance.

- A process must exist to regularly check configurations of devices and alert the Resource Custodian of any changes.

This approach provides a document hierarchy that is easy to navigate for the reader and provides access to increasing levels of detail as needed. Notice also that many of the requirement lines in Figure 4.4 offer links to guidelines. Clicking those links leads to advice to departments subject to this policy that begins with this text:

> UC Berkeley security policy mandates compliance with Minimum Security Standards for Electronic Information for devices handling covered data. The recommendations below are provided as optional guidance.

This is a perfect example of three elements of the information security policy framework working together. The policy sets out the broad objectives of the security program and requires compliance with standards, which includes details of required security controls. Guidelines, discussed later in this chapter, provide advice to organizations seeking to comply with the policy and standards.

In some cases, organizations may encounter industry-specific standards. These best practices, developed by industry groups, are custom-tailored to the needs of the industry. In some heavily regulated industries, compliance with these standards may be required by law or contractual agreement. In other fields, the standards are just helpful resources. Failure to follow industry best practices may be seen as negligence and can cause legal liability for the organization.

Cybersecurity Procedures

Procedures are detailed, step-by-step processes that individuals and organizations must follow in specific circumstances. Similar to checklists, procedures ensure a consistent process for achieving a security objective. Organizations may create procedures for building new systems, releasing code to production environments, responding to security incidents, and many other tasks. Compliance with procedures is mandatory.

For example, Visa publishes a document titled *What To Do If Compromised* (https://usa.visa.com/dam/VCOM/download/merchants/cisp-what-to-do-if-compromised.pdf) that lays out a mandatory process that merchants who suspect a credit card compromise must follow. Although the document doesn't contain the word *procedure* in the title, the introduction clearly states that the document "establishes procedures and timelines for reporting and responding to a suspected or confirmed Compromise Event." The document provides requirements covering the following areas of incident response:

- Notify Visa of the incident within three days.

- Provide Visa with an initial investigation report.

- Provide notice to other relevant parties.
- Provide exposed payment account data to Visa.
- Conduct PCI forensic investigation.
- Conduct independent investigation.
- Preserve evidence.

Each of these sections provides detailed information on how Visa expects merchants to handle incident response activities. For example, the forensic investigation section describes the use of Payment Card Industry Forensic Investigators (PFI) and reads as follows:

> Upon discovery of an account data compromise, or receipt of an independent forensic investigation notification, an entity must:
>
> - Engage a PFI (or sign a contract) within five (5) business days.
> - Provide Visa with the initial forensic (i.e. preliminary) report within ten (10) business days from when the PFI is engaged (or the contract is signed).
> - Provide Visa with a final forensic report within ten (10) business days of the completion of the review.

There's not much room for interpretation in this type of language. Visa is laying out a clear and mandatory procedure describing what actions the merchant must take, the type of investigator they should hire, and the timeline for completing different milestones.

Organizations commonly include the following procedures in their information security policy frameworks:

- *Monitoring procedures* that describe how the organization will perform security monitoring activities, including the possible use of continuous monitoring technology
- *Evidence production procedures* that describe how the organization will respond to subpoenas, court orders, and other legitimate requests to produce digital evidence
- *Patching procedures* that describe the frequency and process of applying patches to applications and systems under the organization's care

Of course, cybersecurity teams may decide to include many other types of procedures in their frameworks, as dictated by the organization's operational needs.

Cybersecurity Guidelines

Guidelines provide best practices and recommendations related to a given concept, technology, or task. Compliance with guidelines is not mandatory, and guidelines are offered in the spirit of providing helpful advice. That said, the "optionality" of guidelines may vary significantly depending on the organization's culture.

In April 2016, the chief information officer (CIO) of the state of Washington published a 25-page document providing guidelines on the use of electronic signatures by state agencies. The document is not designed to be obligatory but, rather, offers advice to agencies seeking to adopt electronic signature technology. The document begins with a purpose section that outlines three goals of the guidelines:

1. Help agencies determine if, and to what extent, their agency will implement and rely on electronic records and electronic signatures.

2. Provide agencies with information they can use to establish policy or rules governing their use and acceptance of digital signatures.

3. Provide direction to agencies for sharing their policies with the Office of the Chief Information Officer (OCIO) pursuant to state law.

The first two stated objectives line up completely with the function of a guideline. Phrases like "help agencies determine" and "provide agencies with information" are common in guideline documents. There is nothing mandatory about them, and in fact, the guidelines explicitly state that Washington state law "does not mandate that any state agency accept or require electronic signatures or records."

The third objective might seem a little strange to include in a guideline. Phrases like "provide direction" are more commonly found in policies and procedures. Browsing through the document, the text relating to this objective is only a single paragraph within a 25-page document:

> The Office of the Chief Information Officer maintains a page on the OCIO .wa.gov website listing links to individual agency electronic signature and record submission policies. As agencies publish their policies, the link and agency contact information should be emailed to the OCIO Policy Mailbox. The information will be added to the page within 5 working days. Agencies are responsible for notifying the OCIO if the information changes.

Reading this paragraph, the text does appear to clearly outline a mandatory procedure and would not be appropriate in a guideline document that fits within the strict definition of the term. However, it is likely that the committee drafting this document thought it would be much more convenient for the reader to include this explanatory text in the related guideline rather than drafting a separate procedure document for a fairly mundane and simple task.

> The full Washingtons state document, *Electronic Signature Guidelines*, is available for download from the Washington State CIO's website at https://ocio.wa.gov/sites/default/files/Electronic_ Signature_Guidelines_FINAL.pdf.

Exceptions and Compensating Controls

When adopting new security policies, standards, and procedures, organizations should also provide a mechanism for exceptions to those rules. Inevitably, unforeseen circumstances will arise that require a deviation from the requirements. The policy framework should lay out the specific requirements for receiving an exception and the individual or committee with the authority to approve exceptions.

The state of Washington uses an exception process that requires the requestor to document the following information:

- Standard/requirement that requires an exception

- Reason for noncompliance with the requirement

- Business and/or technical justification for the exception

- Scope and duration of the exception

- Risks associated with the exception

- Description of any supplemental controls that mitigate the risks associated with the exception

- Plan for achieving compliance

- Identification of any unmitigated risks

Many exception processes require the use of *compensating controls* to mitigate the risk associated with exceptions to security standards. The Payment Card Industry Data Security Standard (PCI DSS) includes one of the most formal compensating control processes in use today. It sets out three criteria that must be met for a compensating control to be satisfactory:

1. The control must meet the intent and rigor of the original requirement.

2. The control must provide a similar level of defense as the original requirement such that the compensating control sufficiently offsets the risk that the original PCI DSS requirement was designed to defend against.

3. The control must be "above and beyond" other PCI DSS requirements.

For example, an organization might find that it needs to run an outdated version of an operating system on a specific machine because the software necessary to run the business will only function on that operating system version. Most security policies would prohibit using the outdated operating system because it might be susceptible to security vulnerabilities. The organization could choose to run this system on an isolated network with either very little or no access to other systems as a compensating control.

The general idea is that a compensating control finds alternative means to achieve an objective when the organization cannot meet the original control requirement. Although PCI DSS offers a very formal process for compensating controls, the use of compensating controls is a common strategy in many different organizations, even those not subject to PCI DSS. Compensating controls balance the fact that it simply isn't possible to implement every required security control in every circumstance with the desire to manage risk to the greatest feasible degree.

In many cases, organizations adopt compensating controls to address a temporary exception to a security requirement. In those cases, the organization should also develop remediation plans designed to bring the organization back into compliance with the letter and intent of the original control.

Developing Policies

When developing new policies, cybersecurity managers should align their work with any other policy development mechanisms that may exist within their organizations. The more that a leader can align cybersecurity policy efforts with existing processes, the easier it will be to gain traction for those initiatives. In any event, cybersecurity managers should follow a few key principles when working on policy development initiatives:

Obtain input from all relevant stakeholders. Think carefully about all of the leaders and teams that might be affected by the policy and work to understand their perspectives while crafting the policy. This doesn't mean that everyone in the organization must agree with a proposed policy but that everyone should feel that their input was solicited and heard during the process.

Follow the chain of command. Knowledge of the organizational structure is essential to the success of a policy initiative. Cybersecurity managers must be aware of both the formal governance lines of authority and as the informal mechanisms of the organization for getting things done.

Accommodate the organizational culture. There's a good reason that there isn't a one-size-fits-all security policy that every organization can adopt. That's because every organization is different. Make sure that the policies you create fit into the organizational culture and match the "tone at the top" from other leaders.

Meet internal and external requirements. Cybersecurity programs are often heavily regulated by both internal governance processes and external laws and regulations. In many cases, these requirements may dictate some of the contents of security policies. At the very least, security policies should not contradict these requirements.

After a policy is drafted, it should move through the policy approval mechanisms used by the organization. After receiving a final sign-off, the cybersecurity manager may then communicate the policy to affected individuals and teams and begin the process of implementing the new policy. Depending on the nature of the change, this may involve using a phased approach that allows the organization to gradually adapt to the new requirements.

Identity and Access Management

Protecting data from unauthorized disclosure is a critical component of preserving privacy. *Identity and access management (IAM)* programs provide the framework used to ensure that users are who they claim to be and limit their access to data in a way that allows them to perform their duties. Privacy professionals are responsible for coordinating closely with cybersecurity teams on implementing appropriate access controls for physical and virtual systems.

Least Privilege

Least privilege is the core principle at the heart of identity and access management. It states that an individual should only have the minimum set of privileges necessary to complete their assigned job duties. Least privilege is important for two reasons:

- Least privilege minimizes the potential damage from an insider attack. If an employee acts in a malicious way, the damage they can cause will be limited by the privileges assigned to them by their job or role. It's unlikely, for example, that an accountant would be able to deface the company website because an accountant's job responsibilities have nothing to do with updating web content.

- Least privilege limits the ability of an external attacker to quickly gain privileged access when compromising an employee's account. Unless they happen to compromise a system administrator's account, they will find themselves limited by the privileges of the account that they steal.

When it comes to access to information, security and privacy professionals often summarize least privilege as requiring a *need to know*. Individuals should not be able to access information unless there is a valid business requirement that gives them a need to know that information.

Identification, Authentication, and Authorization

The access control process consists of three steps that you must understand. These steps are identification, authentication, and authorization.

During the first step of the process, *identification*, an individual makes a claim about their identity. The person trying to gain access doesn't present any proof at this point—they simply make an assertion. It's important to remember that the identification step is only a claim and the user could certainly be making a false claim!

Imagine a physical world scenario where you want to enter a secure office building where you have an appointment. During the identification step of the process, I might walk up to the security desk and say: "Hi, I'm Mike Chapple."

Proof comes into play during the second step of the process: *authentication*. During the authentication step, the individual proves their identity to the satisfaction of the access control system. In our office building example, the guard would likely wish to see my driver's license to confirm my identity.

Simply proving your identity isn't enough to gain access to a system, however. The access control system also needs to be satisfied that you are allowed to access the system. That's the third step of the access control process: *authorization*. In our office building example, the security guard might check a list of that day's appointments to see if it includes my name.

Exam Tip

When you get ready for the exam, it's very important that you remember the distinction between the identification and authentication phases. Be ready to identify the phase associated with an example of a mechanism.

So far, we've talked about identification, authentication, and authorization in the context of gaining access to a building. Let's talk about how they work in the electronic world. When we go to log in to a system, we most often identify ourselves using a username, most likely composed of some combination of the letters from our names.

When we reach the authentication phase, we're commonly asked to enter a password. There are many other ways to authenticate, and we'll talk about those later in this chapter.

Finally, in the electronic world, authorization often takes the form of access control lists that itemize the specific filesystem permissions granted to an individual user or group of users. Users proceed through the identification, authentication, and authorization processes when they request access to a resource.

Authentication Techniques

Computer systems offer many different authentication techniques that allow users to prove their identity. Let's take a look at three different authentication factors: something you know, something you are, and something you have.

Something You Know

Passwords are the most common example of a "something you know" authentication factor. The user remembers their password and enters it into a system during the authentication process.

Users should choose strong passwords consisting of as many characters as possible and combine characters from multiple classes, such as uppercase and lowercase letters, digits, and symbols.

Something You Are

The second authentication factor is something you are, otherwise known as *biometric* authentication. Biometrics measure one of your physical characteristics, such as a fingerprint, eye pattern, face, or voice. Using biometric authentication requires specialized readers, such as the retinal scanner shown in Figure 4.5(a) or the fingerprint reader shown in Figure 4.5(b).

Something You Have

The third authentication factor, something you have, requires the user to have physical possession of a device, such as a smartphone or authentication token keyfob like the one shown in Figure 4.6.

Multifactor Authentication

When used alone, any one authentication factor provides some security for systems. However, each one has its drawbacks. For example, an attacker might steal a user's password through a phishing attack. Once they have the password, they can then use that password to assume the user's identity. Other authentication factors aren't foolproof, either. If you use smartcard authentication to implement something you have, the user may lose the smartcard. Someone coming across it may then impersonate the user.

FIGURE 4.5 Biometric authentication with a (a) retinal scanner (b) fingerprint scanner

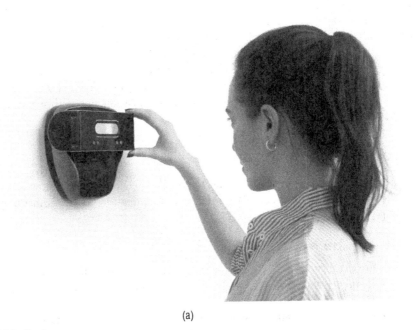

(a)

demphoto / Adobe Stock

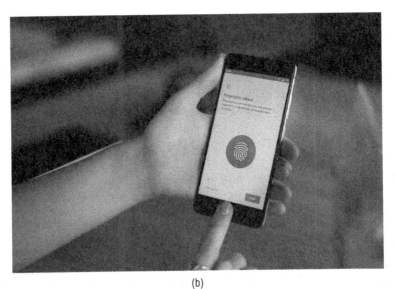

(b)

artiemedvedev / Adobe Stock

The solution to this problem is to combine authentication techniques from multiple factors, such as combining something you know with something you have. This approach is known as *multifactor authentication.*

FIGURE 4.6   Authentication token

Matteo F. / Adobe Stock

Take the two techniques we just discussed: passwords and smartcards. When used alone, either one is subject to hackers either gaining knowledge of the password or stealing a smartcard. However, if an authentication system requires both a password (something you know) and a smartcard (something you have) it brings added security. If the hacker steals the password, they don't have the required smartcard, and vice versa. It suddenly becomes much more difficult for the attacker to gain access to the account. Something you know and something you have are different factors, so this is an example of multifactor authentication.

We can combine other authentication factors as well. For example, a fingerprint reader (something you are) might also require the entry of a PIN (something you know).

When evaluating multifactor authentication, remember that the techniques must be *different* factors. An approach that combines a password with the answer to a security question is *not* multifactor authentication because both factors are something you know.

Provisioning and Deprovisioning

Account administrators are responsible for managing the *provisioning* and *deprovisioning* of user accounts. When a new user joins the organization, administrators ensure that they go through the appropriate onboarding process and then provision a user account for that user. This involves creating authentication credentials and granting the user appropriate authorizations based on their job function.

When that user leaves the organization, administrators ensure that they go through an offboarding process that includes deprovisioning the account to remove their credentials and authorizations at the appropriate time. Administrators must act quickly to remove the user's access to computer systems. This prevents the user from accessing sensitive information or resources after their departure and is especially important when a user leaves the organization under unfavorable circumstances.

Security professionals should ensure that the organization has a strong process designed to remove access, preferably in an automated or semiautomated fashion. This process may have several workflows.

The normal workflow, for a planned departure, should automatically begin when a supervisor informs the Human Resources department that an employee is resigning or retiring.

The account administration team should configure the user's account to automatically expire on the date they are leaving the organization.

An emergency workflow may be used when a user is suddenly terminated. This may occur under adverse circumstances when a user is fired. In those cases, the IT department should carefully coordinate with Human Resources to time the account termination precisely.

If account administrators fail to precisely time the access revocation, two undesirable situations may occur. First, if the account is terminated before the employee is informed of their termination, the employee may gain advance notice of the impending termination and take retaliatory action against the employer. Second, if the account is not terminated immediately upon the user being informed of their termination, the user may gain access to the system after being fired and take retaliatory action.

Suspending and terminating accounts in a timely manner boosts enterprise security by reducing the risk of unauthorized access.

Account and Privilege Management

Security administrators must pay careful attention to the permissions and use of end-user accounts to protect against security incidents. Let's take a look at some account monitoring practices that organizations should put in place.

The first is inaccurate permissions assigned to accounts that either prevent a user from doing their work or violate the principle of least privilege. These permissions are often the result of *privilege creep*, a condition that occurs when users switch jobs and gain new permissions but never have their old permissions revoked.

To protect against inaccurate permissions, administrators should perform regular user account reviews in cooperation with managers from around the organization. During each of these manual reviews, the administrators should pull a listing of all the permissions assigned to each account and then review that listing with managers to ensure that it is appropriate for the user's role, making any necessary adjustments. Administrators should pay careful attention to users who switched jobs since the last account review.

Another issue is the unauthorized use of permissions, either by someone other than the legitimate user accessing the account or by the user performing some illegitimate action. Protecting against unauthorized use of permissions is tricky because it can be hard to detect. This requires the use of continuous account monitoring systems that watch for suspicious activity and alert administrators to strange actions.

For example, a continuous account monitoring system may flag violations of access policies, such as the following:

- Logons from strange geographic locations such as a user connecting from both the home office and a remote location in Eastern Europe at the same time; cases like this are known as impossible travel time logins and should be treated as risky logins.

- Logins from unusual network locations, such as a user who always logs in from the HR network suddenly appearing on a guest network.

- Logons at unusual times of day, such as a mail clerk logging into the system in the middle of the night.

- Deviations from normal behavior, such as users accessing files that they do not normally access.

- High volumes of activity that may represent bulk downloading of sensitive information. The specific circumstances that merit attention will vary from organization to organization, but performing this type of behavior-based continuous account monitoring is an important security control.

Privacy by Design

The discipline of *privacy by design (PbD)* (see Chapter 2, "Privacy Program Framework") seeks to incorporate strong privacy practices into the design and implementation of technology systems, rather than seeking to "bolt on" privacy controls after a system is already in place. This approach leads to more effective privacy controls, more efficient design and implementation processes, and reduced rework.

Ann Cavoukian, the Information and Privacy Commissioner of Ontario, Canada, developed the concept of PbD and outlined seven foundational principles that are crucial to ensuring that individuals retain control over their personal information. These principles are as follows:

Proactive, Not Reactive; Preventive, Not Remedial   Systems should be designed to prevent privacy risks from occurring in the first place, not to respond to privacy lapses that do occur.

Privacy as the Default Setting   Systems should protect the privacy of individuals even if they do not act in any way. The default approach of any system should be to protect privacy unless the user specifically chooses to take actions that reduce the level of privacy.

Privacy Embedded into Design   Privacy should be a primary design consideration, not a "bolted-on" afterthought. Privacy is a core requirement of the system.

Full Functionality—Positive Sum, not Zero Sum   Privacy should not be treated as requiring trade-offs with the business, security, or other objectives. Privacy by design seeks "win-win" situations where privacy objectives may be achieved alongside other objectives.

End-to-End Security—Full Life Cycle Protection   Security practices should persist throughout the entire information life cycle. Information should be securely collected, retained, and disposed of to preserve individual privacy.

Visibility and Transparency—Keep It Open   The component parts of systems preserving PbD should be open for inspection by users and providers alike.

Respect for User Privacy—Keep It User-Centric   Privacy is about protecting personal information, and personal information belongs to individual people. Therefore, PbD practices maintain a focus on the individual, empowering data subjects with user-friendly privacy practices.

The principles of privacy by design offer an outstanding starting point for integrating privacy thinking into a systems engineering practice. Privacy and security professionals should work together to communicate to all relevant stakeholders the importance of integrating these principles into the work of the organization.

Privacy and the SDLC

The *Systems Development Life Cycle (SDLC)* describes the steps in a model for systems and software development. Every mature technology organization uses an SDLC approach to managing the creation of software and systems. Privacy professionals must understand the SDLC used by their organizations and work to integrate privacy requirements throughout the SDLC.

As shown in Figure 4.7, the SDLC maps system creation from an idea to requirements gathering and analysis to design, coding, testing, and rollout. Once a system is in production, it also includes user training, maintenance, and decommissioning at the end of the system's useful life.

FIGURE 4.7   High-level SDLC view

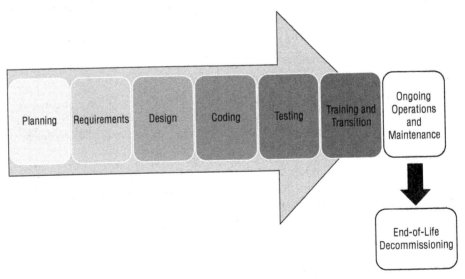

Development does not always follow a formal model, but most enterprise development for major applications does follow most, if not all, of these phases. In some cases, developers may even use elements of an SDLC model without realizing it!

The SDLC is useful for organizations and developers because it provides a consistent framework to structure workflow and provides planning for the development process. Despite these advantages, simply picking an SDLC model to implement may not always be the best choice. Each SDLC model has certain types of work and projects that it fits better than others, making choosing an SDLC model that fits the work an important part of the process.

System Development Phases

Regardless of which SDLC or process is chosen by your organization, a few phases appear in most SDLC models:

1. The *planning* phase is where initial investigations into whether the effort should occur are conducted. Feasibility also looks at alternative solutions and high-level costs for each solution proposed. It results in a recommendation with a plan to move forward.

2. Once an effort has been deemed feasible, it will typically go through an *analysis and requirements definition* phase. In this phase, customer input is sought to determine what the desired functionality is, what the current system or application currently does and what it doesn't do, and what improvements are desired. Requirements may be ranked to determine which are most critical to the success of the project.

Exam Tip

Privacy requirements definition is an important part of the analysis and requirements definition phase. It ensures that the system is designed to protect the privacy of PII.

---

3. The *design* phase includes design for functionality, architecture, integration points and techniques, dataflows, business processes, and any other elements that require design consideration.

4. The actual creation of the system occurs during the *coding* phase. This phase may involve the testing of parts of the system, including *unit testing*, and the testing of small components individually to ensure they function properly.

5. While some testing is likely to occur in the development phase, formal testing with customers or others outside of the development team occurs in the *testing* phase. Individual units or software components are integrated and then tested to ensure proper functionality. In addition, connections to outside services, data sources, and other integration

may occur during this phase. During this phase, *user acceptance testing (UAT)* occurs to ensure that the users of the system are satisfied with its functionality.

6. The important task of ensuring that the end users are trained on the system and that the system has entered general use occurs in the *training and transition* phase. This phase is sometimes called the acceptance, installation, and deployment phase.

7. Once a project reaches completion, the system will enter what is usually the longest phase: *ongoing operations and maintenance.* This phase includes patching, updating, minor modifications, and other work that goes into daily support.

8. The *end-of-life* phase occurs when a product or system reaches the end of its life. Although disposition is often ignored in the excitement of developing new products, it is an important phase for a number of reasons: shutting down old products can produce cost savings, replacing existing tools may require specific knowledge or additional effort, and data and systems may need to be preserved or properly disposed of.

The order of the phases may vary, with some progressing in a simple linear fashion and others taking an iterative or parallel approach. You will still see some form of each of these phases in successful life cycles.

One common way to ensure that privacy requirements are met is to implement a series of "privacy gates" in the organization's project process. When projects reach different stages of the SDLC, they are not permitted to advance "through" the privacy gate unless they have met key privacy requirements and documented their work.

System Development Models

The SDLC can be approached in many ways, and over time a number of formal models have been created to help provide a common framework for development. While formal SDLC models can be very detailed, with specific practices, procedures, and documentation, many organizations choose the elements of one or more models that best fit their organizational style, workflow, and requirements.

Waterfall

The *Waterfall* methodology is a sequential model in which each phase is followed by the next phase. Phases do not overlap, and each logically leads to the next. A typical six-phase Waterfall process is shown in Figure 4.8. In Phase 1, requirements are gathered and documented. Phase 2 involves analysis intended to build business rules and models. In Phase 3, a software architecture is designed, and coding and integration of the software occurs in Phase 4. Once the software is complete, Phase 5 occurs, with testing and debugging completed in this phase. Finally, the software enters an operational phase, with support, maintenance, and other operational activities happening on an ongoing basis.

FIGURE 4.8   The Waterfall SDLC model

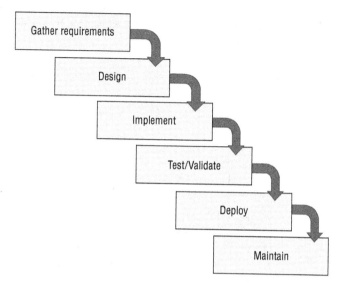

Waterfall has been replaced in many organizations because it is seen as relatively inflexible, but it remains in use for complex systems. Since Waterfall is not highly responsive to changes and does not account for internal iterative work, it is typically recommended for development efforts that involve a fixed scope and a known time frame for delivery and that are using a stable, well-understood technology platform.

Spiral

The *Spiral* model uses the linear development concepts from the Waterfall model and adds an iterative process that revisits four phases multiple times during the development life cycle to gather more detailed requirements, design functionality guided by the requirements, and build based on the design. In addition, the Spiral model puts significant emphasis on risk assessment as part of the SDLC, reviewing risks multiple times during the development process.

The Spiral model shown in Figure 4.9 uses four phases, which it repeatedly visits throughout the development life cycle:

1. Identification, or requirements gathering, which initially gathers business requirements, system requirements, and more detailed requirements for subsystems or modules as the process continues.

2. Design, conceptual, architectural, logical, and sometimes physical or final design.

3. Build, which produces an initial proof of concept and then further development releases until the final production build is produced.

4. Evaluation, which involves risk analysis for the development project intended to monitor the feasibility of delivering the software from a technical and managerial viewpoint. As the development cycle continues, this phase also involves customer testing and feedback to ensure customer acceptance.

FIGURE 4.9   The Spiral SDLC model

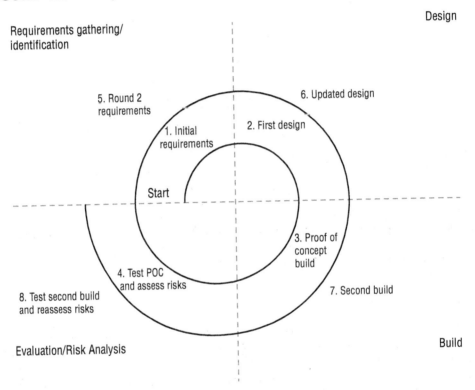

The Spiral model provides greater flexibility to handle changes in requirements as well as external influences such as the availability of customer feedback and development staff. It also allows the software development life cycle to start earlier in the process than Waterfall does. Because Spiral revisits its process, it is possible for this model to result in rework or to identify design requirements later in the process that require a significant design change due to more detailed requirements coming to light.

Agile

Agile software development is an iterative and incremental process, rather than the linear processes that Waterfall and Spiral use. Agile is rooted in the Manifesto for Agile Software Development, a document that has four basic premises:

- Individuals and interactions are more important than processes and tools.

- Working software is preferable to comprehensive documentation.
- Customer collaboration replaces contract negotiation.
- Responding to change is key, rather than following a plan.

If you are used to a Waterfall or Spiral development process, Agile is a significant departure from the planning, design, and documentation-centric approaches that Agile's predecessors use. Agile methods tend to break work up into smaller units, allowing work to be done more quickly and with less up-front planning. It focuses on adapting to needs, rather than predicting them, with major milestones identified early in the process but subject to change as the project continues to develop.

Work is typically broken up into short working sessions, called *sprints*, that can last days to a few weeks. Figure 4.10 shows a simplified view of an Agile project methodology with multiple sprints conducted. When the developers and customer agree that the task is done or when the time allocated for the sprints is complete, the development effort is completed.

FIGURE 4.10   Agile sprints

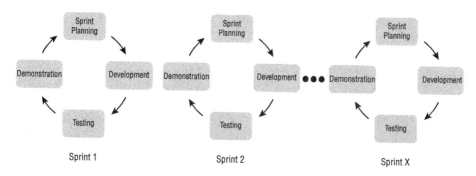

The Agile methodology is based on 12 principles:

- Ensure customer satisfaction via early and continuous delivery of the software.
- Welcome changing requirements, even late in the development process.
- Deliver working software frequently (in weeks rather than months).
- Ensure daily cooperation between developers and businesspeople.
- Projects should be built around motivated individuals who get the support, trust, and environment they need to succeed.
- Face-to-face conversations are the most efficient way to convey information inside the development team.
- Progress is measured by having working software.
- Development should be done at a sustainable pace that can be maintained on an ongoing basis.
- Pay continuous attention to technical excellence and good design.

- Simplicity—the art of maximizing the amount of work not done—is essential.
- The best architectures, requirements, and designs emerge from self-organizing teams.
- Teams should reflect on how to become more effective and then implement that behavior at regular intervals.

These principles drive an SDLC process that is less formally structured than Spiral or Waterfall but that has many opportunities for customer feedback and revision. It can react more nimbly to problems and will typically allow faster customer feedback—an advantage when security or privacy issues are discovered.

Integrating Privacy with Business Processes

As you work to integrate privacy into your organization's business practices, be sure to address each of the key areas that likely collect, use, store, or process PII. You'll want to ensure that each of these groups has privacy requirements integrated into their practices and that they are represented in organization-wide privacy processes. The most common areas to include are:

- Information Technology
- Information Security
- Human Resources
- Marketing
- Legal and Contracts
- Mergers, Acquisitions & Divestitures

 Information security teams are also responsible for building and maintaining cybersecurity incident response processes. We will discuss these processes in more detail in Chapter 6, "Privacy Operational Life Cycle: Respond."

Vulnerability Management

Cybersecurity is a cat-and-mouse game where information technology professionals seek to combat the new vulnerabilities discovered by adversaries on an almost daily basis. Modern enterprises consist of hardware and software of almost unfathomable complexity, and buried within those systems are thousands of undiscovered security vulnerabilities waiting for an attacker to exploit them.

Vulnerability management programs seek to identify, prioritize, and remediate these vulnerabilities before an attacker exploits them to undermine the confidentiality, integrity, or availability of enterprise information assets. Effective vulnerability management programs use an organized approach to scanning enterprise assets for vulnerabilities, using a defined workflow to remediate those vulnerabilities and perform continuous assessments to provide technologists and managers with insight into the current state of enterprise cybersecurity.

Vulnerability Scanning

Cybersecurity professionals depend on automation to help them perform their duties in an efficient, effective manner. Vulnerability scanning tools allow the automated scheduling of scans to take the burden off administrators. Administrators may designate a schedule that meets their security, compliance, vendor patch release frequency, and business requirements.

Administrators should configure these scans to provide automated alerting when they detect new vulnerabilities. Many security teams configure their scans to produce automated email reports or service tickets from scan results.

Many different factors influence how often an organization decides to conduct vulnerability scans against its systems. These include the following:

- The organization's *risk appetite* is its willingness to tolerate risk within the environment. If an organization is extremely risk averse, it may choose to conduct scans more frequently to minimize the amount of time between when a vulnerability comes into existence and when it is detected by a scan.

- *Regulatory requirements,* such as PCI DSS or other compliance requirements, may dictate a minimum frequency for vulnerability scans. These requirements may also come from corporate policies.

- *Technical constraints* may limit the frequency of scanning. For example, the scanning system may only be capable of performing a certain number of scans per day, and organizations may need to adjust scan frequency to ensure that all scans complete successfully.

- *Business constraints* may limit the organization's ability to conduct resource-intensive vulnerability scans during periods of high business activity to avoid disruption of critical processes.

- *Licensing limitations* may curtail the bandwidth consumed by the scanner or the number of scans that may be conducted simultaneously.

Cybersecurity professionals must balance each of these considerations when planning a vulnerability scanning program. It is usually wise to begin small and slowly expand the scope and frequency of vulnerability scans over time to avoid overwhelming the scanning infrastructure or enterprise systems.

Vulnerability Remediation

Vulnerability scans often produce a fairly steady stream of security issues that require attention from cybersecurity professionals, system engineers, software developers, network engineers, and other technologists. A vulnerability scan will typically produce several priorities of risk, like critical, high, medium, low, or informational. The initial scans of an environment can produce an overwhelming number of issues requiring prioritization and eventual remediation. Organizations should develop a remediation workflow that allows for the prioritization of vulnerabilities and the tracking of remediation through the cycle of detection, remediation, and testing shown in Figure 4.11.

This remediation workflow should be as automated as possible, given the tools available to the organization. Many vulnerability management products include a built-in workflow mechanism that allows cybersecurity experts to track vulnerabilities through the remediation process and automatically close out vulnerabilities after testing confirms that the remediation was successful. Although these tools are helpful, other organizations often choose not to use them in favor of tracking vulnerabilities in the IT service management (ITSM) tool that the organization uses for other technology issues. This approach avoids asking technologists to use two different issue tracking systems and improves compliance with the remediation process. However, it also requires selecting vulnerability management tools that integrate natively with the organization's ITSM tool (or vice versa) or building an integration between the tools if one does not already exist.

FIGURE 4.11 Vulnerability management life cycle

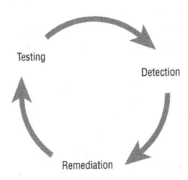

An important trend in vulnerability management is a shift toward *ongoing scanning* and *continuous monitoring*. Ongoing scanning moves away from the scheduled scanning approach that tested systems on a scheduled weekly or monthly basis and instead configures scanners to simply scan systems on a rotating basis, checking for vulnerabilities as often as scanning resources permit. This approach can be bandwidth and resource intensive, but it does provide earlier detection of vulnerabilities. Continuous monitoring incorporates data from agent-based approaches to vulnerability detection and reports security-related configuration changes to the vulnerability management platform as soon as they occur, providing the ability to analyze those changes for potential vulnerabilities.

Data Policies

Organizations building security and privacy programs will need to create a set of specific policies that guide the organization's use of data. These policies should be tailored to the unique needs of the organization and cover all types of data processing, including the collection, use, retention, disclosure, and disposal of the organization's data holdings. They should also incorporate both legal and ethical requirements for the appropriate handling of data.

Implementing these policies is an important administrative safeguard to preserve the privacy of personal information. Policies should be backed up with procedures that define specific privacy practices. Policies and procedures ensure that everyone in the organization understands their privacy responsibilities, and they provide recourse when an individual or team fails to meet its privacy obligations.

Data Sharing

Data sharing policies focus on defining roles and responsibilities within the organization for managing the sharing and disclosure of personal information. These policies should define processes for authorizing and carrying out data sharing with both internal and external parties.

While you should have policies and procedures that address generic sharing and disclosure of data, you may also wish to create specialized policies that cover specific situations normally encountered in your organization. For example, if you commonly share data sets with internal and/or external researchers, you may wish to have policies that specifically cover data sharing for research purposes.

Exam Tip

Any data sharing with external organizations should be done under the terms of a formal, written contract that defines the privacy and security responsibilities of both parties to the agreement.

Data Retention

Data retention policies specify what types of data the organization will store and the appropriate length of time for that data to be preserved before it is destroyed. These policies ensure that the organization retains data as long as it is needed to meet business and legal requirements but that they destroy data as soon as they no longer have a valid need to preserve it.

Data Destruction

When data reaches the end of its life span, destroying the media that contains it is an important physical security measure. Secure data destruction helps prevent data breaches, including intentional attacks like dumpster diving as well as unintentional losses via reuse of media, systems, or other data storage devices. Table 4.1 shows some of the most common options for the destruction of paper records, media like hard drives, tapes, flash-based devices, and even complete computers.

TABLE 4.1 Secure data destruction options

Destruction method	Description	Notes
Burning	Most often done in a high-temperature incinerator. Primarily used for paper records, although some incinerators may support electronic devices.	Typically done offsite through a third-party service, leaves no recoverable materials.
Shredding	Can be done on site, and can support paper or devices using an industrial shredder.	Traditional paper shredders may allow for the recovery of documents, even from cross-cut shredded documents. For high-security environments, burning or pulping may be required.
Pulping	Breaks paper documents into wood pulp, removing ink. Materials can be recycled.	Completely destroys documents, preventing recovery.
Pulverizing	Breaks devices down into very small pieces, preventing recovery.	The size of the output material can determine the potential for recovery of data, typically pulverizing results in very small fragments of material.
Degaussing	Magnetically wipes data from tapes and traditional hard magnetic media hard drives.	Only effective on magnetic media and will not work on SSDs, flash media, optical media (such as CDs or DVDs), or paper.

While physical destruction is the most secure way to ensure data destruction, nondestructive options are often desirable in a business environment to allow for the reuse of media or devices. Secure drive or media wiping options can be used when the potential for exposure is low or the risks of remnant data exposure are not a significant concern for the organization.

A final option that many organizations choose to put into place for secure destruction is the use of third-party solutions. Contracted document and device destruction companies will pick up and remove sensitive documents and media for shredding at their facility or will perform the same service on site. Organizations may opt for a thoroughly documented destruction process, including photos of the devices and per-device destruction certification, depending on their security needs. Third-party destruction services are a good fit for many organizations with typical security needs, since they ensure appropriate destruction without requiring internal investment in the tools and time to securely destroy media and systems.

Exam Tip

When using a third-party data destruction service, the provider should give customers a certificate of destruction that certifies that the data they collected was properly destroyed.

Summary

Protecting the confidentiality, integrity, and availability of information is critical to preserving its privacy. For this reason, cybersecurity and privacy programs are closely related to each other, sharing many common goals. In this chapter, you learned about many of the controls that cybersecurity professionals use to achieve their objectives and the ways that privacy professionals can implement additional controls designed to achieve privacy objectives.

Exam Essentials

Know that security and privacy programs are closely related. Security programs have three main goals: confidentiality, integrity, and availability. Confidentiality ensures that unauthorized individuals are not able to gain access to sensitive information. Integrity ensures that there are no unauthorized modifications to information or systems, either intentionally or unintentionally. Availability ensures that information and systems are ready to meet the needs of legitimate users at the time those users request them.

Be able to define privacy by design (PbD). PbD, which integrates privacy requirements into the systems development process, has seven guiding principles:

- Proactive, not reactive; preventive, not remedial
- Privacy as the default setting
- Privacy embedded into design

- Full functionality—positive sum, not zero sum
- End-to-end security—full life cycle protection
- Visibility and transparency—keep it open
- Respect for user privacy—keep it user-centric

Know how identity and access management programs regulate access to data.   Identity and access management systems perform three major functions: identification, authentication, and authorization. Identification is the process of a user making a claim of identity, such as by providing a username. Authentication allows the user to prove their identity. Authentication may be done using something you know, something you have, or something you are. Multifactor authentication combines different authentication techniques to provide stronger security. Authorization ensures that authenticated users may only perform actions necessary to carry out their assigned responsibilities.

Know the purpose of policy frameworks.   Policies, which consist of policies, standards, procedures, and guidelines, are high-level statements of management intent for the information security program. Standards describe the detailed implementation requirements for policy. Procedures offer step-by-step instructions for carrying out security activities. Compliance with policies, standards, and procedures is mandatory. Guidelines offer optional advice that complements other elements of the policy framework.

Know that the end of the data life cycle may require secure destruction.   When a device or media is retired, it may need to be securely destroyed to prevent data loss. A variety of techniques exist, including burning, shredding, or pulping paper media, or shredding, pulverizing, or degaussing devices and magnetic media. Using the appropriate solution will help prevent data from being exposed when a system or media is retired or sold. Third parties perform these services and can provide destruction receipts and other documentation to ensure that the destruction was done properly without organizations having to maintain the capability on their own.

Review Questions

1. Gordon is concerned that one of his coworkers recently left a laptop on a train and that laptop contained sensitive personal information. Which one of the following security controls, if in place, would best protect this information from disclosure?

   A. Full-disk encryption

   B. Transport Layer Security

   C. Degaussing

   D. Pulverizing

2. Which one of the following data protection techniques is reversible when conducted properly?

   A. Tokenization

   B. Masking

   C. Hashing

   D. Shredding

3. Joe is authoring a document that explains to system administrators one way in which they might comply with the organization's requirement to encrypt all laptops. What type of document is Joe writing?

   A. Policy

   B. Guideline

   C. Procedure

   D. Standard

4. Which one of the following items is *not* normally included in a request for an exception to security policy?

   A. Description of a compensating control

   B. Description of the risks associated with the exception

   C. Proposed revision to the security policy

   D. Business justification for the exception

5. Kevin is a privacy professional and is reviewing his organization's identity and access management program and finds that some team members have full access to all data stored on the organization's servers. Which one of the following statements is most likely correct?

   A. The access is likely appropriate as long as the affected employees are managers.

   B. The access is likely appropriate as long as the affected employees have appropriate security clearance.

   C. The access is likely appropriate and Kevin should not have questioned it without more knowledge.

   D. The access is most likely a violation of the principle of least privilege.

6. Which one of the following activities is not part of the vulnerability management life cycle?

    A. Detection

    B. Remediation

    C. Reporting

    D. Testing

7. Amanda wants to securely destroy data held on DVDs. Which of the following options is not a suitable solution for this?

    A. Degaussing

    B. Burning

    C. Pulverizing

    D. Shredding

8. Which one of the following factors is least likely to impact vulnerability scanning schedules?

    A. Regulatory requirements

    B. Technical constraints

    C. Business constraints

    D. Staff availability

9. Gwen is developing a new security policy for her organization. Which one of the following statements does not reflect best practices for policy development?

    A. All stakeholders should agree with the proposed policy.

    B. The policy should follow normal corporate policy approval processes.

    C. Policies should match the "tone at the top" from senior business leaders.

    D. Cybersecurity managers are typically responsible for communicating and implementing approved security policies.

10. What type of backup involves always storing copies of all files modified since the most recent full backup?

    A. Differential backups

    B. Partial backup

    C. Incremental backups

    D. Database backup

11. Matthew is concerned that his organization may have Social Security numbers stored in many different locations that are unknown to the privacy team. He would like to search systems for that data. What technology can best be used to meet his goal?

    A. TLS

    B. HSM

    C. FDE

    D. DLP

12. Which one of the following is the best example of data in motion?

A. Data in a cloud service

B. Data in memory

C. Data on a network

D. Data on a hard drive

13. Under the privacy by design philosophy, which statement is correct?

A. Organizations should design systems to respond to privacy lapses that occur.

B. Privacy should be treated as requiring trade-offs with business objectives.

C. Organizations should strictly limit the disclosure of their privacy practices.

D. Privacy should be embedded into design.

14. Gary is logging into a system and is providing his fingerprint to gain access. What step of the IAM process is he performing?

A. Identification

B. Authorization

C. Authentication

D. Accounting

15. Tom is building a multifactor authentication system that requires users to enter a passcode and then verifies that their face matches a photo stored in the system. What two factors is this system using?

A. Something you know and something you have

B. Something you know and something you know

C. Something you have and something you are

D. Something you know and something you are

16. Nolan is writing an after-action report on a security breach that took place in his organization. The attackers stole thousands of customer records from the organization's database. What cybersecurity principle was most impacted in this breach?

A. Availability

B. Nonrepudiation

C. Confidentiality

D. Integrity

17. Greg recently conducted an assessment of his organization's security controls and discovered a potential gap: the organization does not use full-disk encryption on laptops. What type of control gap exists in this case?

A. Detective

B. Corrective

C. Deterrent

D. Preventive

18. What term best describes an organization's desired security state?

    A. Control objectives

    B. Security priorities

    C. Strategic goals

    D. Best practices

19. Tina is tuning her organization's intrusion prevention system to prevent false positive alerts. What type of control is Tina implementing?

    A. Technical control

    B. Physical control

    C. Managerial control

    D. Operational control

20. Tonya is concerned about the risk that an attacker will attempt to gain access to her organization's database server. She is searching for a control that would discourage the attacker from attempting to gain access. What type of security control is she seeking to implement?

    A. Preventive

    B. Detective

    C. Corrective

    D. Deterrent

Chapter 5

Privacy Operational Life Cycle: Sustain

THE CIPM EXAM OBJECTIVES COVERED IN THIS CHAPTER INCLUDE:

Throughout this book, we have explored strategies for developing a privacy program, tools for assessing privacy risks, and methods for protecting private information. Privacy managers employ these strategies to get a healthy privacy program off the ground and into operation. Privacy programs, however, require continual management and attention to remain healthy. These processes are required to *sustain* a privacy program.

Internally, privacy programs may falter if employees become lax about following procedures. Business practices may also change, leading to new technologies, jurisdictional considerations, and new data processing activities. Externally, regulatory obligations may change, causing unmonitored privacy programs to suddenly become outdated. Threats to information security and privacy are constantly evolving, as is the public attitude toward the importance of data privacy.

Effective privacy managers manage their privacy programs with the goal of continual improvement. Sustaining a privacy program should prevent errors by ensuring internal compliance with the privacy program. At the same time, the privacy program itself needs to be managed and updated in response to external regulations and risks. Privacy managers have several important tools at their disposal to ensure their programs are sustained. In this chapter, we will explore techniques for monitoring programs and for conducting program audits.

Monitor

Program monitoring is a management process that aims to ensure that a privacy program stays effective and up to date. Privacy program elements should be monitored to make sure the program responds to major changes in regulations or privacy risk. Business processes and employee practices should be monitored to ensure compliance with privacy protection requirements.

Another benefit of robust monitoring is ongoing communication regarding the privacy program. In order to conduct monitoring of the program, privacy managers must communicate regularly with functional managers, contractors, and employees in general. These communications keep the privacy program top of mind for everyone involved and continue to reinforce policies, procedures, standards, and expectations.

Monitoring activities also generate findings that enable the celebration of success as well as suggestions for improvement. These findings must be communicated with an organization's executive leadership in order to aid in decision-making, risk management, and strategic planning. Communication is, by necessity, a beneficial companion to privacy program monitoring.

Monitoring the Environment

In today's digital world, even small businesses typically employ an array of complex technologies for collecting, storing, using, and sharing data. Cloud service, payment card processing, customer databases, point-of-sale systems, advertising, websites, apps, and more all represent information systems that interact with data in some way.

To ensure that critical information systems are securely managed, the privacy function must rely on the information security function. An organization's information security program must ensure the ongoing confidentiality, integrity, and availability of information, systems, and applications.

 The confidentiality, integrity, and availability of information is known as the CIA Triad, discussed in more detail in Chapter 4, "Privacy Operational Life Cycle: Protect."

The information security function also manages compliance risk for security-related regulatory requirements. The information security program, however, should never be taken for granted. Privacy managers must work closely with information security managers to align their programs and ensure that each program is meeting the needs of the other.

Documenting the privacy program baseline, discussed in Chapter 3, "Privacy Operational Life Cycle: Assess," should help in identifying the systems that an organization uses to process private information. These may range from paper files to modern customer relationship management (CRM) platforms running online. As part of sustaining the privacy program, it is important to implement procedures that monitor changes in the organization's privacy environment.

When an organization is planning to adopt new systems for data processing, several tools can help analyze the privacy implications and update privacy controls as needed. Chapter 3 covered several such tools. For example, privacy threshold analyses (PTAs) help determine whether systems interact with private information, and privacy impact assessments (PIAs) analyze the potential privacy risks that may arise when adopting new systems.

Without a process for monitoring changes in the IT environment, however, new information systems can appear in the environment without proper due diligence. Proper monitoring ensures that changes to the IT environment are proactively assessed so that privacy protections may be updated accordingly.

It can be surprisingly challenging to monitor the IT environment for changes, especially in a large and complex organization. IT system changes sometimes occur rapidly, are often outsourced, and are often invisible to users. To monitor for these changes, a combination of approaches is often necessary:

- Develop written policies and procedures for the changes to IT systems and applications that include privacy protection procedures and assessments.

- Identify employees responsible for authorizing changes to the IT environment and deliver targeted training.

- Add procedures to existing business processes to ensure that new information systems and applications are not implemented without due diligence. The process of allocating resources to new IT projects is one important way to monitor for changes in the IT environment. The process for procuring new systems and applications is another.

- Connect with IT service and product management functions across the organization. These functions typically have detailed change management procedures that should include privacy assessment.

Monitor Compliance with Privacy Policies

A privacy policy is meaningless unless people follow it. Internal compliance with a privacy policy is often less of a problem when a privacy program is first implemented. In most cases, employees and executives have helped construct the program and are freshly trained in the policy. Over time, however, employees come and go, people get busy, and compliance may start to slip. Ongoing monitoring allows functional leadership, as well as privacy managers, to ensure that employees continue to adhere to the privacy policy over time.

For example, most privacy programs require that all employees complete a basic privacy awareness education program on a periodic basis. This is usually managed by the Human Resources (HR) function. HR should have a system for keeping records of which employees have completed the requirement and have some mechanism for enforcing the policy.

Other forms of monitoring may include making privacy policy compliance part of annual performance reviews or requiring employees to sign off on checklists when completing key procedures. Technology tools can also help monitor compliance with privacy policies. Some technologies, for example, can scan internal IT systems for confidential data and flag any data stored in unauthorized systems or formats.

Monitor Regulatory Changes

As discussed in previous chapters, it is critical for healthy privacy programs to respond to changes in regulations. Sometimes regulations change, sometimes jurisdictions change, and sometimes organizations enter new jurisdictions. Monitoring the regulatory environment begins by identifying all the jurisdictions in which an organization operates, then monitoring regulatory changes within those jurisdictions.

Common sources of regulation that must be monitored include:

National Legislation   Examples include GLBA or HIPAA in the United States or GDPR in the European Union (EU).

Enforcement Agency Rules and Enforcement Actions   Agencies such as the FTC in the United States and DPAs in the EU have broad authority for rulemaking and enforcement. Tracking enforcement actions, for example, helps privacy managers to understand how regulations are currently interpreted.

Judicial Decisions   Court decisions, such as the *Schrems II* decision (discussed in Chapter 2, "Privacy Program Framework") in the EU, have a significant impact on the application and scope of privacy regulations.

State Laws   Unlike other nations, the United States does not have a comprehensive federal privacy law. As a result, privacy rules in the U.S. are partially determined by a patchwork of rapidly evolving state laws, such as California's CCPA (discussed in Chapter 2).

Municipal Regulations   Some major cities and counties are enacting regulations that impact privacy, particularly in areas such as preemployment background screening. This is less common but must still be monitored.

Self-Regulatory Systems   Many organizations participate in voluntary frameworks or programs for self-regulation. Such frameworks may be industry specific or intended to facilitate international data transfer.

Compliance Monitoring

While monitoring for changes in applicable rules and regulations is critical, it is also important to monitor the privacy program framework to make sure the program enables the organization to remain in compliance with those regulations. Several areas worth monitoring for compliance are as follows:

Privacy Policy   Privacy policies should detail controls and handling procedures related to data control and processing. The privacy policy should ensure compliance with applicable regulations for the collection, storage, usage, disclosure, and destruction of private information. The privacy policy should also document how the organization protects the privacy rights of individuals under applicable laws.

Records Retention   Records retention policies and procedures must align with the privacy policy and manage how information is collected, stored, and ultimately purged. Several laws contain specific requirements that impact records retention. For example, GDPR includes the right to be forgotten, which requires organizations to purge an individual's personal data upon request.

Training and Awareness   Many regulations require appropriate privacy training and awareness programs for employees who handle private information. Such programs must typically include general privacy awareness training for all employees as well as targeted role-based training for employees with specific responsibilities for privacy controls.

Incident Response and Notification   Virtually every privacy law includes provisions requiring procedures for managing incidents and breaches. These provisions usually include a definition of what constitutes private information, when a privacy incident is legally considered a breach, and requirements for notification of individuals affected by a breach as well as notifications to regulatory authorities.

Exam Tip

For the exam, you will not be expected to know the various incident response and notification requirements for all laws and regulations in detail. However, it is a good idea to be familiar with the notification requirements of major comprehensive privacy regulations, such as GDPR.

Privacy Risk Assessment   Specific privacy risk assessments such as DPIAs are required under regulations such as the GDPR. Other assessments, such as legitimate interest assessments (LIAs) and transfer risk assessments (TRAs), may not be explicitly required by law but help organizations check for ongoing compliance with privacy regulations when making decisions. Ongoing monitoring ensures that privacy assessment processes are well documented, that the processes are triggered when appropriate, and that the resulting reports are used as required.

Internal Audit   Internal audit is a tool for management and helps to ensure that a privacy program is operating effectively. Internal audit is an important tool for ensuring ongoing compliance, but the internal audit process, in itself, must be monitored as well. As with privacy risk assessments, ongoing monitoring checks to ensure that internal audits are conducted as required and the resulting internal audit reports are shared with management, acted upon, and retained according to the records retention policy.

Audit

Audits are more formal tools for ensuring that a privacy program is properly maintained. While regular monitoring may be performed by functional managers and privacy program personnel, audits are performed by somebody else who is not responsible for the success of the area being reviewed. Audits can be more objective and, and the same time, provide a measure of accountability for those responsible for data privacy protection. Chapter 3 covered two different types of audits, internal and external. Internal audits are often referred to as *first-party audits*, and external audits are also called *third-party audits*.

There is also another common type of audit, called *second-party audits*. Second-party audits occur when an organization audits a third-party vendor, data processor, or other data sharing partner. Organizations may want the right to conduct second-party privacy audits to ensure that vendors, contractors, suppliers, and other partners sustain data privacy protections as promised in their contracts. The right to perform second-party audits is usually established in the contract as well.

No matter which category of audit is employed, the purpose of privacy-related auditing is to make sure that data protection policies and procedures are implemented and maintained, and adequately meet standards set by policies, rules, and regulations. Audits vary in scope and objective. The scope of an audit may be a narrow examination of something like record retention practices or target an entire privacy program. Audit objectives vary as well. Some audits are required by law, such as an annual GLBA audit, to ensure compliance with a set legal standard.

Aligning with Audits

Although audits can be intimidating, they are an important tool for program assurance and are intended to help keep everything working as it should. Audits often delve deeply into organizational records. For this reason, it is best to manage privacy program functions as if they are always being audited. Audits are designed to support program assurance, so aligning operations to audit requirements should be synonymous with aligning to the privacy program's objectives.

The various audit processes must also be aligned with one another. Internal audits should be conducted to align with second- and third-party audits. Internal audits can help an organization maintain a state of compliance in advance of more formal audits. For example, an organization that serves as a third-party data processor knows they may be audited by the controller based on the terms of their contract. In this case, they should use their internal audit practice to ensure they are continually meeting the standards set by that contract.

Audit Processes and Audit Trails

Audits look not only for documentation of policies and procedures but also for evidence that policies and procedures have been followed. Consider the example of privacy assessments. An auditor is likely to look for documented procedures for performing DPIAs when required. But they might also look for the reports from individual DPIAs and records to show that DPIAs were conducted appropriately in advance of changes to data processing activities.

If a procedure is subject to audit, then it is important to keep written records each time those procedures are followed. For example, if an IT manager makes a phone call to alert the privacy manager of the need to perform a DPIA, it is critical to create a written record of that phone call, including the date and time, to show that a DPIA was triggered when required. Keeping written transactional records related to following privacy protection procedures is also known as maintaining an *audit trail*. Audit trail records should be produced in real time and kept well organized. This improves ongoing accountability and enables a smoother audit process.

To produce privacy-related audit trail records, personnel with privacy responsibilities must understand the audit processes in place at their organizations. They need to know which procedures may be audited and what sort of records auditors expect to be able to see.

Assess Against Industry Standards

The output of an audit is an audit report that summarizes findings from the audit. Along with qualitative analyses, audits commonly provide numeric scores, percentages, or ratings, such as letter grades, to help the organization understand its own performance. To make sense of these results, audits usually assess operations against some sort of standard. Sometimes, a standard of performance is relatively straightforward. For example, a regulation may require personal data to be fully encrypted. An audit result may be a simple yes or no. Either the organization is compliant with the legal standard or it isn't.

More frequently, however, audit findings are more nuanced. Performance in some areas may be perfect most of the time, but an audit may detect occasional lapses. Perhaps all appropriate procedures are performed just as they should be, but the documentation is out of date or partially missing. For these reasons, many privacy program frameworks include performance standards to help organizations understand their audit findings in context.

The American Institute of Certified Public Accountants (AICPA), which maintains its own privacy management framework (PMF) and related maturity model, has an Auditing Standards Board (ASB). Other industry frameworks for data security and privacy, such as ISO 27001 (information security) and ISO 27701 (managing PII and personal data processing) also define industry standards that can be audited. Organizations should carefully define which industry standard best applies to their operations and align internal and external audit programs with the selected standards.

Regulatory Compliance Assessment Tools

Managing all the information needed to respond effectively to audits can be complicated. In addition to maintaining the audit trail described above, it is important to keep inventories of all privacy program policies and procedures, current compliance obligations, risk inventories, privacy risk assessments, and decision-making processes. Organizations must manage the workflows around completing, approving, and recording compliance management activities and easily produce compliance reports in response to audits.

Thankfully, there is a growing category of software products for this purpose. This product category is known broadly as *governance, risk, and compliance (GRC)* software. It is also sometimes referred to as compliance or risk management software. GRC software tools serve as document management systems for policies, procedures, and records as well as workflow engines to automate compliance processes. Some more advanced GRC tools can even integrate with other information systems to perform automated scans to ensure that system configurations, such as encryption or multifactor authentication settings, conform with the privacy policy. Some GRC systems can also help to manage other compliance activities, such as records retention, employee training, and more.

Audit Focus

Audits generally have defined objectives for assessment. Sometimes, these objectives are dictated by regulations or industry standards as discussed earlier. This section explores commonly targeted areas for privacy audits.

Audit Compliance with Privacy Policies and Standards

Audits in this category focus on examining the potential gaps between documented policy and actual practice. This provides assurance that the business practices follow the written privacy policy and that employees comply with the policy as they go about their work. If an organization's business practices don't match its privacy policy, then the risk of privacy and compliance problems may increase.

For example, if a company is selling customer data even though their privacy policy says they don't, then that company may be at risk of an FTC investigation into unfair or deceptive practices (UDAPs). Ideally, regular compliance monitoring prevents such misalignment between policy and practice, but formal audits provide more objective assurance.

Audit Data Integrity and Quality and Communicate Audit Findings with Stakeholders

Audits of data quality and integrity examine information systems, controls, safeguards, and other data management practices. In close alignment with the information security program, these data management practices are intended to ensure that all data is up to date, complete, and accurate. Sustaining rigorous data integrity and quality is a pillar of building trust with stakeholders. For this reason, audit findings related to data integrity should be communicated to appropriate stakeholders clearly and in a timely manner. Even if an audit reveals problems, covering those problems up does far more damage to reputation and trust.

Data quality and integrity are necessary for managing good business processes as well as for complying with data privacy regulations. In jurisdictions such as the EU and the state of California, organizations are required to disclose the personal data they hold about an individual and correct or delete it upon request. Assuring such privacy rights requires that data integrity and quality are maintained in the first place.

Audit Information Access, Modification, and Disclosure Accounting

Access controls may be technological, administrative, and physical. Technical controls include authentication methods, like passwords, as well as systems and procedures for managing employee accounts and levels of access within information systems. Administrative controls include practices such as training and oversight. Physical controls include facility security, locks, and monitoring or surveillance systems. Organizations should have policies that control access to private data and procedures for managing that access.

Additionally, organizations should have processes for logging and monitoring changes to private information. If private information is altered, deleted, extracted, or moved inappropriately, then the organization relies on logs to track the changes and, ideally, to restore data to the proper state. If data integrity or quality is damaged, either accidentally or maliciously, then logging and monitoring allow the organization to detect the problem and intervene.

Disclosure accounting is the practice of keeping records of any disclosures of private information made as an exception to the privacy policy or applicable regulations.

This does not necessarily mean that a privacy breach has occurred, since many regulations do include allowable exceptions. For example, the federal Privacy Act of 1974 requires federal government agencies to keep a history of disclosures of PII, including the date, time, and purpose of the disclosure and information about the party who received the disclosure.

The HIPAA privacy rule also requires that covered entities keep records of any PHI disclosures that aren't related to treatment, payment, or healthcare operations. As described in Chapter 2, HIPAA allows such disclosures in certain circumstances, such as when a disclosure is required by law. Audits in this area seek to ensure that all nonstandard disclosures have been reported as required.

Targeted Employee Training

Organizations should also audit all required training and awareness policies, programs, and procedures. Since training is typically managed by HR, Human Resources personnel will likely lead the response to training audits. Organizations must have appropriate policies in place that detail which employees are required to complete which training programs.

Training programs should be up to date and relevant to the requirements of the privacy program. Training should also be offered in multiple modalities and at multiple times and locations to ensure that all employees can fulfill training requirements. All employees with any access to private information should receive basic privacy awareness education on an ongoing basis. Customized, or targeted, training should be required for specific roles.

- Managers often have responsibility for specific parts of the privacy policy. For example, HR managers are often responsible for implementing, tracking, and enforcing privacy training requirements. IT managers are usually responsible for compliance with system configurations. Call center managers may be responsible for processing requests from data subjects.

- Contractors are easily overlooked when it comes to training. As employees, they should receive equivalent training, depending on their roles. Contractors also work remotely in different jurisdictions and require compliance training on regulations that might not affect regular employees. Finally, contractors should be trained on compliance with any contract-specific privacy requirements.

In addition to managers and contractors, many other employees serve in specialized roles that require specific training. As mentioned earlier, some level of general privacy awareness training should be required of nearly every employee. Several areas of focus for privacy training and awareness are as follows:

Privacy Policies   Awareness of organization-wide privacy policies should be included in basic privacy awareness training. However, some organizations also have multiple privacy policies specific to certain departments or products.

Operational Privacy Practices   Standard operating procedures and instructions are essential for ensuring that privacy policies are implemented across the organization. These procedures should be well documented, and employees should be trained regularly according to their roles. In addition to regular instruction through classes or reading materials, tabletop drills and simulations are important elements of successful training. Common role-based procedural areas include:

- Data management, including procedures for each phase of the DLM life cycle
- Access control, including procedures for granting, monitoring, and removing access to private information, as well as record-keeping of access control activities for audits and compliance
- Incident response, including a focus on training employees to spot the signs of potential privacy incidents and to report such incidents immediately
- Knowing key roles and responsibilities, including where to report incidents, concerns, and who is responsible for the various parts of the privacy program

Training is essential to the success of any privacy program. It is no surprise, therefore, that training programs are a common focus for audits. Organizations should maintain a system for monitoring compliance with training requirements. Organizations must also be able to produce reports for audits and for monitoring internal operations.

Summary

Sustaining a privacy program relies on ongoing monitoring and auditing. Privacy program activities should always be monitored continually. Monitoring enables privacy managers to oversee complex cross-functional programs that span the organization. Key programmatic areas to monitor include the organization's information environment, internal compliance with the privacy policy, changes to regulatory requirements, and regulatory compliance.

Monitoring the environment helps to ensure the confidentiality, integrity, and availability of information. Privacy program managers should work closely with information security program managers to ensure that systems and applications are protected and in compliance with information security regulations and standards. At the same time, changes to information systems must be monitored as well to ensure that appropriate risk assessments and mitigations are implemented whenever systems and applications change.

Privacy policies are only effective when employees adhere to them. Organizations must rigorously monitor internal compliance with the requirements of the privacy policy. Examples include ensuring employee training is completed as required or that records are stored and purged according to the record retention policy.

Even the most well-executed privacy program may become out of date, or even out of compliance, when regulations change. To avoid this, organizations must monitor the regulatory environment for changes to laws, court decisions, industry self-regulatory frameworks, or other rule changes that might alter compliance requirements. In addition, organizations must monitor changes to its own practices that might bring new compliance requirements. For example, entering new markets or completing a corporate merger may place an organization in a new jurisdiction with new requirements.

An organization should monitor its own compliance activities. Monitoring helps ensure that an organization is meeting the proper requirements for the use and retention of data, as well as other key areas, such as record retention and incident response. Compliance monitoring should include internal audit processes while also monitoring the internal audit process itself.

Ongoing monitoring keeps a program on track and in sync with compliance requirements. Audits, on the other hand, are periodic formal evaluations of data privacy protection. Common types of audits include internal audits, second-party audits, and external third-party audits. Audits are conducted by people outside the functional area being audited to increase objectivity and hold functional areas accountable to set standards. Audits assure management, partners, regulators, or other stakeholders that a privacy program is effective, that controls are adequate and effective, and that compliance obligations are met.

Since audits are designed to ensure a privacy program is operating properly, it is a good idea to align a privacy program with the audit process. This includes keeping documentation updated and maintaining written records to create an "audit trail" as evidence of compliance. The organization must also know which audits to expect and what sort of records must be produced for those audits to maintain the audit trail. In addition, audits typically assess privacy programs against some set industry standard, so these standards should be adopted internally as performance standards. Finally, governance, risk, and compliance (GRC) software tools are available to help organizations manage all information and workflows related to audit processes.

Audits vary in both scope and objective. They may target only a single functional area or an entire program. Audits also have different objectives for assessment. Common areas of audit focus include the privacy policy, data integrity and quality, information access and disclosure accounting, and training. When audit processes are communicated to appropriate stakeholders, they help to increase overall trust in an organization's privacy practices.

Exam Essentials

Understand what it means to sustain a privacy program.   Once up and running, privacy programs are sustained via ongoing monitoring, training, and communication. Ongoing monitoring keeps the program on track and audits assure stakeholders that requirements continue to be met. Once a program is developed and running, privacy managers can focus on sustaining activities to continue to maintain and improve the program.

Focus on training.   Training features prominently in this domain. Training is a key activity for sustaining a privacy program. Sustaining a program requires monitoring, and training is also a key area to monitor. Audits also often assess training and expect to find repeated programs that include role-based training.

Know what to monitor.   Monitoring is a multifaceted activity that is intended to ensure that the privacy program is being followed, that the privacy program itself is up to date, and that the organization remains in compliance. It is therefore important to monitor employee compliance with privacy policies, changes to laws and regulations, and whether the organization itself remains in compliance.

Define the auditing process.   The purpose of an audit is to evaluate whether privacy programs are adequate, effective, and in compliance. Audits should be objective and unbiased, measure performance against set industry standards, and be reported to the appropriate stakeholders. There are multiple types of audits, including internal audits, second-party audits, and external audits.

Review Questions

1. Gia is a privacy manager at a growing data processing company that has just launched services to provide contract-based processing for clients around the world. Gia worked hard to put processes in place to facilitate international data transfer for all the countries where her company does business. But Gia is concerned about making sure the company remains rigorous about international compliance as they expand into new territories over time. Which of the following would help address Gia's concern?

   A. Improving training on transfer risk assessments (TRAs)

   B. Implementing a policy that the company will only do business under safe harbor programs

   C. Implementing compliance monitoring

   D. Improving training for all employees working on contracts in other countries

2. Mallory is the CFO at her company, and she is pleased with the privacy training program her company has just instituted. Mallory trusts the HR director, who reports to her, to get the job done and make sure employees comply with the requirement. Still, Mallory thinks her boss, the CEO, will want more assurance that the program is working as it should. What process might help Mallory with this?

   A. Creating an audit trail

   B. Compliance monitoring

   C. Third-party audit

   D. Internal audit

3. Samit is a privacy manager at a data processing company. He is disturbed to learn that a major IT database was just moved to the cloud without his knowledge. Samit has a robust privacy program in place with a clear privacy policy that covers this. What might have gone wrong in this case?

   A. Lack of specificity in the privacy policy

   B. Failure to audit the IT function

   C. Failure to complete DPIAs

   D. Failure to monitor the environment

4. Why should a privacy manager care about general monitoring of court decisions?

   A. Court decisions may result in financial penalties for the organization.

   B. Courts frequently strike down important provisions of privacy laws.

   C. Court decisions sometimes change the scope and application of privacy laws.

   D. Court decisions assign liability for privacy violations.

5. Yuping is responding to an audit of her company's record retention policy. As the process began, she felt confident because her policy and procedures were detailed and updated, and all employees are trained on them regularly. However, the auditor started asking for evidence that specific records had been archived or deleted. Yuping found herself poring through emails and paper files to try to piece together the details the auditor needed. What may have been missed?

    A. Training for audits

    B. Creating an audit trail

    C. Monitoring for internal compliance with record retention

    D. Role-based retention training

6. You have spent the last year implementing a privacy program at your new company. You have an established privacy policy, documented procedures, controls are in place, and employees are trained. Where should you put your focus to continue improving the program?

    A. Protect

    B. Sustain

    C. Optimize

    D. Assess

7. Which of the following is an example of disclosure accounting?

    A. A financial institution publishes a privacy notice disclosing privacy protections in accounting practices.

    B. A medical records company produces reports whenever PHI is disclosed in response to court orders.

    C. A company keeps careful records of all violations of its privacy policy.

    D. As part of financial risk assessment, a company calculates the potential costs of privacy breaches.

8. Huan is the new HR manager at her company. During her orientation, she learned that she would have some role in monitoring the company's privacy program. What might Huan's monitoring responsibilities include?

    A. Auditing the privacy training process

    B. Tracking which employees have completed privacy training

    C. Ensuring employees fully comply with the privacy policy

    D. Tracking data subject requests

9. Why might ISO 27701 be relevant in the context of a privacy audit?

    A. ISO 27701 compliance is a legal requirement in most U.S. states.

    B. ISO 27701 is an example of a set of industry standards for assessing performance.

    C. ISO 27701 contains a requirement for annual external auditing.

    D. Violations of ISO 27701 may result in severe penalties.

10. LearnMost is a company that sells educational software to schools. In order to scale up operations, LearnMost has decided to offer its software online as a cloud service so that school districts will no longer have to install software on individual computers. LearnMost has decided to contract with a private cloud provider to host their applications. Because privacy is so important to LearnMost, they want contractual language that would allow them to formally inspect the cloud provider for privacy compliance every year. Which of the following best describes such a process?

    A. Third-party audit

    B. External audit

    C. Second-party audit

    D. Due diligence

11. Which of the following is not part of environmental monitoring?

    A. Aligning with the information security program

    B. Monitoring information system vulnerabilities

    C. Managing information security breaches

    D. Detecting changes in the IT systems and applications

12. Erich is a new CEO and looks forward to requesting his first internal audit of the company's privacy program. How should Erich interpret the findings to understand whether to be concerned or pleased with the company's privacy performance?

    A. Rely on the objective judgment of the auditor.

    B. Determine whether his competitors had better or worse findings on similar audits.

    C. Evaluate the company's track record on past privacy audits.

    D. Apply an industry standard for privacy program performance.

13. Sue is an attorney representing a French company in a case where a data subject is accusing the company of keeping their personal information after it was no longer needed for processing or any other legitimate purpose. The privacy policy requires compliance with data subject rights. When Sue interviews the manager in charge of the customer database, the manager claims she had to preserve the data because she was following the company's data archiving procedures. Where might the privacy program be falling short in this case?

    A. Compliance monitoring

    B. Training and awareness

    C. Destruction of records

    D. Monitoring the regulatory environment

14. In addition to making sure that a privacy program functions effectively over the long term, what is another benefit of ongoing privacy program monitoring?

    A. Less frequent auditing of monitored programs

    B. Improved communication

    C. Reduced liability in case of litigation

    D. Due diligence demonstrated to data controllers

15. Which of the following is the best indicator of an external audit?

- **A.** Conducted for management purposes
- **B.** Conducted by data controllers as per contractual terms
- **C.** Not conducted by line of business or unit in question
- **D.** Reports to the board

16. Which of the following is *not* a potential source of regulatory change?

- **A.** Board bylaws
- **B.** Court decisions
- **C.** Legislation
- **D.** Municipal regulation

17. Which of the following best describes an audit trail?

- **A.** Documentation of updated policies and procedures for compliance
- **B.** Records showing that policies and procedures have been followed
- **C.** Documentation of the audit process
- **D.** Alignment of the privacy program with the audit process

18. Which of the following best describes the Sustain phase of the privacy operational life cycle?

- **A.** Continually improve through monitoring, training, and audit.
- **B.** Implement privacy controls and safeguards.
- **C.** Develop governance and metrics for the privacy program.
- **D.** Respond to privacy incidents as they occur.

19. Marco is proud of his privacy program and feels ready for his next audit. His documentation of policy and procedures is updated and clear, employees are trained, he has program monitoring in place, and record-keeping is ongoing to create an audit trail. His only concern is that, with so much to manage, he can barely keep up with all the processes, records, and organization. He's worried that it might take him a long time to gather all the information an auditor requests. What might help Marco with this?

- **A.** Records management
- **B.** GRC software
- **C.** Role-based training on record-keeping
- **D.** Better alignment between privacy program and audit process

20. Day-to-day compliance with training requirements is usually monitored by which role?

- **A.** Privacy manager
- **B.** HR
- **C.** Internal audit
- **D.** Functional manager

Chapter

6

Privacy Operational Life Cycle: Respond

THE CIPM EXAM OBJECTIVES COVERED IN THIS CHAPTER INCLUDE:

The final phase of the privacy operational life cycle, Respond, covers two significant activities undertaken by privacy professionals: handling requests from data subjects and responding to privacy incidents as they arise. Mature privacy programs have well-thought-out processes in place to manage both activities. In this chapter, you will learn how to design appropriate response mechanisms for your organization.

Data Subject Rights

In Chapter 2, "Privacy Program Framework," you learned about many of the laws governing the ways that organizations collect, store, process, and use personally identifiable information (PII). Those laws protect the rights of the *data subject*: the person who is described in the PII. The rights granted by each law vary between jurisdictions and data types, so privacy professionals should be aware of the broad principles that many of these laws share. Additionally, many organizations choose to go above and beyond statutory requirements to demonstrate concern for the privacy rights of individuals.

In general, legal compliance issues impose five categories of requirements on organizations:

- Preventing harm to data subjects
- Limiting the collection of personal information
- Providing accountability for data controllers and processors
- Monitoring and enforcing compliance with requirements
- Requiring reporting of privacy incidents

Because these laws vary between jurisdictions, we use the European General Data Protection Regulation (GDPR) as the primary example in this chapter.

Exam Tip

When you're taking the exam, watch out for questions that ask you about legal compliance situations. Remember that privacy professionals may be privacy experts, but many are not attorneys. If you suspect that your organization may be in legal or regulatory jeopardy, you should always consult an attorney.

Access

One of the most significant privacy rights granted to individuals under most privacy laws is the right of access. This means that individuals must be provided with access to and copies of any information that the organization maintains about them. Under Article 15 of GDPR, data subjects have the right to access virtually any information that a controller maintains, as well as information about how the organization uses that data. Here is the relevant text:

> The data subject shall have the right to obtain from the controller confirmation as to whether or not personal data concerning him or her are being processed and, where that is the case, access to the personal data and the following information:
>
> > the purposes of the processing;
> >
> > the categories of personal data concerned;
> >
> > the recipients or categories of recipient to whom the personal data have been or will be disclosed, in particular recipients in third countries or international organisations;
> >
> > where possible, the envisaged period for which the personal data will be stored, or, if not possible, the criteria used to determine that period;
> >
> > the existence of the right to request from the controller rectification or erasure of personal data or restriction of processing of personal data concerning the data subject or to object to such processing;
> >
> > the right to lodge a complaint with a supervisory authority;
> >
> > where the personal data are not collected from the data subject, any available information as to their source;
> >
> > the existence of automated decision-making, including profiling, referred to in Article 22 and, at least in those cases, meaningful information about the logic involved, as well as the significance and the envisaged consequences of such processing for the data subject.
>
> Where personal data are transferred to a third country or to an international organisation, the data subject shall have the right to be informed of the appropriate safeguards pursuant to Article 46 relating to the transfer.
>
> The controller shall provide a copy of the personal data undergoing processing. For any further copies requested by the data subject, the controller may charge a reasonable fee based on administrative costs. Where the data subject makes the request by electronic means, and

unless otherwise requested by the data subject, the information shall be provided in a commonly used electronic form.

The right to obtain a copy referred to in paragraph 3 shall not adversely affect the rights and freedoms of others.

Managing Data Integrity

Privacy regulations also provide individuals with the means to ensure that the information that organizations maintain about them is correct. This is known as ensuring the *integrity* of the information. In cases where information is incorrect, data subjects must have the ability to redress those inaccuracies by requesting that records be corrected.

The right to data integrity and redress is addressed by Article 16 of the GDPR, which reads:

> The data subject shall have the right to obtain from the controller without undue delay the rectification of inaccurate personal data concerning him or her. Taking into account the purposes of the processing, the data subject shall have the right to have incomplete personal data completed, including by means of providing a supplementary statement.

Right of Erasure

Many laws also provide individuals with the *right of erasure* of PII maintained about them by an organization. This right is commonly known as the *right to be forgotten*.

Erasure of Personal Information

One of the primary rights granted by many privacy laws is the right of individuals to request that a data controller erase any PII maintained about them.

Under GDPR, the right of a data subject to request the erasure of personal information is covered by paragraph 1 of Article 17, which reads:

> The data subject shall have the right to obtain from the controller the erasure of personal data concerning him or her without undue delay and the controller shall have the obligation to erase personal data without undue delay where one of the following grounds applies:
>
> the personal data are no longer necessary in relation to the purposes for which they were collected or otherwise processed;
>
> the data subject withdraws consent on which the processing is based according to point (a) of Article 6, or point (a) of Article 9, and where there is no other legal ground for the processing;
>
> the data subject objects to the processing pursuant to Article 21 and there are no overriding legitimate grounds for the processing, or the data subject objects to the processing pursuant to Article 21;

the personal data have been unlawfully processed;

the personal data have to be erased for compliance with a legal obligation in Union or Member State law to which the controller is subject;

the personal data have been collected in relation to the offer of information society services referred to in Article 8.

Passing on Requests

Privacy laws may also require that organizations pass along erasure requests to other entities under certain circumstances. Under GDPR, this requirement is encapsulated in paragraph 2 of Article 17, which reads:

> Where the controller has made the personal data public and is obliged pursuant to paragraph 1 to erase the personal data, the controller, taking account of available technology and the cost of implementation, shall take reasonable steps, including technical measures, to inform controllers which are processing the personal data that the data subject has requested the erasure by such controllers of any links to, or copy or replication of, those personal data.

Exceptions to the Right of Erasure

Although the right of erasure granted to data subjects is broad, it is not absolute. There are circumstances where organizations are permitted to reject erasure requests. Paragraph 3 of GDPR Article 17 outlines the circumstances under which a data controller may reject or partially reject a request for erasure from a data subject. It reads:

> Paragraphs 1 and 2 shall not apply to the extent that processing is necessary:

for exercising the right of freedom of expression and information;

for compliance with a legal obligation which requires processing by Union or Member State law to which the controller is subject or for the performance of a task carried out in the public interest or in the exercise of official authority vested in the controller;

for reasons of public interest in the area of public health in accordance with points (h) and (i) of Article 9;

for archiving purposes in the public interest, scientific or historical research purposes or statistical purposes in accordance with Article 89 in so far as the right referred to in paragraph 1 is likely to render impossible or seriously impair the achievement of the objectives of that processing; or

for the establishment, exercise or defence of legal claims.

Right to Be Informed

GDPR and other privacy regulations codify the right of data subjects to be informed about circumstances where they request the correction of records, the erasure of records, or they wish to impose restrictions on processing their PII. This right is embodied in Article 19 of GDPR, which reads:

> The controller shall communicate any rectification or erasure of personal data or restriction of processing carried out in accordance with Article 16, Article 17, and Article 18 to each recipient to whom the personal data have been disclosed, unless this proves impossible or involves disproportionate effort. The controller shall inform the data subject about those recipients if the data subject requests it.

Control over Use

Data subjects also have control over the use and processing of their PII. They may request that data controllers stop or restrict the processing of their information under certain circumstances. Data subject rights to the restriction of processing are found in Article 18 of GDPR, which reads:

> The data subject shall have the right to obtain from the controller restriction of processing where one of the following applies:
>
> > a) the accuracy of the personal data is contested by the data subject, for a period enabling the controller to verify the accuracy of the personal data;
> >
> > the processing is unlawful and the data subject opposes the erasure of the personal data and requests the restriction of their use instead;
> >
> > the controller no longer needs the personal data for the purposes of the processing, but they are required by the data subject for the establishment, exercise or defence of legal claims;
> >
> > the data subject has objected to processing pursuant to Article 21 pending the verification whether the legitimate grounds of the controller override those of the data subject.
> >
> > Where processing has been restricted under paragraph 1, such personal data shall, with the exception of storage, only be processed with the data subject's consent or for the establishment, exercise or defence of legal claims or for the protection of the rights of another natural or legal person or for reasons of important public interest of the Union or of a Member State.

A data subject who has obtained restriction of processing pursuant to paragraph 1 shall be informed by the controller before the restriction of processing is lifted.

GDPR also provides an explicit right for data subjects to opt out of the use of *automated decision-making technologies* on their data. This subject is addressed by Article 22 of GDPR, which reads, in part:

The data subject shall have the right not to be subject to a decision based solely on automated processing, including profiling, which produces legal effects concerning him or her or similarly significantly affects him or her.

Complaints

Privacy laws also provide mechanisms for data subjects to file complaints with government agencies and/or the courts when they believe that their privacy rights have been violated.

Article 77 of GDPR provides data subjects with the right to file complaints with the supervisory authority in their nation of residence, work, or the place where the infringement took place. This article reads:

Without prejudice to any other administrative or judicial remedy, every data subject shall have the right to lodge a complaint with a supervisory authority, in particular in the Member State of his or her habitual residence, place of work or place of the alleged infringement if the data subject considers that the processing of personal data relating to him or her infringes this Regulation.

The supervisory authority with which the complaint has been lodged shall inform the complainant on the progress and the outcome of the complaint including the possibility of a judicial remedy pursuant to Article 78.

Data subjects also have escalating rights to bring matters to court for a judicial remedy if they are not satisfied with the administrative outcome reached by the supervisory governmental authority.

Handling Information Requests

Many of the privacy rights protected by various regulatory schemes require that organizations receive, process, and respond to requests made by data subjects. For example, when an individual invokes their right to access information, the organization must have procedures in place to receive that request; track it through the various stages of information identification, retrieval, and production; and then maintain records documenting the organization's compliance with the data subject's rights.

Complying with data subject requests imposes a significant burden on organizations. Therefore, it is a good idea to introduce processes that make handling these requests more efficient. First and foremost, organizations should build a *personal information inventory* that documents the types of personally identifiable information that they maintain and the locations where that type of data is stored. This inventory may then be used to fully comply with data subject requests. For example, when the organization receives a request from an individual for all personal information maintained about them, they can turn to the inventory to identify possible locations for that information, rather than having to laboriously hunt through all of their records. Similarly, the inventory provides a roadmap for complying with information erasure requests.

Many organizations choose to use a ticket-based tracking system for handling these requests. This approach assigns a unique tracking number to each request, tracks requests through their workflow, and notifies managers of failures to meet time requirements.

Exam Tip

Most IT organizations already have an incident tracking system that is used for managing internal user requests for assistance. Customer contact centers and Human Resource departments also require this type of technology. Privacy programs may be able to reduce costs by piggybacking on existing technology already in use by other areas of the organization.

Incident Response Planning

No matter how well an organization prepares its privacy program and security program, the time will come that it suffers an incident that compromises the privacy and/or security of personal information under its control. This incident may be the loss of a mobile device that is quickly remediated or a serious breach of personal information that ultimately comes into the national media spotlight. In either event, the organization must be prepared to conduct a coordinated, methodical response effort. By planning in advance, business leaders, technology leaders, privacy professionals, information security experts, and technologists can decide how they will handle these situations and prepare a well-thought-out response.

Stakeholder Identification

One of the very first steps that you should undertake when developing a privacy incident response plan is identifying the key stakeholders from around the business that should be involved in the development, implementation, and execution of the plan. Some of the key business stakeholders include:

- **Privacy** professionals provide the core subject matter expertise necessary to address privacy incidents.

- **Information security** professionals offer important expertise in both incident handling and cybersecurity controls.

- **Legal** teams, including attorneys, and **compliance officials** help incident response teams understand their legal and regulatory obligations.

- **Audit** teams (both internal and external) should be advised of privacy incidents so that they may assess their impact on other operations.

- **Human Resources** teams may be required to take adverse personnel actions, when warranted, and may participate in communications with employees affected by privacy incidents.

- **Marketing** and **business development** teams should understand the scope and impact of incidents so that they may carry on their normal customer relationships in an appropriate manner.

- **Communications** and **public relations** teams must understand incidents so that they may better communicate with **external parties** and other stakeholders who require information.

Building an Incident Oversight Team

Organizations should establish a *privacy incident oversight team* that is responsible for managing the end-to-end response to privacy incidents. Many different roles should be represented on this team. Depending on the organization and its technical needs, some of these roles may be core team members who are always activated, whereas others may be called in as needed on an incident-by-incident basis. For example, a database administrator might be crucial when investigating the aftermath of a technical database breach but would probably not be very helpful when responding to a case of personal information inadvertently emailed to a group of customers.

The core incident response team normally consists of privacy and information security professionals with specific expertise in incident response. In larger organizations, these may be full-time employees dedicated to incident response, whereas smaller organizations may call on experts who fill other roles for their "day jobs" to step into response roles in the aftermath of an incident.

The Role of Management

Management should have an active role in incident response efforts. The primary responsibility of managers and senior leadership is to provide the authority, resources, and time required to respond appropriately to a privacy incident. This includes ensuring that the team has the budget and staff required to plan for incidents and access to subject matter experts during a response.

Management may also be called on during incident response to make crucial business decisions about the need to shut down critical operations, communicate with law enforcement or the general public, and assess the impact of an incident on essential stakeholders.

In addition to the core team members, the privacy incident response team may include representation from the following:

- Technical subject matter experts whose knowledge may be required during a response. This includes system engineers, network administrators, database administrators, desktop experts, and application experts.

- IT support staff, who may be needed to carry out actions directed by the team.

- Legal counsel responsible for ensuring that the team's actions comply with legal, policy, and regulatory requirements and who can advise team leaders on compliance issues and communication with regulatory bodies.

- Public relations and marketing staff, who can coordinate communications with the media and general public.

The team should be run by a designated leader with clear authority to direct incident response efforts and serve as a liaison to management. This leader should be a skilled incident responder who is either assigned to lead the team as a full-time responsibility or who serves in a privacy leadership position.

Building the Incident Response Plan

One of the major responsibilities that organizations have during the preparation phase of incident response is building a solid incident response plan that will guide the program. This creates the policies, procedures, and other documentation required to support the program's ongoing efforts and ensure that response efforts are effective and timely.

Policy

The incident response policy serves as the cornerstone of an organization's incident response program. This policy should be written to guide efforts at a high level and provide the authority for incident response. The policy should be approved at the highest level possible within the organization, preferably by the chief executive officer. For this reason, policy authors should attempt to write the policy in a manner that makes it relatively timeless. This means that the policy should contain statements that provide authority for incident response, assign responsibility to the privacy incident oversight team, and describe the role of individuals and state organizational priorities. The policy is *not* the place to describe specific technologies, response procedures, or evidence-gathering techniques. Those details may change frequently and should be covered in more easily changed procedure documents.

The National Institute of Standards and Technology (NIST) recommends that incident response policies contain these key elements:

- Statement of management commitment
- Purpose and objectives of the policy
- Scope of the policy (to whom it applies and under what circumstances)
- Definition of incidents and related terms
- Organizational structure and definition of roles, responsibilities, and level of authority
- Prioritization or severity rating scheme for incidents
- Performance measures for the team
- Reporting and contact forms

Including these elements in the policy provides a solid foundation for the team's routine and crisis activities.

For more information on NIST's incident response recommendations, see NIST Special Publication (SP) 800-61 Rev. 2, "Computer Security Incident Handling Guide" (https://csrc.nist.gov/publications/detail/sp/800-61/rev-2/final).

Procedures and Playbooks

Procedures provide the detailed tactical information that team members need when responding to an incident. They represent the collective wisdom of team members and subject matter experts collected during periods of calm and ready to be applied in the event of an actual incident. Teams often develop *playbooks* that describe the specific procedures that they will follow in the event of a specific type of incident. For example, a financial institution team might develop playbooks that cover the following:

- Breach of personal financial information
- Phishing attacks targeted at customers
- Failure to meet regulatory deadlines
- General privacy incidents not covered by another playbook

This is not an exhaustive list, and each organization will develop playbooks that describe their response to both high severity and frequently occurring incident categories. The idea behind the playbook is that the team should be able to pick it up and find an operational plan for responding to the privacy incident. Playbooks are especially important in the early hours of incident response to ensure that the team has a planned, measured response to the first reports of a potential incident.

Playbooks are designed to be step-by-step recipe-style responses to specific types of incidents. They should guide the team's response, but they are not a substitute for professional judgment. The responders handling an incident should have appropriate professional expertise and the authority to deviate from the playbook when circumstances require a different approach.

Documenting the Incident Response Plan

When developing the incident response plan documentation, organizations should pay particular attention to creating tools that may be useful during an incident response. These tools should provide clear guidance to response teams that may be quickly read and interpreted during a crisis situation. For example, the incident response checklist shown in Figure 6.1 provides a high-level overview of a cybersecurity incident response process in checklist form. The team leader may use this checklist to ensure that the team doesn't miss an important step in the heat of the crisis environment.

FIGURE 6.1   Incident response checklist

	Action	Completed
	Detection and Analysis	
1.	Determine whether an incident has occurred	
1.1	Analyze the precursors and indicators	
1.2	Look for correlating information	
1.3	Perform research (e.g., search engines, knowledge base)	
1.4	As soon as the handler believes an incident has occurred, begin documenting the investigation and gathering evidence	
2.	Prioritize handling the incident based on the relevant factors (functional impact, information impact, recoverability effort, etc.)	
3.	Report the incident to the appropriate internal personnel and external organizations	
	Containment, Eradication, and Recovery	
4.	Acquire, preserve, secure, and document evidence	
5.	Contain the incident	
6.	Eradicate the incident	
6.1	Identify and mitigate all vulnerabilities that were exploited	
6.2	Remove malware, inappropriate materials, and other components	
6.3	If more affected hosts are discovered (e.g., new malware infections), repeat the Detection and Analysis steps (1.1, 1.2) to identify all other affected hosts, then contain (5) and eradicate (6) the incident for them	
7.	Recover from the incident	
7.1	Return affected systems to an operationally ready state	
7.2	Confirm that the affected systems are functioning normally	
7.3	If necessary, implement additional monitoring to look for future related activity	
	Post-Incident Activity	
8.	Create a follow-up report	
9.	Hold a lessons learned meeting (mandatory for major incidents, optional otherwise)	

Source: NIST SP 800-61: *Computer Security Incident Handling Guide*

The National Institute of Standards and Technology publishes a *Computer Security Incident Handling Guide* (SP 800-61) that contains a wealth of information that is useful to both government agencies and private organizations developing incident response plans. The current version of the guide, NIST SP 800-61 revision 2, is available online at http://nvlpubs.nist.gov/nistpubs/SpecialPublications/NIST.SP.800-61r2.pdf.

Integrating the Plan with Other Functions

Incident response plans developed by privacy teams should be tightly integrated with the incident response plans developed by other business functions. For example, many privacy incidents are also cybersecurity incidents. For this reason, the privacy incident response plan should be closely aligned with the cybersecurity incident response plan. The same is true for aligning the organization's privacy incident response plan with its business continuity plan, a topic discussed later in this chapter.

Incident Detection

One of the most critical components of an organization's incident response plan is its ability to detect incidents in the first place. This capability is responsible for triggering the remaining actions under the organization's response plan.

Security and Privacy Incidents

Cybersecurity and privacy incidents are closely related to each other. This is because many privacy incidents have cybersecurity issues as their root cause and many cybersecurity incidents have privacy implications. However, not every cybersecurity incident is a privacy incident and not every privacy incident is a cybersecurity incident. Let's explore that through the use of three different examples:

- John maintains a database of customer records that includes PII. He learns that an external attacker compromised the security of that database and stole customer records. This is both a cybersecurity incident and a privacy incident. It is a cybersecurity incident because the security of the technology system was compromised. It is a privacy incident because it involved the unauthorized access of PII.

- Mary was recently traveling on a public train when her backpack, including her corporate laptop, was stolen. The laptop contained sensitive company records but did not include PII. This is a cybersecurity incident but not a privacy incident. The theft of the laptop resulted in the unauthorized loss of sensitive information, making it a cybersecurity incident, but no PII was involved, so it is not a privacy incident.

- Renee processes "right to be forgotten" requests for her organization and is backlogged in her work. She recently fell far enough behind that the organization is not meeting its legal obligation to process these requests. This is a privacy incident but not a cybersecurity incident. It is a privacy incident because the organization is failing to meet its obligations for processing PII. It is not a cybersecurity incident because the confidentiality, integrity, and availability of the PII were not undermined.

Security Events and Incidents

Many IT professionals use the terms *security event* and *security incident* casually and interchangeably, but this is not correct. Members of a cybersecurity incident response team should use these terms carefully and according to their precise definitions within the organization. The National Institute for Standards and Technology (NIST) offers the following standard definitions for use throughout the U.S. government, and many private organizations choose to adopt them as well:

- An event is any observable occurrence in a system or network. A security event includes any observable occurrence that relates to a security function. For example, a user accessing a file stored on a server, an administrator changing permissions on a shared folder, and an attacker conducting a port scan are all examples of security events.

- An adverse event is any event that has negative consequences. Examples of adverse events include a malware infection on a system, a server crash, and a user accessing a file that they are not authorized to view.

- A security incident is a violation or imminent threat of violation of computer security policies, acceptable use policies, or standard security practices. Examples of security incidents include the accidental loss of sensitive information, an intrusion into a computer system by an attacker, the use of a keylogger on an executive's system to steal passwords, and the launch of a denial-of-service attack against a website.

Every security incident includes one or more security events, but not every security event is a security incident.

Computer security incident response teams (CSIRTs) are responsible for responding to computer security incidents that occur within an organization by following standardized response procedures and incorporating their subject matter expertise and professional judgment.

Privacy Incidents

Privacy incidents occur when an organization fails to meet its privacy obligations under legal or regulatory requirements or the organization's own policies. The exact definition of privacy incidents may vary from organization to organization. For example, many organizations consider any breach of privacy obligations to be a privacy incident, regardless of whether there was an unauthorized access to PII, while other organizations may restrict the definition of a privacy incident to cases where PII was compromised.

For example, here is the definition of a privacy incident used by the U.S. Department of Homeland Security:

> The loss of control, compromise, unauthorized disclosure, unauthorized acquisition, or any similar occurrence when (1) a person other than the authorized user accesses or potentially accesses PII or (2) an authorized user accesses or potentially accesses PII for an unauthorized purpose.

Security incidents and privacy incidents are closely related. Many security incidents are also privacy incidents and many privacy incidents are also security incidents. However, there are exceptions. Some security incidents are not privacy incidents. For example, if an attacker can take control of an organization's web server and remove critical product information, that is clearly a security incident. It is not, however, a privacy incident unless PII was involved. Remember, some privacy incidents are not security incidents. For example, if an organization fails to respond promptly to a data subject information request, that qualifies as a privacy incident, but there was never any breach of security.

Reporting Privacy Incidents

Organizations may have an obligation to report privacy incidents to data subjects and/or regulators. These obligations may come as a result of national, state/province, and/or local laws.

For example, the GDPR contains two related articles: Article 33 and Article 34.

GDPR Article 33

Article 33 requires that data controllers notify the supervisory authority of a personal data breach. It reads, in part:

> In the case of a personal data breach, the controller shall without undue delay and, where feasible, not later than 72 hours after having become aware of it, notify the personal data breach to the supervisory authority ... unless the personal data breach is unlikely to result in a risk to the rights and freedoms of natural persons.

Article 33 also includes four requirements for these notifications. They must:

> Describe the nature of the personal data breach including where possible, the categories and approximate number of data subjects concerned and the categories and approximate number of personal data records concerned;

> Communicate the name and contact details of the data protection officer or other contact point where more information can be obtained;

> Describe the likely consequences of the personal data breach;

> Describe the measures taken or proposed to be taken by the controller to address the personal data breach, including, where appropriate, measures to mitigate its possible adverse effects.

Article 34

GDPR Article 34 requires that data controllers notify data subjects of breaches under some circumstances. Article 34 reads, in part:

> When the personal data breach is likely to result in a high risk to the rights and freedoms of natural persons, the controller shall communicate the personal data breach to the data subject without undue delay.

Notifications made under Article 34 must contain information similar to the supervisory authority notifications made under Article 33, with the exception that the notice need not include details of the nature of the data breach.

Article 34 does contain three important exceptions. If any of the following circumstances apply, the controller is not obligated to notify data subjects of a breach:

> The controller has implemented appropriate technical and organisational protection measures, and those measures were applied to the personal data affected by the personal data breach, in particular those that render the personal data unintelligible to any person who is not authorised to access it, such as encryption;

> The controller has taken subsequent measures which ensure that the high risk to the rights and freedoms of data subjects referred to in paragraph 1 is no longer likely to materialise;

> It would involve disproportionate effort. In such a case, there shall instead be a public communication or similar measure whereby the data subjects are informed in an equally effective manner.

Data processors often handle information on behalf of data controllers. In many cases, laws that affect data controllers extend to data processors as well. In all cases, data processors should include language in vendor contracts that contains explicit privacy incident notification requirements.

Coordination and Information Sharing

During a privacy incident response effort, team members often need to communicate and share information with both internal and external partners. Smooth information sharing is essential to effective and efficient incident response, but it must be done within the established parameters of an incident communication plan. The organization's incident response policies should limit communication to trusted parties and put controls in place to prevent the inadvertent release of sensitive information outside of those trusted partners.

Internal Communications

Internal communications among the privacy incident oversight team and with other employees within the organization should take place over secure communications channels that are designated in advance and tested for security. This may include email, instant messaging, message boards, and other collaboration tools that pass security muster. The key is to evaluate and standardize those communications tools in advance so that responders are not left to their own devices to identify tools in the heat of an incident.

Developing strong internal communications capabilities and practices improves coordination within the organization. In particular, privacy teams should ensure that they coordinate incident detection capabilities with the following:

- Information technology teams
- Information security teams
- Physical security teams
- Human resources teams
- Investigation teams
- Vendors

Incidents detected by any of those teams may have privacy implications that are not readily apparent. For example, a physical security team may note that a records room was breached by an intruder. If the physical security response plan is well coordinated with the privacy incident response plan, this physical breach will trigger an evaluation as to whether a privacy incident also occurred.

External Communications

Team members, business leaders, public relations teams, and legal counsel may all bring to the table requirements that may justify sharing limited or detailed information with external entities. The incident response plan should guide these efforts. Types of external communications may include the following:

- Law enforcement may wish to be involved when an incident appears to be criminal in nature. The organization may choose to cooperate or decline participation in an investigation but should always make this decision with the advice of legal counsel.
- Information sharing partners, such as Information Sharing and Analysis Centers (ISACs), provide community-based warnings of cybersecurity risks. The organization may choose to participate in one of these consortiums and, in some cases, share information about ongoing and past incidents with partners in that consortium.

- Vendors may be able to provide information crucial to the response. The manufacturers of hardware and software used within the organization may be able to provide patches, troubleshooting advice, or other guidance crucial to the response effort.

- Other organizations may be actual or potential victims of the same attack. Team members may wish to coordinate their incident response with other organizations.

- Communications with the media and the general public may be mandatory under regulatory or legislative reporting requirements, voluntary, or forced by media coverage of a privacy incident.

It is incumbent upon the team leader to control and coordinate external communications in a manner that meets regulatory requirements and best serves the response effort.

Breach Notification

Organizations may also have a responsibility under national and regional laws to make public notifications and disclosures in the wake of a data breach involving certain types of PII. This responsibility may be limited to notifying the individuals involved or, in some cases, may require notification of government regulators and/or the news media. The purpose of these notifications is to ensure that individuals are aware of the potential breach and can take appropriate action to protect themselves.

Every U.S. state has a data breach notification law, with different requirements for triggering notifications. The GDPR also includes the breach notification requirements discussed earlier in this chapter. The United States lacks a federal law requiring broad notification for all security breaches but does have industry-specific laws and requirements that require notification in some circumstances.

The bottom line is that breach notification requirements vary by industry and jurisdiction, and an organization experiencing a breach may be required to untangle many overlapping requirements. For this reason, organizations experiencing a data breach should consult with an attorney who is well versed in this field.

Incident Handling

When handling privacy incidents, teams should follow a standard process that includes four steps:

- Risk assessment
- Containment
- Remediation
- Communications

Every individual involved in the privacy effort must understand their role and responsibilities in responding to a privacy incident.

Risk Assessment

The first step in handling a privacy incident is conducting a *risk assessment* that identifies the potential harm caused to both the organization and data subjects. This risk assessment should examine the following key characteristics:

- Nature of the PII involved
- Risk of harm to data subjects and the organization
- Likelihood that the information is accessible and usable to unauthorized parties
- Number of individuals affected

Containment Activities

Containment should begin as quickly as possible after analysts determine that an incident is underway. Containment activities are designed to isolate the incident and prevent it from spreading further. If that phrase sounds somewhat vague, that's because containment means very different things in the context of different types of security incidents. For example, if the organization is experiencing active exfiltration of data from a credit card processing system, incident responders might contain the damage by disconnecting that system from the network, preventing the attackers from continuing to exfiltrate information.

Exam Tip

When you take the exam, remember that containment is a critical priority. You want to stop the spread of any potential threats before you worry about eradicating the damage or recovering operations.

Containment activities typically aren't perfect and often cause some collateral damage that disrupts normal business activity. Consider the example described in the previous paragraph. Disconnecting a credit card processing system from the network may bring transactions to a halt, causing potentially significant losses of business. Incident responders undertaking containment strategies must understand the potential side effects of their actions while weighing them against the greater benefit to the organization. Decisions such as these are one of the reasons that senior management may want to have input into the organization's incident response strategies and tactics.

Containment Strategy Criteria

Selecting appropriate containment strategies is one of the most difficult tasks facing incident responders. Containment approaches that are too drastic may have an unacceptable impact on business operations. On the other hand, responders who select weak containment approaches may find that the incident escalates to cause even more damage.

In the *Computer Security Incident Handling Guide*, NIST recommends using the following criteria to develop an appropriate containment strategy and weigh it against business interests:

- Potential damage to and theft of resources

- Need for evidence preservation

- Service availability (e.g., network connectivity, services provided to external parties)

- Time and resources needed to implement the strategy

- Effectiveness of the strategy (e.g., partial containment, full containment)

- Duration of the solution (e.g., an emergency workaround to be removed in four hours, a temporary workaround to be removed in two weeks, a permanent solution)

Unfortunately, there's no formula or decision tree that guarantees responders will make the "right" decision while responding to an incident. Incident responders should understand these criteria, the intent of management, and their technical and business operating environment. Armed with this information, responders will be well positioned to follow their best judgment and select an appropriate containment strategy.

Remediation Measures

The *remediation* phase of incident response focuses on restoring normal capabilities and services. This includes making changes to the organization's privacy practices that make it less likely that an incident will recur in the future. For example, the organization might update its personal information inventory, modify privacy policies and procedures, or add new checks and balances to ensure privacy controls are properly maintained. This phase also includes reconstituting resources and correcting security control deficiencies that may have led to the incident. This could include rebuilding and patching systems, reconfiguring firewalls, updating malware signatures, and similar activities. The goal of recovery is not just to rebuild the organization's network but to do so in a manner that reduces the likelihood of a successful future attack.

During the remediation effort, cybersecurity analysts should develop a clear understanding of the incident's *root cause*. This is critical to implementing a secure recovery that corrects control deficiencies that led to the original attack. After all, if you don't understand how an attacker breached your security controls in the first place, it will be hard to correct those controls so the attack doesn't reoccur!

Root cause analysis also helps an organization identify other systems they operate that might share the same vulnerability. For example, if an attacker compromises a Cisco router and root cause analysis reveals an error in that device's configuration, administrators may correct the error on other routers they control to prevent a similar attack from compromising those devices.

Ongoing Communications

Incident response teams should also define their standard notification and escalation procedures. Remember that anyone in the organization may be the first to identify a potential privacy incident. Procedures should clearly define how first responders report a potential incident to the incident response team, the process for notifying team members of activation, and the criteria for escalating incident reports to management, as warranted.

The ongoing communications that take place during an incident should include appropriate communications to privacy incident response team members, regulators, impacted individuals, and/or responsible data controllers.

Focus on Process

Organizations should standardize their incident response processes as much as possible. Creating standardized plans makes it easier to ensure that the organization meets jurisdictional, global, and business requirements. For example, a high-level process might include the following steps that begin when the organization detects a potential privacy incident:

1. Engage the privacy team as quickly as possible.

2. Review the facts of the incident, including gathering additional information necessary to triage the incident. This may require interviews with data owners and stakeholders.

3. Conduct a risk analysis and identify the potential risk of harm.

4. Determine necessary actions to contain the incident and communicate with data owners and stakeholders.

5. Execute those actions.

6. Maintain an incident register and associated records of the incident management.

7. Monitor the incident to ensure that it is appropriately resolved.

8. Review and apply lessons learned to reduce the likelihood of future incidents.

Post-Incident Activity

Privacy incidents don't end after privacy and security professionals have addressed the urgent circumstances of the incident. Once the immediate danger passes and normal operations resume, the incident response team enters the post-incident activity phase of incident response. During this phase, team members conduct a lessons-learned review and ensure that they meet internal and external evidence retention requirements.

Lessons-Learned Review

During the lessons-learned review, responders conduct a thorough review of the incident and their response, with an eye toward improving procedures and tools for the next incident. This review is most effective if conducted during a meeting where everyone is present for the discussion (physically or virtually). Although some organizations try to conduct lessons-learned reviews in an offline manner, this approach does not lead to the back-and-forth discussion that often yields the greatest insight.

The lessons-learned review should be facilitated by an independent facilitator who was not involved in the incident response and who is perceived by everyone involved as an objective outsider. This allows the facilitator to guide the discussion productively without participants feeling that they are advancing a hidden agenda. NIST recommends that lessons-learned processes answer the following questions:

- Exactly what happened and at what times?
- What was the root cause of the incident?
- How well did staff and management perform in responding to the incident?
- Were the documented procedures followed? Were they adequate?
- What information was needed sooner?
- Were any steps or actions taken that might have inhibited the recovery?
- What would the staff and management do differently the next time a similar incident occurs?
- How could information sharing with other organizations have been improved?
- What corrective actions can prevent similar incidents in the future?
- What precursors or indicators should be watched for in the future to detect similar incidents?
- What additional tools or resources are needed to detect, analyze, and mitigate future incidents?

Once the group answers these questions, management must ensure that the organization takes follow-up actions, as appropriate. Lessons-learned reviews are only effective if they surface needed changes and those changes then occur to improve future incident response efforts.

The lessons-learned effort may result in the organization making changes to its privacy and security programs to reduce the risk of future incidents. In cases where these remediations occur, the organization should reassess its level of risk after those remedial actions.

Evidence Retention

At the conclusion of an incident, the team has often gathered large quantities of evidence. The team leader should work with staff to identify both internal and external evidence retention requirements. If the incident may result in civil litigation or criminal prosecution, the team should consult organizational attorneys before discarding any evidence. If there is no likelihood that the evidence will be used in court, the team should follow any retention policies that the organization has in place.

 If the organization does not have an existing evidence retention policy for privacy incidents, now would be a good time to create one. Many organizations choose to implement a two-year retention period for evidence not covered by other requirements. This allows incident handlers time to review the evidence at a later date during incident-handling program reviews or while handling future similar incidents.

After the post-incident activity phase, the team deactivates, and the incident-handling cycle returns to the preparation and detect and analyze phases.

 U.S. federal government agencies must retain all incident-handling records for at least three years. This requirement appears in the National Archives General Records Schedule 3.2, Item 20. See www.archives .gov/files/records-mgmt/grs/grs03-2.pdf for more information.

Developing a Final Report

Every incident that activates the privacy incident oversight team should conclude with a formal written report that documents the incident for posterity. This serves several important purposes. First, it creates an institutional memory of the incident that is useful when developing new privacy controls and training new privacy team members. Second, it may serve as an important record of the incident if there is ever legal action that results from the incident. Finally, the act of creating the written report can help identify previously undetected deficiencies in the incident response process that may feed back through the lessons-learned process.

Important elements that the team should cover in a post-incident report include the following:

- Chronology of events for the incident and response efforts
- Root cause of the incident
- Location and description of evidence collected during the incident response process

- Specific actions taken by responders to contain, eradicate, and recover from the incident, including the rationale for those decisions

- Estimates of the impact of the incident on the organization and its stakeholders, including an attempt to quantify the cost of the incident and maintain ongoing metrics

- Documentation of issues identified during the lessons-learned review

Incident summary reports should be classified in accordance with the organization's classification policy and stored in an appropriately secured manner. The organization should also have a defined retention period for incident reports and destroy old reports when they exceed that period.

Measuring the Effectiveness of Incident Response Programs

Privacy leaders should continually evaluate the effectiveness of their incident response programs, and it's important that they use appropriate metrics when performing these evaluations.

It's tempting to simply use the number of privacy incidents as the core metric, but this can be a very misleading figure. In organizations with immature (or even no!) privacy incident response plans, many incidents may simply go undetected. As the organization becomes more effective in its response to privacy incidents, this may cause an increase in the number of reported incidents. If you use the number of reported incidents as a metric, a program that is improving may actually look like it is decreasing in effectiveness.

While you should track the number of incidents that occur, a more important metric for a developing privacy program is the amount of time that it takes to resolve privacy incidents. The more mature the incident response program, the more quickly it will be able to detect and resolve privacy incidents.

Planning for Business Continuity

Business continuity planning involves assessing the risks to organizational processes and creating policies, plans, and procedures to minimize the impact those risks might have on the organization if they were to occur. The product of the business continuity planning process is the *business continuity plan (BCP)*. The BCP is used to maintain the continuous operation of a business in the event of an emergency. The goal of BCP developers is to implement a combination of policies, procedures, and processes such that a potentially disruptive event has as little impact on the business as possible.

Business continuity plans should be closely linked to privacy and security programs because they share many common goals. The BCP focuses on maintaining business operations with reduced or restricted infrastructure capabilities or resources. As long as the continuity of the organization's ability to perform its mission-critical work tasks is maintained, the BCP can be used to manage and restore the environment.

Business Continuity Planning vs. Disaster Recovery Planning

CIPM candidates often become confused about the difference between business continuity planning and disaster recovery planning. They might try to sequence them in a particular order or draw firm lines between the two activities. The reality of the situation is that these lines are blurry in real life and don't lend themselves to neat and clean categorization.

The distinction between the two is one of perspective. Both activities help prepare an organization for a disaster. They intend to keep operations running continuously, when possible, and recover functions as quickly as possible if a disruption occurs. The perspective difference is that business continuity activities are typically strategically focused and center themselves on business processes and operations. Disaster recovery plans tend to be more tactical and describe technical activities such as recovery sites, backups, and fault tolerance.

In any event, don't get hung up on the difference between the two. We've yet to see an exam question force anyone to draw a solid line between the two activities. It's much more important that you understand the processes and technologies involved in these two related disciplines.

The overall goal of business continuity planning is to provide a quick, calm, and efficient response in the event of an emergency and to enhance a company's ability to recover from a disruptive event promptly. The BCP process has four main steps:

1. Project scope and planning
2. Business impact analysis
3. Continuity planning
4. Plan approval and implementation

The next four sections of this chapter cover each of these phases in detail. The last portion of this chapter will introduce some of the critical elements you should consider when compiling documentation of your organization's business continuity plan.

Exam Tip

The top priority of both business continuity and disaster recovery planning is always *people*. The primary concern is to get people out of harm's way; then you can address recovery and restoration issues.

Project Scope and Planning

As with any formalized business process, the development of a resilient business continuity plan requires the use of a proven methodology. Organizations should approach the planning process with several goals in mind:

- Perform a structured review of the business's organization from a crisis planning point of view.

- Create a BCP team with the approval of senior management.

- Assess the resources available to participate in business continuity activities.

- Analyze the legal and regulatory landscape that governs an organization's response to a catastrophic event.

The exact process you use will depend on the size and nature of your organization and its business. There isn't a "one-size-fits-all" guide to business continuity project planning. You should consult with project planning professionals in your organization and determine the approach that will work best within your organizational culture.

The purpose of this phase is to ensure that the organization dedicates sufficient time and attention to both developing the project scope and plan and then documenting those activities for future reference.

Organizational Review

One of the first tasks of the team responsible for business continuity planning is to perform an analysis of the business organization to identify all departments and individuals who have a stake in the BCP process. Here are some areas to consider:

- Operational departments that are responsible for the core services the business provides to its clients

- Critical support services, such as the IT department, facilities, and maintenance personnel, and other groups responsible for the upkeep of systems that support the operational departments

- Security teams that are responsible for physical security, since they often are the first responders to an incident and are also responsible for the physical safeguarding of the primary facility and alternate processing facility

- Senior executives and other key individuals essential for the ongoing viability of the organization

This identification process is critical for two reasons. First, it provides the groundwork necessary to help identify potential members of the BCP team (see the next section). Second, it builds the foundation for the remainder of the BCP process.

Typically, the team spearheading the BCP effort performs the business organization analysis. Some organizations employ a dedicated business continuity manager to lead these efforts, whereas others treat it as a part-time responsibility for another IT leader. Either approach is acceptable because the output of the analysis commonly guides the selection of the remaining BCP team members. However, a thorough review of this analysis should be one of the first tasks assigned to the full BCP team when it convenes. This step is critical because the individuals performing the initial analysis may have overlooked critical business functions known to BCP team members that represent other parts of the organization. If the team were to continue without revising the organizational analysis, the entire BCP process might be negatively affected, resulting in the development of a plan that does not fully address the emergency-response needs of the organization as a whole.

Exam Tip

When developing a business continuity plan, be sure to consider the location of both your headquarters and any branch offices. The plan should account for a disaster that occurs at any location where your organization conducts its business, including your own physical locations and those of your cloud service providers.

BCP Team Selection

In some organizations, the IT and/or security departments bear sole responsibility for business continuity planning, and no other operational or support departments provide input. Those departments may not even know of the plan's existence until a disaster looms on the horizon or actually strikes the organization. This is a critical flaw! The isolated development of a business continuity plan can spell disaster in two ways. First, the plan itself may not take into account knowledge possessed only by the individuals responsible for the day-to-day operation of the business. Second, it keeps operational elements "in the dark" about plan specifics until implementation becomes necessary. These two factors may lead to disengaged units disagreeing with the provisions of the plan and failing to implement it properly. They also deny organizations the benefits achieved by a structured training and testing program for the plan.

To prevent these situations from adversely impacting the BCP process, the individuals responsible for the effort should take special care when selecting the BCP team. The team should include, at a minimum, the following individuals:

- Representatives from each of the organization's departments that are responsible for the core services performed by the business
- Business unit team members from the functional areas identified by the organizational analysis
- IT subject matter experts with technical expertise in areas covered by the BCP
- Cybersecurity and privacy team members with knowledge of the BCP process
- Physical security and facility management teams responsible for the physical plant

- Attorneys familiar with corporate legal, regulatory, and contractual responsibilities
- Human resources team members who can address staffing issues and the impact on individual employees
- Public relations team members who need to conduct similar planning for how they will communicate with stakeholders and the public in the event of a disruption
- Senior management representatives with the ability to set the vision, define priorities, and allocate resources

---

Tips for Selecting an Effective BCP Team

Select your team carefully! You need to strike a balance between representing different points of view and creating a team with explosive personality differences. Your goal should be to create a group that is as diverse as possible and still operates in harmony.

Take some time to think about the BCP team membership and who would be appropriate for your organization's technical, financial, and political environment. Who would you include?

Each team member brings a unique perspective to the BCP process and will have individual biases. For example, representatives from operational departments will often consider their department the most critical to the organization's continued viability. Although these biases may at first seem divisive, the leader of the BCP effort should embrace them and harness them productively. If used effectively, the biases will help achieve a healthy balance in the final plan as each representative advocates the needs of their department. On the other hand, without effective leadership, these biases may devolve into destructive turf battles that derail the BCP effort and harm the organization as a whole.

Resource Requirements

After the team validates the organizational review, it should turn to an assessment of the resources required by the BCP effort. This assessment involves the resources needed by three distinct BCP phases:

BCP Development   The BCP team will require some resources to perform the four elements of the BCP process (project scope and planning, business impact analysis, continuity planning, and approval and implementation). It's more than likely that the major resource consumed by this BCP phase will be the effort expended by members of the BCP team and the support staff they call on to assist in the development of the plan.

BCP Testing, Training, and Maintenance   The testing, training, and maintenance phases of BCP will require some hardware and software commitments. Still, once again, the major commitment in this phase will be the effort of the employees involved in those activities.

BCP Implementation   When a disaster strikes and the BCP team deems it necessary to conduct a full-scale implementation of the business continuity plan, the implementation will require significant resources. Those resources include a large amount of effort (BCP will likely become the focus of a large part, if not all, of the organization) as well as direct financial expenses. For this reason, the team must use its BCP implementation powers judiciously yet decisively.

An effective business continuity plan requires the expenditure of significant resources, ranging from the purchase and deployment of redundant computing facilities to the pencils and paper used by team members scratching out the first drafts of the plan. However, as you saw earlier, personnel are one of the most significant resources consumed by the BCP process. Many security professionals overlook the importance of accounting for labor, but you can rest assured that senior management will not. Business leaders are keenly aware of the effect that time-consuming side activities have on the operational productivity of their organizations and the real cost of personnel in terms of salary, benefits, and lost opportunities. These concerns become especially paramount when you are requesting the time of senior executives.

You should expect that leaders responsible for resource utilization management will put your BCP proposal under a microscope, and you should prepare to defend the necessity of your plan with coherent, logical arguments that address the business case for BCP.

Legal and Regulatory Requirements

Many industries may find themselves bound by federal, state, and local laws or regulations that require them to implement various degrees of BCP. We've already discussed one example in this chapter—the officers and directors of publicly traded firms have a fiduciary responsibility to exercise due diligence in the execution of their business continuity duties. In other circumstances, the requirements (and consequences of failure) might be even more severe. Emergency services, such as police, fire, and emergency medical operations, have a responsibility to the community to continue operations in the event of a disaster. Indeed, their services become even more critical in an emergency that threatens public safety. Failure to implement an effective BCP could result in the loss of life or property and decrease public confidence in the government.

In many countries, financial institutions, such as banks, brokerages, and the firms that process their data, are subject to strict government and international banking and securities regulations. These regulations are necessarily strict because their purpose is to ensure the continued operation of the institution as a crucial part of the economy. When pharmaceutical manufacturers must produce products in less-than-optimal circumstances following a disaster or in response to a rapidly emerging pandemic, they are required to certify the purity of their products to government regulators. There are countless other examples of industries that are necessary to continue operating in the event of an emergency by various laws and regulations.

Even if you're not bound by any of these considerations, you might have contractual obligations to your clients that require you to implement sound BCP practices. If your contracts include commitments to customers expressed as SLAs, you might find yourself in breach of those contracts if a disaster interrupts your ability to service your clients. Many clients may feel sorry for you and want to continue using your products/services, but their own business requirements might force them to sever the relationship and find new suppliers.

On the flip side of the coin, developing a strong, documented business continuity plan can help your organization win new clients and additional business from existing clients. If you can show your customers the sound procedures you have in place to continue serving them in the event of a disaster, they'll place greater confidence in your firm and might be more likely to choose you as their preferred vendor. That's not a bad position to be in!

All of these concerns point to one conclusion—it's essential to include your organization's legal counsel in the BCP process. They are intimately familiar with the legal, regulatory, and contractual obligations that apply to your organization. They can help your team implement a plan that meets those requirements while ensuring the continued viability of the organization to the benefit of all—employees, shareholders, suppliers, and customers alike.

Laws regarding computing systems, business practices, and disaster management change frequently. They also vary from jurisdiction to jurisdiction. Be sure to keep your attorneys involved throughout the lifetime of your BCP, including the testing and maintenance phases. If you restrict their involvement to a pre-implementation review of the plan, you may not become aware of the impact that changing laws and regulations have on your corporate responsibilities.

Business Impact Analysis

Once your BCP team completes the project scope and planning process, it's time to dive into the heart of the work—the *business impact analysis (BIA)*. The BIA identifies the business processes and tasks that are critical to an organization's ongoing viability and the threats posed to those resources. It also assesses the likelihood that each threat will occur and the impact those occurrences will have on the business. The results of the BIA provide you with quantitative measures that can help you prioritize the commitment of business continuity resources to the various local, regional, and global risk exposures facing your organization.

It's important to realize that there are two different types of analyses that business planners use when facing a decision:

Quantitative Impact Assessment Involves the use of numbers and formulas to reach a decision. This type of data often expresses options in terms of the dollar value to the business.

Qualitative Impact Assessment Takes non-numerical factors, such as reputation, investor/customer confidence, workforce stability, and other concerns, into account. This type of data often results in categories of prioritization (such as high, medium, and low).

 Quantitative analysis and qualitative assessment both play an essential role in the BCP process. However, most people tend to favor one type of analysis over the other. When selecting the individual members of the BCP team, try to achieve a balance between people who prefer each strategy. This approach helps develop a well-rounded BCP and will benefit the organization in the long run.

The BIA process described in this chapter approaches the problem from both quantitative and qualitative points of view. However, it's tempting for a BCP team to "go with the numbers" and perform a quantitative assessment while neglecting the somewhat more subjective qualitative assessment. The BCP team should perform a qualitative analysis of the factors affecting your BCP process. For example, if your business is highly dependent on a few important clients, your management team is probably willing to suffer a significant short-term financial loss to retain those clients in the long term. The BCP team must sit down and discuss (preferably with the involvement of senior management) qualitative concerns to develop a comprehensive approach that satisfies all stakeholders.

Identifying Priorities

The first BIA task facing the BCP team is identifying business priorities. Depending on your line of business, certain activities are essential to your day-to-day operations when disaster strikes. You should create a comprehensive list of critical business functions and rank them in order of importance. Although this task may seem somewhat daunting, it's not as hard as it looks.

These critical business functions will vary from organization to organization, based on each organization's mission. They are the activities that, if disrupted, would jeopardize the organization's ability to achieve its goals. For example, an online retailer would treat the ability to sell products from their website and fulfill those orders promptly as critical business functions.

A great way to divide the workload of this process among the team members is to assign each participant responsibility for drawing up a prioritized list that covers the business functions for which their department is responsible. When the entire BCP team convenes, team members can use those prioritized lists to create a master prioritized list for the organization as a whole. One caution with this approach—if your team is not truly representative of the organization, you may miss critical priorities. Be sure to gather input from all parts of the organization, especially from any areas not represented on the BCP team.

This process helps identify business priorities from a qualitative point of view. Recall that we're describing an attempt to develop both qualitative and quantitative BIAs simultaneously. To begin the quantitative assessment, the BCP team should develop a list of organization assets and then assign an *asset value (AV)* in monetary terms to each asset. Teams creating this list may draw on other existing documentation within the organization, such as accounting information, insurance policies, and configuration management systems. These values form the basis of risk calculations performed later in the BIA.

The second quantitative measure that the team must develop is the *maximum tolerable downtime (MTD)*, sometimes also known as *maximum tolerable outage (MTO)*. The MTD is the maximum length of time a business function can tolerate a disruption before suffering irreparable harm. The MTD provides valuable information when you're performing both BC and DR planning. The organization's list of critical business functions plays a crucial role in this process. The MTD for critical business functions should be lower than the MTD for activities not identified as critical. Returning to the example of an online retailer, the MTD for the website selling products may be only a few minutes, whereas the MTD for their internal email system might be measured in hours.

The *recovery time objective (RTO)* for each business function is the amount of time in which you think you can feasibly recover the function in the event of a disruption. This value is closely related to the MTD. Once you have defined your recovery objectives, you can design and plan the procedures necessary to accomplish the recovery tasks.

As you conduct your BCP work, ensure that your RTOs are less than your MTDs, resulting in a situation in which a function should never be unavailable beyond the maximum tolerable downtime.

While the RTO and MTD measure the time to recover operations and the impact of that recovery time on operations, organizations must also pay attention to the potential data loss that might occur during an availability incident. Depending on the way that information is collected, stored, and processed, some data loss may take place.

The *recovery point objective (RPO)* is the data loss equivalent to the time-focused RTO. The RPO defines the maximum amount of data that the organization can tolerate losing. For example, an organization might perform database transaction log backups every 15 minutes. In that case, the RPO would be 15 minutes, meaning that the organization may lose up to 15 minutes' worth of data after an incident. If an incident takes place at 8:30 a.m., the last transaction log backup must have occurred sometime between 8:15 a.m. and 8:30 a.m. Depending on the precise timing of the incident and the backup, the organization may have irretrievably lost between 0 and 15 minutes of data.

Risk Identification

The next phase of the BIA is the identification of risks posed to your organization. During this phase, you'll have an easy time identifying some common threats, but you might need to exercise some creativity to come up with more obscure (but very real!) risks.

Risks come in two forms: natural risks and person-made risks. The following list includes some events that pose natural threats:

- Violent storms/hurricanes/tornadoes/blizzards
- Lightning strikes/fires

- Earthquakes
- Mudslides/avalanches
- Volcanic eruptions
- Pandemics

Person-made threats include the following events:

- Terrorist acts/wars/civil unrest
- Theft/vandalism
- Fires/explosions
- Prolonged power outages
- Building collapses
- Transportation failures
- Internet disruptions
- Service provider outages
- Economic crises

Remember, these are by no means all-inclusive lists. They merely identify some common risks that many organizations face. You may want to use them as a starting point, but a full listing of risks facing your organization will require input from all members of the BCP team.

The risk identification portion of the process is purely qualitative. At this point in the process, the BCP team should not be concerned about the likelihood that each type of risk will materialize or the amount of damage such an occurrence would inflict upon the continued operation of the business. The results of this analysis will drive both the qualitative and quantitative portions of the remaining BIA tasks.

Business Impact Analysis and the Cloud

As you conduct your business impact analysis, don't forget to take into account any cloud vendors on which your organization relies. Depending on the nature of the cloud service, the vendor's own business continuity arrangements may have a critical impact on your organization's business operations as well.

Consider, for example, a firm that outsourced email and calendaring to a third-party software-as-a-service (SaaS) provider. Does the contract with that provider include details about the provider's SLA and commitments for restoring operations in the event of a disaster?

Also, remember that a contract is not normally sufficient due diligence when choosing a cloud provider. You should also verify that they have the controls in place to deliver on their contractual commitments. Although it may not be possible for you to physically visit the vendor's facilities to verify their control implementation, you can always do the next best thing—send someone else!

Now, before you go off identifying an emissary and booking flights, realize that many of your vendor's customers are probably asking the same question. For this reason, the vendor may have already hired an independent auditing firm to conduct an assessment of its controls. They can make the results of this assessment available to you in the form of a Service Organization Control (SOC) report.

Keep in mind that there are three different versions of the SOC report. The simplest of these, a SOC 1 report, covers only internal controls over financial reporting. If you want to verify the security, privacy, and availability controls, you'll want to review either a SOC 2 or SOC 3 report. The AICPA sets and maintains the standards surrounding these reports to maintain consistency between auditors from different accounting firms.

For more information on this topic, see the AICPA's document comparing the SOC report types at www.aicpa.org/interestareas/frc/assuranceadvisoryservices/serviceorganization-smanagement.html.

Likelihood Assessment

The preceding step consisted of the BCP team's drawing up a comprehensive list of the events that can be a threat to an organization. You probably recognized that some events are much more likely to happen than others. For example, an earthquake is a much more plausible risk than a tropical storm for a business located in Southern California. A company based in Florida might have the exact opposite likelihood that each risk would occur.

To account for these differences, the next phase of the business impact analysis identifies the likelihood that each risk will occur. First, we determine the *annualized rate of occurrence (ARO)* that reflects the number of times a business expects to experience a given disaster each year. This annualization process simplifies comparing the magnitude of very different risks.

The BCP team should determine an ARO for each risk identified in the previous section. Base these numbers on corporate history, professional experience of team members, and advice from experts, such as meteorologists, seismologists, fire prevention professionals, and other consultants, as needed.

Exam Tip

In addition to the government resources identified in this chapter, insurance companies develop large repositories of risk information as part of their actuarial processes. You may be able to obtain this information from them to assist in your BCP efforts. After all, you have a mutual interest in preventing damage to your business!

In many cases, you may be able to find likelihood assessments for some risks prepared by experts at no cost to you. For example, the U.S. Geological Survey (USGS) developed an earthquake hazard map that illustrates the ARO for earthquakes in various regions of the United States. Similarly, the Federal Emergency Management Agency (FEMA) coordinates the development of detailed flood maps of local communities throughout the United States. These resources are available online and offer a wealth of information to organizations performing a business impact analysis.

Impact Analysis

As you may have surmised based on its name, the impact analysis is one of the most critical portions of the business impact analysis. In this phase, you analyze the data gathered during risk identification and likelihood assessment and attempt to determine what impact each one of the identified risks would have on the business if it were to occur.

From a quantitative point of view, we will cover three specific metrics: the exposure factor, the single loss expectancy, and the annualized loss expectancy. Each one of these values describes a particular risk/asset combination evaluated during the previous phases.

The *exposure factor (EF)* is the amount of damage that the risk poses to the asset, expressed as a percentage of the asset's value (AV). For example, if the BCP team consults with fire experts and determines that a building fire would destroy 70 percent of the building, the exposure factor of the building to fire is 70 percent.

The *single loss expectancy (SLE)* is the monetary loss expected each time the risk materializes. You can compute the SLE using the following formula:

$$SLE = AV \times EF$$

Continuing with the preceding example, if the building is worth $500,000, the single loss expectancy would be 70 percent of $500,000, or $350,000. You can interpret this figure to mean that you could expect a single fire in the building would cause $350,000 worth of damage.

The *annualized loss expectancy (ALE)* is the monetary loss that the business expects to incur as a result of the risk harming the asset during a typical year. The SLE is the amount of damage you expect each time a disaster strikes, and the ARO (from the likelihood analysis) is the number of times you expect a disaster to occur each year. You compute the ALE by simply multiplying those two numbers:

$$ALE = ARO \times SLE$$

Returning once again to our building example, fire experts might predict that a fire will occur in the building approximately once every 30 years, specifically determining that there is a 0.03 chance of a fire in any given year. The ALE is then 3 percent of the $350,000 SLE, or $10,500. You can interpret this figure to mean that the business should expect to lose $10,500 each year due to a fire in the building.

Obviously, a fire will not occur each year—this figure represents the average cost over the approximately 30 years between fires. It's not especially useful for budgeting considerations but proves invaluable when attempting to prioritize the assignment of BCP resources to a given risk. Of course, a business leader may decide that the risk of a fire remains unacceptable and take actions that contradict the quantitative analysis. That's where qualitative assessment comes into play.

Exam Tip

Be sure you're familiar with the quantitative formulas contained in this chapter, and the concepts of asset value, exposure factor, the annualized rate of occurrence, single loss expectancy, and annualized loss expectancy. Know the formulas and be able to work through a scenario.

From a qualitative point of view, you must consider the nonmonetary impact that interruptions might have on your business. For example, you might want to consider the following:

- Loss of goodwill among your clients
- Loss of employees to other jobs after prolonged downtime
- Social/ethical responsibilities to the community
- Negative publicity

It's difficult to put dollar values on items like these to include them in the quantitative portion of the impact analysis, but they are equally important. After all, if you decimate your client base, you won't have a business to return to when you're ready to resume operations!

Resource Prioritization

The final step of the BIA is to prioritize the allocation of business continuity resources to the various risks that you identified and assessed in earlier phases of the BIA.

From a quantitative point of view, this process is fairly straightforward. You take the risks you analyzed during the BIA process and sort them in descending order according to the ALE computed during the impact analysis phase. This step provides you with a prioritized list of the risks that you should address. Select as many items as you're willing and able to handle simultaneously from the top of the list and work your way down. Eventually, you'll reach a point at which you've exhausted either the list of risks (unlikely!) or all your available resources (much more likely!).

Recall from the previous section that we also stressed the importance of addressing qualitatively important concerns. In earlier sections about the BIA, we treated quantitative and qualitative analysis as mainly separate functions with some overlap in the analysis. Now it's time to merge the two prioritized lists, which is more of an art than a science. You must work with the BCP team and representatives from the senior management team and combine the two lists into a single prioritized list.

Qualitative concerns may justify elevating or lowering the priority of risks that already exist on the ALE-sorted quantitative list. For example, if you run a fire suppression company, your number-one priority might be the prevention of a fire in your principal place of business even though an earthquake might cause more physical damage. The potential loss of reputation within the business community resulting from the destruction of a fire suppression company by fire might be too challenging to overcome and result in the eventual collapse of the business, justifying the increased priority.

Continuity Planning

The first two phases of the BCP process (project scope and planning and the business impact analysis) focus on determining how the BCP process will work and prioritizing the business assets that you must protect against interruption. The next phase of BCP development, continuity planning, focuses on developing and implementing a continuity strategy to minimize the impact realized risks might have on protected assets.

In this section, you'll learn about the subtasks involved in continuity planning:

- Strategy development
- Provisions and processes
- Plan approval
- Plan implementation
- Training and education

Strategy Development

The strategy development phase bridges the gap between the business impact analysis and the continuity planning phases of BCP development. The BCP team must now take the prioritized list of concerns raised by the quantitative and qualitative resource prioritization exercises and determine which risks will be addressed by the business continuity plan. Fully addressing all the contingencies would require the implementation of provisions and processes that maintain a zero-downtime posture in the face of every possible risk. For obvious reasons, implementing a policy this comprehensive is impossible.

The BCP team should look back at the MTD estimates created during the early stages of the BIA and determine which risks are deemed acceptable and which must be mitigated by BCP continuity provisions. Some of these decisions are obvious—the risk of a blizzard striking an operations facility in Egypt is negligible and constitutes an acceptable risk. The risk of a monsoon in New Delhi is severe enough that BCP provisions must mitigate it.

Once the BCP team determines which risks require mitigation and the level of resources that will be committed to each mitigation task, they are ready to move on to the provisions and processes phase of continuity planning.

Provisions and Processes

The provisions and processes phase of continuity planning is the meat of the entire business continuity plan. In this task, the BCP team designs the specific procedures and mechanisms that will mitigate the risks deemed unacceptable during the strategy development stage. Three categories of assets must be protected through BCP provisions and processes: people, buildings/facilities, and infrastructure. In the next three sections, we'll explore some of the techniques you can use to safeguard these categories.

People

First, you must ensure that the people within your organization are safe before, during, and after an emergency. Once you've achieved that goal, you must make provisions to allow your employees to conduct both their BCP and operational tasks in as normal a manner as possible, given the circumstances.

Don't lose sight of the fact that people are your most valuable asset. The safety of people must always come before the organization's business goals. Be sure that your business continuity plan makes adequate provisions for the security of your employees, customers, suppliers, and any other individuals who may be affected.

Management should provide team members with all the resources they need to complete their assigned tasks. At the same time, if circumstances dictate that people be present in the workplace for extended periods, arrangements must be made for shelter and food. Any continuity plan that requires these provisions should include detailed instructions for the BCP team in the event of a disaster. The organization should maintain stockpiles of provisions sufficient to feed the operational and support groups for an extended time in an accessible location. Plans should specify the periodic rotation of those stockpiles to prevent spoilage.

Buildings and Facilities

Many businesses require specialized facilities to carry out their critical operations. These might include standard office facilities, manufacturing plants, operations centers, warehouses, distribution/logistics centers, and repair/maintenance depots, among others. When you perform your BIA, you will identify those facilities that play a critical role in your organization's continued viability. Your continuity plan should address two areas for each critical facility:

Hardening Provisions Your BCP should outline mechanisms and procedures that can be put in place to protect your existing facilities against the risks defined in the strategy development phase. Hardening provisions might include steps as simple as patching a leaky roof or as complex as installing reinforced hurricane shutters and fireproof walls.

Alternate Sites If it's not feasible to harden a facility against a risk, your BCP should identify alternate sites where business activities can resume immediately (or at least in a time that's shorter than the maximum tolerable downtime for all affected critical business functions). Typically, an alternate site is associated with disaster recovery planning (DRP) rather than BCP. The organization might identify the need for an alternate site during BCP development, but it takes an actual interruption to trigger the use of the site, making it fall under the DRP.

Technology Infrastructure

Every business depends on some sort of technology infrastructure for its critical processes. For many companies, a vital part of this infrastructure is an IT backbone of communications and computer systems that process orders, manage the supply chain, handle customer interaction, and perform other business functions. This backbone consists of servers, workstations, and critical communications links between sites. The BCP must address how the organization will protect these systems against risks identified during the strategy development phase. As with buildings and facilities, there are two main methods of providing this protection:

Physically Hardening Systems   You can protect systems against the risks by introducing protective measures such as computer-safe fire suppression systems and uninterruptible power supplies.

Alternative Systems   You can also protect business functions by introducing redundancy (either redundant components or completely redundant systems/communications links that rely on different facilities).

These same principles apply to whatever infrastructure components serve your critical business processes—transportation systems, electrical power grids, banking and financial systems, water supplies, and so on.

As organizations move many of their technology operations to the cloud, this doesn't reduce their reliance on physical infrastructure. Although the company may no longer operate the infrastructure themselves, they still rely on the physical infrastructure of their cloud service providers and should take measures to ensure they are comfortable with the level of continuity planning conducted by those providers. A disruption at a key cloud provider that affects one of the organization's critical business functions can be just as damaging as a failure of the organization's own infrastructure.

Plan Approval and Implementation

Once the BCP team completes the design phase of the BCP document, it's time to gain top-level management endorsement of the plan. If you were fortunate enough to have senior management involvement throughout the development phases of the plan, this should be a relatively straightforward process. On the other hand, if this is your first time approaching management with the BCP document, you should be prepared to provide a lengthy explanation of the plan's purpose and specific provisions.

Senior management buy-in is essential to the success of the overall BCP effort.

Plan Approval

If possible, you should attempt to have the plan endorsed by the top executive in your business—the chief executive officer, chairperson, president, or similar business leader. This move demonstrates the importance of the plan to the entire organization and showcases the business leader's commitment to business continuity. The signature of such an individual on the plan also gives it much greater weight and credibility in the eyes of other senior managers, who might otherwise brush it off as a necessary but trivial IT initiative.

Plan Implementation

Once you've received approval from senior management, it's time to dive in and start implementing your plan. The BCP team should get together and develop an implementation schedule that utilizes the resources dedicated to the program to achieve the stated process and provision goals in as prompt a manner as possible, given the scope of the modifications and the organization's attitude toward continuity planning.

After fully deploying resources, the BCP team should supervise the design and implementation of a BCP maintenance program. This program ensures that the plan remains responsive to evolving business needs.

Training and Education

Training and education are essential elements of the BCP implementation. All personnel who will be involved in the plan (either directly or indirectly) should receive some sort of training on the overall plan, as well as on their individual responsibilities.

Everyone in the organization should receive at least a plan overview briefing. These briefings provide employees with the confidence that business leaders have considered the possible risks posed to the continued operation of the business and have put a plan in place to mitigate the impact on the organization should a disruption occur.

People with direct BCP responsibilities should be trained and evaluated on their specific BCP tasks to ensure that they can complete them efficiently when disaster strikes. Furthermore, at least one person should be trained as a backup for every BCP task to provide redundancy in the event personnel are injured or cannot reach the workplace during an emergency.

BCP Documentation

Documentation is a critical step in the business continuity planning process. Committing your BCP methodology to paper provides several significant benefits:

- It ensures that BCP personnel have a written continuity document to reference in the event of an emergency, even if senior BCP team members are not present to guide the effort.

- It provides a historical record of the BCP process that will be useful to future personnel seeking to both understand the reasoning behind various procedures and implement necessary changes in the plan.

- It forces the team members to commit their thoughts to paper—a process that often facilitates the identification of flaws in the plan. Having the plan on paper also allows draft documents to be distributed to individuals not on the BCP team for a "sanity check."

In the following sections, we'll explore some of the essential components of the written business continuity plan.

Continuity Planning Goals

First, the plan should describe the goals of continuity planning as set forth by the BCP team and senior management. These goals should be decided at or before the first BCP team meeting and will most likely remain unchanged throughout the life of the BCP.

The most common goal of the BCP is quite simple: to ensure the continuous operation of the business in the face of an emergency. Other goals may also be inserted in this section of the document to meet organizational needs. For example, you might have an objective that your customer call center experience no more than 15 consecutive minutes of downtime or that your backup servers be able to handle 75 percent of your processing load within one hour of plan activation.

Statement of Importance

The *statement of importance* reflects the criticality of the BCP to the organization's continued viability. This document commonly takes the form of a letter to the organization's employees, stating the reason that the organization devoted significant resources to the BCP development process and requesting the cooperation of all personnel in the BCP implementation phase.

Here's where the importance of senior executive buy-in comes into play. If you can put out this letter under the signature of the chief executive officer (CEO) or an officer at a similar level, the plan will carry tremendous weight as you attempt to implement changes throughout the organization. If you have the signature of a lower-level manager, you may encounter resistance as you try to work with portions of the organization outside of that individual's direct control.

Statement of Priorities

The *statement of priorities* flows directly from the "identify priorities" phase of the business impact analysis. It simply involves listing the functions considered critical to continued business operations in a prioritized order. When listing these priorities, you should also include a statement that they were developed as part of the BCP process and reflect the importance of the functions to continued business operations in the event of an emergency and nothing more. Otherwise, the list of priorities could be used for unintended purposes and result in a political turf battle between competing organizations to the detriment of the business continuity plan.

Statement of Organizational Responsibility

The *statement of organizational responsibility* also comes from a senior-level executive and can be incorporated into the same letter as the statement of importance. It echoes the sentiment that "business continuity is everyone's responsibility!" The statement of organizational responsibility restates the organization's commitment to business continuity planning. It informs employees, vendors, and affiliates that the organization expects them to do everything they can to assist with the BCP process.

Statement of Urgency and Timing

The *statement of urgency and timing* expresses the criticality of implementing the BCP and outlines the implementation timetable decided on by the BCP team and agreed to by upper management. The wording of this statement will depend on the actual urgency assigned to the BCP process by your organization's leadership. Consider including a detailed implementation timeline to foster a sense of urgency.

Risk Assessment

The *risk assessment* portion of the BCP documentation essentially recaps the decision-making process undertaken during the business impact analysis. It should include a discussion of all the critical business functions considered during the BIA as well as the quantitative and qualitative analyses performed to assess the risks to those functions. Include the actual AV, EF, ARO, SLE, and ALE figures in the quantitative analysis. Also, describe the thought process behind the analysis to the reader. Finally, keep in mind that the assessment reflects a point-in-time evaluation, and the team must update it regularly to reflect changing conditions.

Risk Acceptance/Mitigation

The *risk acceptance/mitigation* section of the BCP documentation contains the outcome of the strategy development portion of the BCP process. It should cover each risk identified in the risk analysis portion of the document and outline one of two thought processes:

- For risks that were deemed acceptable, it should outline the reasons the risk was considered acceptable as well as potential future events that might warrant a reconsideration of this determination.

- For risks that were deemed unacceptable, it should outline the risk management provisions and processes put into place to reduce the risk to the organization's continued viability.

WARNING   It's far too easy to look at a difficult risk mitigation challenge and say, "We accept this risk" before moving on to less difficult things. Business continuity planners should resist these statements and ask business leaders to document their risk acceptance decisions formally. If auditors later scrutinize your business continuity plan, they will most certainly look for formal artifacts of any risk acceptance decisions made in the BCP process.

Vital Records Program

The BCP documentation should also outline a vital records program for the organization. A vital records program identifies and protects records containing vital information necessary for an organization to continue its key functions and activities in case of an emergency/disaster.

 The BC and DR plans themselves are also vital records that should be protected as part of this effort!

One of the biggest challenges in implementing a vital records program often is identifying the essential records in the first place. As many organizations transitioned from paper-based to digital workflows, they often lost the rigor that existed around creating and maintaining formal file structures. Vital records may now be distributed among a wide variety of IT systems and cloud services. Some may be stored on central servers accessible to groups, whereas others may be located in digital repositories assigned to an individual employee.

If that messy state of affairs sounds like your current reality, you may want to begin your vital records program by identifying the records that are truly critical to your business. Sit down with functional leaders and ask, "If we needed to rebuild our organization today in a completely new location without access to any of our computers or files, what records would you need?" Asking the question in this way forces the team to visualize the actual process of re-creating operations and, as they walk through the steps in their minds, will produce an inventory of the organization's vital records. This inventory may evolve as people remember other important information sources, so you should consider using multiple conversations to finalize it.

Once you've identified the records that your organization considers vital, the next task is a formidable one: find them! You should be able to identify the storage locations for each document identified in your vital records inventory. Once you've completed this task, you can then use this vital records inventory to inform the rest of your business continuity planning efforts.

Emergency Response Guidelines

The emergency response guidelines outline the organizational and individual responsibilities for immediate response to an emergency. This document provides the first employees to detect an emergency with the steps they should take to activate provisions of the BCP that do not start automatically. These guidelines should include the following:

- Immediate response procedures (security and safety procedures, fire suppression procedures, notification of appropriate emergency-response agencies, and so on)

- A list of the individuals to notify of the incident (executives, BCP team members, and so on)

- Secondary response procedures that first responders should take while waiting for the BCP team to assemble

Your guidelines should be easily accessible to everyone in the organization who may be among the first responders to a crisis incident. Any time a disruption strikes, time is of the essence. Slowdowns in activating your business continuity procedures may result in undesirable downtime for your business operations.

Maintenance

The BCP documentation and the plan itself must be living documents. Every organization encounters nearly constant change, and this dynamic nature ensures that the business's continuity requirements will also evolve. The BCP team should not disband after the plan is developed but should still meet periodically to discuss the plan and review the results of plan tests to ensure that it continues to meet organizational needs.

Minor changes to the plan do not require conducting the full BCP development process from scratch; the BCP team may make them at an informal meeting by unanimous consent. However, keep in mind that drastic changes in an organization's mission or resources may require going back to the BCP drawing board and beginning again.

Any time you make a change to the BCP, you must practice reasonable version control. All older versions of the BCP should be physically destroyed and replaced by the most current version so that no confusion exists as to the correct implementation of the BCP.

It is also a good practice to include BCP components in job descriptions to ensure that the BCP remains fresh and to increase the likelihood that team members carry out their BCP responsibilities correctly. Including BCP responsibilities in an employee's job description also makes them fair game for the performance review process, allowing the organization to more accurately assess an employee's total contribution to the business.

Testing and Exercises

The BCP documentation should also outline a formalized exercise program to ensure that the plan remains current. Exercises also verify that team members receive adequate training to perform their duties in the event of a disaster. The BC plan should be tested annually as part of the normal BC process.

Summary

Mature privacy programs must have robust processes and procedures in place to respond to privacy events as they occur. This includes handling data subject requests received by the organization in a manner that complies with policies and regulations and responding to potential privacy incidents promptly to contain the damage and minimize the harm to data subjects and the organization. By maintaining an appropriate privacy incident response process, organizations may stay on top of both of these obligations. Organizations also must put strong business continuity and disaster recovery programs in place to limit the risk of disruption to data processing and increase the speed of recovery after disruptions occur.

Exam Essentials

Understand the organization's requirement to respond to data subject requests. Data subjects have a set of rights that vary based on the type of information and jurisdiction. Privacy teams must ensure that they understand and comply with a data subject's right to access information, request the correction of records that contain errors, and request the erasure of personal information under the right to be forgotten. Organizations must also comply with data subject restrictions on the processing of their information and maintain a process for handling data subject complaints.

Know the legal compliance obligations of an organization in response to privacy issues. Legal obligations center around five core requirements: preventing harm to data subjects, limiting the collection of personal information, providing accountability for data controllers and processors, monitoring and enforcing compliance with requirements, and requiring reporting of privacy incidents.

Explain the provisions of the major articles of the GDPR. Article 15 of the GDPR provides data subjects with the right to access information that an organization maintains about them. Article 16 provides for the right of data integrity and correction. Article 17 contains the right to be forgotten — the right to request the erasure of personal information maintained by a data controller. Article 18 allows data subjects to restrict the processing of their personal information. Article 19 requires the communication of the rectification or erasure of personal information. Article 22 provides data subjects with the right to opt out of the use of automated decision-making technologies. Article 33 requires the notification of supervisory authorities after a breach. Article 34 requires the notification of data subjects after a breach. Article 77 provides data subjects with the right to file complaints with supervisory authorities.

Know the key stakeholders in a privacy incident response plan. The key stakeholders in a privacy incident response plan are privacy professionals, information security professionals, legal teams, compliance officials, audit teams, human resources teams, marketing and business development teams, communications and public relations teams, and external parties.

Understand the differences between privacy and security incidents. A security incident is a violation or imminent threat of violation of computer security policies, acceptable use policies, or standard security practices. Privacy incidents occur when an organization fails to meet its privacy obligations under legal or regulatory requirements or the organization's own policies. Security incidents and privacy incidents are closely related. Many (but not all) security incidents are also privacy incidents and many (but not all) privacy incidents are also security incidents.

Explain the four steps of the incident handling process. The first step in handling a privacy incident is conducting a *risk assessment* that identifies the potential harm caused to both the organization and data subjects. The second step is to conduct containment activities that are designed to isolate the incident and prevent it from spreading further. The third step is to conduct remediation activities that include reconstituting resources and correcting security control deficiencies that may have led to the incident. The fourth step is to conduct ongoing communication with appropriate stakeholders.

Know the eight elements of a strong incident response. The elements are as follows:

1. Engage the privacy team as quickly as possible.

2. Review the facts of the incident, including gathering additional information necessary to triage the incident. This may require interviews with stakeholders.

3. Conduct a risk analysis and identify the potential risk of harm.

4. Determine necessary actions to contain the incident and communicate with stakeholders.

5. Execute those actions.

6. Maintain an incident register and associated records of the incident management.

7. Monitor the incident to ensure that it is appropriately resolved.

8. Review and apply lessons learned to reduce the likelihood of future incidents.

Explain the importance of comprehensively documenting an organization's business continuity and disaster recovery plans.

Committing the plan to writing provides the organization with a written record of the procedures to follow when disaster strikes. It prevents the "it's in my head" syndrome and ensures the orderly progress of events in an emergency.

Describe the process used to develop a continuity strategy. During the strategy development phase, the BCP team determines which risks they will mitigate. In the provisions and processes phase, the team designs mechanisms and procedures that will mitigate identified risks. The plan must then be approved by senior management and implemented. Personnel must also receive training on their roles in the BCP process.

Review Questions

1. Which one of the following document types would outline the authority of a team responding to a privacy incident?

   A. Policy

   B. Procedure

   C. Playbook

   D. Baseline

2. Robert is finishing a draft of a proposed incident response policy for his organization. Who would be the most appropriate person to sign the policy?

   A. CEO

   B. Director of security

   C. CIO

   D. CSIRT leader

3. Who is the best facilitator for a post-incident lessons-learned session?

   A. CEO

   B. Privacy incident oversight team leader

   C. Independent facilitator

   D. First responder

4. Under Article 33 of the General Data Protection Regulation, how much time does a data controller have to report a personal data breach to the relevant supervisory authority?

   A. 24 hours

   B. 72 hours

   C. 30 days

   D. 90 days

5. When informing data subjects of a security breach under Article 34 of the GDPR, which of the following is *not* required?

   A. Describing the nature of the breach

   B. Communicating contact information for the DPO

   C. Describing the likely consequences of the breach

   D. Describing the measures taken to address the breach

6. Matthew is participating in the response to a privacy incident. He was informed by his manager that an employee may have lost a spreadsheet containing PII but he has very little detail about the incident. What should be his next action?

   A. Conduct a risk assessment.

   B. Interview the employee.

   C. Contact data subjects.

   D. Contact the supervisory authority.

7. Which one of the following rights is *not* guaranteed to data subjects by the GDPR?

   A. Right to be forgotten

   B. Right to correction

   C. Right to demand encryption

   D. Right to restrict processing

8. Which one of the following metrics would provide the best measure of the effectiveness of an organization's new privacy incident response program?

   A. Number of security breaches

   B. Number of records breached

   C. Time to resolve breaches

   D. Size of the largest breach

9. Gary is a privacy program manager and he receives a request from a data subject to access all information about themselves maintained by the organization. Which one of the following tools, if appropriately maintained, would best help Gary respond to this request?

   A. Privacy breach log

   B. Incident response plan

   C. Business continuity plan

   D. Personal information inventory

10. Which one of the following activities is considered part of the Respond portion of the privacy life cycle?

    A. Answer data subject requests

    B. Document privacy program baseline

    C. Integrate privacy in the SDLC

    D. Audit information access

11. Which one of the following is not a valid reason for an organization to reject an individual's request to be forgotten under GDPR?

    A. Exercising the right of freedom of expression

    B. Difficulty in complying with the request

    C. Archiving purposes in the public interest

    D. Defending a legal claim

12. What type of system can help an organization track data subject information requests?

   A. Ticketing system

   B. Change management system

   C. Version control system

   D. Vulnerability scanning system

13. When developing an incident response plan, where would you normally place the statement of management commitment to the plan?

   A. Procedure

   B. Playbook

   C. Policy

   D. Guidelines

14. Of the individuals listed, who would provide the best endorsement for a business continuity plan's statement of importance?

   A. Vice president of business operations

   B. Chief information officer

   C. Chief executive officer

   D. Business continuity manager

15. Darren is concerned about the risk of a serious power outage affecting his organization's data center. He consults the organization's business impact analysis and determines that the ARO of a power outage is 20 percent. He notes that the assessment took place three years ago and no power outage has occurred. What ARO should he use in this year's assessment, assuming that none of the circumstances underlying the analysis have changed?

   A. 20 percent

   B. 50 percent

   C. 75 percent

   D. 100 percent

16. Jake is conducting a business impact analysis for his organization. As part of the process, he asks leaders from different units to provide input on how long the enterprise resource planning (ERP) system could be unavailable without causing irreparable harm to the organization. What measure is he seeking to determine?

   A. SLE

   B. EF

   C. MTD

   D. ARO

17. Renee is reporting the results of her organization's BIA to senior leaders. They express frustration at all of the detail, and one of them says, "Look, we just need to know how much we should expect these risks to cost us each year." What measure could Renee provide to best answer this question?

A. ARO

B. SLE

C. ALE

D. EF

18. Tracy is preparing for her organization's annual business continuity exercise and encounters resistance from some managers who don't see the exercise as important and feel that it is a waste of resources. She has already told the managers that it will only take half a day for their employees to participate. What argument could Tracy make to best address these concerns?

A. The exercise is required by policy.

B. The exercise is already scheduled and canceling it would be difficult.

C. The exercise is crucial to ensuring that the organization is prepared for emergencies.

D. The exercise will not be very time-consuming.

19. Tommy is the privacy incident oversight team leader for his organization and is responding to a newly discovered privacy incident. What document is most likely to contain step-by-step instructions that he might follow in the early hours of the response effort?

A. Policy

B. Baseline

C. Playbook

D. Textbook

20. Grace is the privacy incident oversight team leader for a business unit within NASA, a federal agency. What is the minimum amount of time that Grace must retain incident-handling records?

A. Six months

B. One year

C. Two years

D. Three years

Appendix

Answers to Review Questions

Chapter 1: Developing a Privacy Program

1. A. All of these records are important to a business and may be considered sensitive. However, this does not mean that they would fall into the scope of a privacy program. Privacy programs are specifically intended to protect personal information, and of the information presented here, only customer records fall into that category. A security program would be interested in protecting all of these elements of information.

2. A. Centralized data governance programs have a core office that directs the data governance efforts of the entire organization. Distributed data governance programs may have organization-wide standards, but each business unit creates its own data governance program that achieves those shared objectives. Hybrid data governance programs combine the centralized and distributed approaches, with a centralized office providing oversight and guidance to distributed teams who focus on particular business units. Oppositional data governance strategies do not exist.

3. C. Industry best practice calls for conducting privacy risk assessments on at least an annual basis. These risk assessments are designed to analyze the organization's current practices in light of the evolving privacy environment.

4. B. The special categories of information under GDPR include information about racial and ethnic origin, political opinions, religious or philosophical beliefs, trade union membership, genetic information, biometric information, health data, and data about a person's sex life or sexual orientation. Other categories of information may be sensitive but do not fit into this definition.

5. C. One of the provisions of the notice principle is that organizations should provide notice to data subjects before they use information for a purpose other than those that were previously disclosed.

6. C. Kara's organization is collecting and processing this information for its own business needs. Therefore, it is best described as the data controller.

7. C. ISO 27701 covers best practices for implementing privacy controls. ISO 27001 and ISO 27002 relate to an organization's information security program. ISO 27702 does not yet exist.

8. D. Unlike assessments, audits are always performed by an independent auditor who does not have a vested interest in the outcome. Audits may be performed at the request of internal management, a board of directors, or regulatory authorities.

9. A. The mission of a privacy program should be written at a high level as an enduring document. The goals, objectives, and procedures of a privacy program may change frequently as business needs and privacy requirements change.

10. C. Protect includes information security practices designed to safeguard information, the implementation of privacy by design (PbD) principles, the integration of privacy requirements into functional areas of the organization, and technical and organizational measures used to protect data.

11. C. All of these statements are true, with the exception of the requirement to retain a third-party dispute resolution service. While organizations should definitely maintain a dispute resolution process, there is no requirement that it be run by a third party.

12. B. The chief privacy officer is a senior executive who should be involved in strategic privacy tasks. It would be quite unusual for someone in this role to be involved in the actual encryption of personal information.

13. B. The gap analysis is the formal process of identifying deficiencies that prevent an organization from achieving its privacy objectives. The results of the gap analysis may be used to design new controls.

14. B. The current governance structure allows these subsidiaries to remain independent. Therefore, it is not appropriate to include them in the parent organization's program or replace their programs. Instead, Abe should limit the portion of the organization included in his program, which is a limitation of scope.

15. D. Respond covers how the organization reacts to data subject information requests and privacy rights and how the organization responds to privacy incidents.

16. C. The best-case scenario is that expenses are close to the budgeted amount but do not exceed the actual budget. Budget overages are difficult because funds may not be available to cover all expenses. When expenses are significantly under budget, the organization suffers an opportunity cost because those funds could have been used for other purposes or returned to shareholders as profit.

17. B. Privacy program charters commonly contain high-level organizational items, such as a scope statement, statement of roles and responsibilities, and description of the governance structure. A project schedule is a more tactical document that would not normally be included in a program-level charter due to its changing nature.

18. D. This is an operational expense, since it is a payroll expenditure, rather than a large purchase of capital equipment. The cost of hiring an employee is a recurring cost, rather than a one-time cost. The scenario does not identify whether the expense was budgeted or unbudgeted.

19. A. Justice Louis Brandeis used the term "right to be let alone" in a dissenting opinion in *Olmstead v. United States*. This opinion was later cited in *Roe v. Wade, Katz v. United States*, and *Carpenter v. United States*.

20. C. This is an example of aggregation, a technique that only reports summary information about a population in a manner that avoids disclosing information that may be traced back to a single person.

Chapter 2: Privacy Program Framework

1. C. Unlike the EU, the United States does not have a single comprehensive law protecting individual data privacy rights.

2. D. The right to rectification is, in fact, a data subject right under the GDPR, not the APEC Privacy Framework.

3. B. While all the possible answers refer to important steps in the planning process, this example involves executives who cannot agree on how to measure the success of the program. The privacy manager is measuring compliance with training, the CFO is measuring audit performance, and the CEO is measuring customer satisfaction. A few key metrics should be defined when a privacy program is first implemented to avoid this sort of confusion.

4. A. An ROI calculation would help the CFO determine whether the cost of the additional training programs would be justified by the value of not having those programs in place.

5. B. For smaller companies developing direct contracts with EU companies, standard contractual clauses are probably simplest and most effective to implement.

6. B. Dataflow mapping is the process of documenting how data flows throughout an organization from the point of collection to the point of purging.

7. C. In this case, Aidan has completed his initial risk assessment and noted specific issues with vendor risk. The lack of a contract means that Aidan can't be certain that the company is in compliance with PCI DSS rules. It makes sense for Aidan to implement a contract to manage the risk as an early priority.

8. B. Privacy by design (PbD) is compatible with FIPPS but goes further by encouraging more respect for individual choice, consent, and other end-user privacy protections. The U.S. Privacy Act only applies to the U.S. federal government and Annie wants to choose a framework to align with company values, not compliance requirements.

9. B. The AICPA's maturity model defines programs where procedures exist, but are not well documented, as "repeatable." An ad hoc program has only informal and inconsistent procedures and a defined program's procedures are fully documented and comprehensive. "Adequate" is not a term associated with a program maturity level.

10. C. The NIST framework includes the defining of profiles, or areas of focus selected from the NIST core. Under the NIST framework, organizations first define a "current profile" that documents the activities of the profile as they are. Then a "target profile" is set, which documents the goals the organization wants to achieve in those areas.

11. C. Since Melinda is running a healthcare operation that conducts electronic transactions, she is subject to HIPAA requirements. HIPAA requires a business associate agreement (BAA) to be in place for any vendor to process HIPAA data.

12. A. The NIST privacy framework's Protect function includes identity management, along with data security, access control, and other important privacy protection activities.

13. C. Since Surfside Rentals has decided to offer a credit card, it may be considered a financial institution and fall under the requirements of GLBA. This means that the FTC may now have subject-matter jurisdiction over the financial operations of the company. In this example, neither the personnel nor the location of the company has changed, so there is probably nothing new to worry about in terms of personal or territorial jurisdiction. Federal jurisdiction is not a formal category of jurisdiction.

14. B. GLBA distinguishes between customers and consumers. Financial institutions have different obligations to each. A customer has an ongoing relationship with a bank, for instance as an account holder. A consumer is a person who has only conducted isolated transactions.

15. D. Jennifer can use a trend analysis to track privacy incidents over time to see if the incidents are declining, increasing, or holding steady as she implements new controls.

16. C. All of the other answers can be quantified as numbers. Good metrics lend themselves to specific measurements. The overall quality of the incident response program is important, but this statement is not specific enough to be measurable.

17. B. Fines for egregious violations of GDPR provisions can be very steep. Data subjects may also seek additional damages for any harm they may have suffered from the violations.

18. D. Privacy impact assessments are performed when a business is considering a major change to technology or other activities that may affect privacy protection. PIAs should be performed in advance to understand and mitigate privacy risks proactively.

19. A. A data privacy agreement obligates the vendor to maintain appropriate privacy protections into the future and holds the vendor accountable for protecting customer data. No matter which vendor Nadya uses, a data privacy agreement is still important, and even a full-time privacy program manager would not be able to monitor the operations of a third-party vendor on a daily basis.

20. A. The CFO and privacy program manager both have direct responsibility for complying with the provisions of GLBA that relate to privacy and the resulting audit performance, so they are both probably primary audiences for this metric. Investors may receive a high-level summary of the audit performance in general and are most likely a tertiary audience. The CIO is the likely secondary audience because that position supports systems that affect audit performance but is not directly responsible.

Chapter 3: Privacy Operational Life Cycle: Assess

1. D. While all the possible answers are good ideas for Nathan to consider, the only way to ensure that Nathan's company won't bear financial responsibility for a breach caused by the vendor is to transfer liability to the vendor in the contract.

2. D. Before the old computers can be donated, it is critical to ensure that no private information remains stored on the hard drives. Companies usually remove and physically destroy the hard drives before transferring the equipment to a new owner.

3. D. External audits are commonly used to certify compliance with external regulations, programs, and frameworks. Internal audits hold a program accountable to management, program assurance could refer to multiple types of audits and reviews, and transfer impact assessments are not used for certification purposes.

4. C. Since Hassan was surprised to learn about cloud computing services, it is most likely that ShoeStop missed this during preacquisition due diligence. Had ShoeStop known about Footbarn's use of third-party cloud services, then Hassan may have had the opportunity to ensure proper contracts were in place and/or work with IT to consider upgrading ShoeStop's infrastructure to align with the new acquisition.

5. C. While all of these answers might help, role-based training for HR staff on record retention would be the most direct way to reduce risk in this area.

6. B.. The GDPR does not specifically mention incident response planning as a required component of a data protection impact assessment. However, incident response procedures could be included as part of plans to mitigate risks.

7. B. A data protection impact analysis is a requirement of GDPR and, since Marcel's company is global, his company is most likely subject to GDPR.

8. B. Since Molly's company will retain all assets of the subsidiary, this will include the subsidiary's data. Molly's company needs to ensure that the data is managed securely and available to retrieve based on her company's record retention policy.

9. D. Performing risk assessments, understanding vendor technologies, and analyzing legal compliance are all important components of evaluating potential vendors. However, it would be highly unusual for a company to implement privacy safeguards on a vendor's systems directly.

10. A. Data lifecycle management (DLM) documents how and where data is collected, stored, used, archived, and destroyed. Well-documented DLM would help Javier quickly identify the data he needs to respond to customer requests.

11. D. While standards for information security are important, they are not specific to privacy protection. While Hassan's program depends on information security for success, his work focuses on privacy-specific functions. The other areas of risk mentioned all represent direct privacy protection and privacy compliance risks that should concern Hassan as the privacy program manager.

12. A. Marla should probably do everything listed. However, it is most urgent to make sure that customer records are not inadvertently left unsecured in areas accessible to the general public. Once access to the records is secured, Marla can spend time implementing additional policies and safeguards.

13. A. Whenever a business is in a rush to engage with a third party, there is a risk of skipping the full vendor evaluation process. The vendor evaluation process would include an understanding of the contractor's training and location. The vendor evaluation would also help determine risks related to the vendor that may inform provisions of the contract.

14. B. A transfer impact assessment will help the company evaluate the implications of cross-border data sharing. Since the company is the EU, there may well be risks related to transferring data to a U.S.-based company, since the EU does not consider that U.S. law provides adequate data privacy protection.

15. B. A privacy program's incident management function includes procedures for breach notification requirements.

16. C. While protecting computers with passwords is an important information security control, passwords are considered a technical control and are not usually included as part of a physical privacy assessment.

17. B. It is important to know where in the world a vendor plans to store private data to assess the need for any cross-border transfer arrangements. It is also important to understand any laws and regulations that might apply based on the jurisdiction(s) in which data is stored.

18. A. All assessments must have a starting point for measurement. That starting point is a baseline against which you can benchmark future performance. Once a baseline is established, risk assessments and audits help identify gaps between the baseline and the desired state.

19. A. While not explicitly required by the GDPR, it would be a good idea for Aiofe to complete a legitimate interest assessment to ensure that she has a good reason for collecting extra personal information via her new website. If she determines there is a legitimate purpose for the collection, she would be required to complete a DPIA before implementation.

20. A. GDPR requires data processors to notify controllers of data privacy incidents promptly. Any organization engaging with a third-party data processor should make sure this requirement is part of any contractual agreement to be certain that data processors comply.

Chapter 4: Privacy Operational Life Cycle: Protect

1. A. Full-disk encryption protects all of the data stored on a disk and is particularly useful in cases where a laptop or mobile device is lost or stolen. Transport Layer Security (TLS) protects data in transit over a network and does not protect data stored on a disk. Degaussing and pulverizing are data destruction techniques that cannot be used after a device has been lost.

2. A. Tokenization techniques use a lookup table and are designed to be reversible. Masking and hashing techniques replace the data with values that can't be reversed back to the original data if performed properly. Shredding, when conducted properly, physically destroys data so that it may not be recovered.

3. B. The key term in this scenario is "one way." This indicates that compliance with the document is not mandatory, so Joe must be authoring a guideline. Policies, standards, and procedures are all mandatory.

4. C. Requests for an exception to a security policy would not normally include a proposed revision to the policy. Exceptions are documented variances from the policy because of specific technical and/or business requirements. They do not alter the original policy, which remains in force for systems not covered by the exception.

5. D. Employees should only have the access necessary to carry out their job responsibilities. It is almost certain that no employee in Kevin's organization needs access to all data as part of their work, so this activity violates the principle of least privilege. As a privacy professional, Kevin should definitely question situations that seem inappropriate.

6. C. While reporting and communication are an important part of vulnerability management, they are not included in the life cycle. The three life cycle phases are detection, remediation, and testing.

7. A. Degaussing only works on magnetic media, and DVDs are optical media. Amanda could burn, pulverize, or even shred the DVDs to ensure that data is properly destroyed.

8. D. Scan schedules are most often determined by the organization's risk appetite, regulatory requirements, technical constraints, business constraints, and licensing limitations. Most scans are automated and do not require staff availability to run on schedule.

9. A. Policies should be developed in a manner that obtains input from all relevant stakeholders, but it is not necessary to obtain agreement or approval from all stakeholders. Policies should follow normal corporate policy approval processes and should be written in a manner that fits within the organizational culture and "tone at the top." Once an information security policy is approved, it commonly falls to the information security manager to communicate and implement the policy.

10. A. Differential backups involve always storing copies of all files modified since the most recent full backup, regardless of any incremental or differential backups created during the intervening time period.

11. D. One of the capabilities of data loss prevention (DLP) systems is the ability to search systems for the presence of sensitive information, such as Social Security numbers. Transport Layer Security (TLS) is used to protect data from unauthorized access when in transit over a network. Full-disk encryption (FDE) is used to protect data stored on a disk from unauthorized access. Hardware security modules (HSMs) are used to manage encryption keys.

12. C. Data being transmitted over a network is the best example of data in motion. Data stored on a hard drive or in a cloud service is not in motion; it is data at rest. Data being actively processed in memory fits into the category of data in use.

13. D. Privacy should be embedded into design, rather than bolted on as an afterthought. Organizations should strive for a positive-sum approach to privacy that does not treat privacy as requiring trade-offs. Organizations should design privacy mechanisms with visibility and transparency in mind. Systems should be designed to prevent privacy risks from occurring in the first place, not to respond to privacy lapses that do occur.

14. C. Gary is proving his identity with his fingerprint, a biometric mechanism. Steps that prove your identity are examples of authentication techniques.

15. D. Facial recognition technology is an example of a biometric authentication technique, or "something you are." A passcode is an example of a knowledge-based authentication technique, or "something you know."

16. C. The disclosure of sensitive information to unauthorized individuals is a violation of the principle of confidentiality.

17. D. The use of full-disk encryption is intended to prevent a security incident from occurring if a device is lost or stolen. Therefore, this is a preventive control gap.

18. A. As an organization analyzes its risk environment, technical and business leaders determine the level of protection required to preserve the confidentiality, integrity, and availability of their information and systems. They express these requirements by writing the control objectives that the organization wishes to achieve. These control objectives are statements of a desired security state.

19. A. Technical controls enforce confidentiality, integrity, and availability in the digital space. Examples of technical security controls include firewall rules, access control lists, intrusion prevention systems, and encryption.

20. D. Deterrent controls are designed to prevent an attacker from attempting to violate security policies in the first place. Preventive controls would attempt to block an attack that was about to take place. Corrective controls would remediate the issues that arose during an attack.

Chapter 5: Privacy Operational Life Cycle: Sustain

1. C. Gia made sure the company was initially in compliance with international data transfer rules as it expanded into new territory. Ongoing monitoring for compliance will ensure that procedures such as completing TRAs are followed if the company enters new territories in the future.

2. D. An internal audit generally reports to company management (the CEO) whereas external audits usually report to the board of directors or regulators. Internal audits provide a more objective form of assurance that a program is meeting expectations. Compliance monitoring ensures that the training requirements comply with policies, laws, and regulations.

3. D. Since Samit has a clear privacy program and policy in place, then he must employ procedures for ongoing monitoring of the IT environment to ensure compliance with the policy when it comes to new IT systems.

4. C. It is true that, in some circumstances, courts may strike down provisions of a law (though this does not happen frequently), assess penalties, or assign liability. However, court decisions do frequently interpret privacy laws in ways that change the scope and application. Privacy managers monitor court decisions to ensure their privacy programs are updated to comply with any guidance issued by the courts.

5. B. Audit trails are records showing that policies and procedures have been followed. For example, if documents are sent out for destruction, then records should be kept that include an inventory of which documents were delivered for destruction and verification of when the documents are destroyed.

6. B. The Sustain phase of the privacy operational life cycle focuses on the continual improvement of an existing program. The Protect and Assess phases are earlier stages in the privacy operational life cycle, and "optimize" refers to a capability maturity model, not the privacy operational life cycle.

7. B. Disclosure accounting is the practice of keeping specific records of nonstandard disclosures of private information. Some regulations, such as HIPAA, have explicit requirements for covered entities to maintain disclosure accounting records.

8. B. HR typically manages the training function and must track employee compliance with training requirements. Auditing would be conducted by someone outside of HR. Compliance with every aspect of the privacy policy is monitored by the privacy program manager with the support of multiple functional areas.

9. B. Audits assess privacy program performance against a set standard that describes a satisfactory program. Such standards make it possible to interpret audit requests to understand whether or not a privacy program's performance is adequate.

10. C. Second-party audits are formal audit processes where one organization audits a supplier, contractor, or other vendor. Third-party and external audits mean the same thing and refer to audits conducted by a dedicated auditor, not a business partner. Due diligence processes occur when vetting a vendor in the first place but do not encompass ongoing inspection.

11. C. Monitoring the privacy environment involves keeping an eye on the systems and applications that control and process data. This means monitoring risks and vulnerabilities in concert with the information security program as well as watching for changes in the systems and applications. Managing information security breaches, however, is handled by the information security function.

12. D. To evaluate audit findings in context, it is important to audit against a predefined industry standard that describes performance expectations for the program.

13. A. Compliance monitoring ensures that key processes, such as records management, are aligned with the privacy policy and comply with current regulations. In this case, the records management strategy had not been adequately monitored for compliance.

14. B. Communication is key to sustaining an effective privacy program. Program monitoring activities are based almost entirely on communication across the organization to check on compliance, implement changes, and share the results of monitoring.

15. D. External audits are usually reported to the board of directors and are conducted by a dedicated third-party auditor with no other business relationship with the organization. Audits conducted by data controllers as per contract terms are most likely examples of second-party audits. Audits should never be conducted by the functional office being audited, so this doesn't narrow down the type of audit.

16. A. Monitoring for regulatory changes refers to external monitoring. An organization's board of directors certainly could adopt bylaws that might affect privacy, but that would not be considered a form of regulation.

17. B. Audits provide assurance that programs are effective, which includes assessing the program itself and checking to see that the program requirements are followed by employees. Audit trails provide evidence that procedures are implemented and followed.

18. A. The Sustain phase of the privacy operational life cycle focuses on managing a program via ongoing monitoring, training, and audit. Implementing privacy controls refers to the Protect phase, governance and metrics are implemented before the operational life cycle begins, and responding to incidents refers to the Respond phase.

19. B. Governance, risk, and compliance (GRC) software helps manage workflows and documents to support compliance activities such as audits. If Marco implements a GRC software system, he will not only be better able to manage the privacy program, he will also be able to rapidly produce information for auditors.

20. B. The human resources department is usually responsible for managing training programs, including ongoing monitoring of employee compliance. An internal audit may also check for compliance with training requirements, but not on a day-to-day basis.

Chapter 6: Privacy Operational Life Cycle: Respond

1. A. An organization's incident response policy should contain a clear description of the authority assigned to the privacy incident oversight team while responding to an active privacy incident.

2. A. The incident response policy provides the team with the authority needed to do their job. Therefore, it should be approved by the highest possible level of authority within the organization, preferably the CEO.

3. C. Lessons-learned sessions are most effective when facilitated by an independent party who was not involved in the incident response effort.

4. B. Article 33 requires that data controllers notify the supervisory authority of a personal data breach. It reads, in part: "In the case of a personal data breach, the controller shall without undue delay and, where feasible, not later than 72 hours after having become aware of it, notify the personal data breach to the supervisory authority ... unless the personal data breach is unlikely to result in a risk to the rights and freedoms of natural persons."

5. A. When notifying data subjects of a breach, GDPR requires that data controllers communicate the name and contact details of the data protection officer, describe the likely consequences of the personal data breach, and describe the measures taken by the controller to address the breach. Controllers are required to inform the supervisory authority of the nature of the breach but are not required to give this information to data subjects.

6. B. Matthew will likely need to conduct all of these actions at some point during the incident response. However, he does not yet have enough information to perform a risk assessment or contact any other stakeholders. He should first interview the employee to gain the basic facts of the incident. Once he has all of the relevant details, he may then move on to a risk assessment.

7. C. GDPR Article 17 provides for the right to be forgotten. GDPR Article 16 provides for the right to data integrity and correction. GDPR Article 18 allows data subjects to restrict the processing of their personal information. GDPR does not contain a requirement that data subjects have the right to demand that their personal information be encrypted.

8. C. It's tempting to simply use the number of privacy incidents as the core metric, but this can be a very misleading figure. In organizations with immature (or even no!) privacy incident response plans, many incidents may simply go undetected. As the organization becomes more effective in its response to privacy incidents, this may cause an increase in the number of reported incidents. If you use the number of reported incidents as a metric, a program that is improving may actually look like it is decreasing in effectiveness! While you should track the number of incidents that occur, a more important metric for a developing privacy program is the amount of time that it takes to resolve privacy incidents. The more mature the incident response program, the more quickly it will be able to detect and resolve privacy incidents.

9. D. Organizations that maintain personal information inventories may use them to facilitate their response to both requests to access records and requests to correct or erase personal information. The inventory helps the organization quickly locate all relevant records.

10. A. Answering data subject requests is one of the core responsibilities of the Respond phase. Documenting a privacy program baseline occurs during the Assess phase. Integrating privacy into the systems development life cycle (SDLC) occurs during the Protect phase. Auditing information access occurs during the Sustain phase.

11. B. Organizations are not permitted to reject a request simply because it is difficult to comply with it. GDPR outlines five reasons that organizations may reject a request:

    For exercising the right of freedom of expression and information

    For compliance with a legal obligation

    For reasons of public interest in the area of public health

    For archiving purposes in the public interest, scientific or historical research purposes, or statistical purposes

    For the establishment, exercise, or defense of legal claims

12. A. Many organizations choose to use a ticket-based tracking system for handling data subject requests. This approach assigns a unique tracking number to each request, tracks requests through their workflow, and notifies managers of failures to meet time requirements.

13. C. The incident response policy should contain statements that provide authority for incident response, assign responsibility to the privacy incident oversight team, and describe the role of individuals and state organizational priorities. Procedures, playbooks, and guidelines should provide more tactical advice.

14. C. You should strive to have the highest-ranking person possible sign the BCP's statement of importance. Of the choices given, the chief executive officer (CEO) is the highest ranking.

15. A. The annualized rate of occurrence (ARO) is the likelihood that the risk will materialize in any given year. The fact that a power outage did not occur in any of the past three years doesn't change the probability that one will occur in the upcoming year. Unless other circumstances have changed, the ARO should remain the same.

16. C. The maximum tolerable downtime (MTD) represents the longest period a business function can be unavailable before causing irreparable harm to the business. This figure is useful when determining the level of business continuity resources to assign to a particular function.

17. C. The annualized loss expectancy (ALE) represents the amount of money a business expects to lose to a given risk each year. This figure is quite useful when performing a quantitative prioritization of business continuity resource allocation.

18. C. This question requires that you exercise some judgment, as do many questions on the CIPM exam. All of these answers are plausible things that Tracy could bring up, but we're looking for the best answer. In this case, that is ensuring that the organization is ready for an emergency—a mission-critical goal. Telling managers that the exercise is already scheduled or required by policy doesn't address their concerns that it is a waste of time. Telling them that it won't be time-consuming is not likely to be an effective argument because they are already raising concerns about the amount of time requested.

19. C. Incident response playbooks contain detailed step-by-step instructions that guide the early response to a privacy incident. Organizations typically have playbooks prepared for high-severity and frequently occurring incident types.

20. D. National Archives General Records Schedule (GRS) 3.2 requires that all U.S. federal agencies retain incident handling records for at least three years.

Index

Comprehensive Online Learning Environment

Register to gain one year of FREE access after activation to the online interactive test bank to help you study for your CIPM certification exam—included with your purchase of this book!

The online test bank includes the following:

- **Assessment Test** to help you focus your study on specific objectives
- **Chapter Tests** to reinforce what you've learned
- **Practice Exams** to test your knowledge of the material
- **Digital Flashcards** to reinforce your learning and provide last-minute test prep before the exam
- **Searchable Glossary** to define the key terms you'll need to know for the exam

Register and Access the Online Test Bank

To register your book and get access to the online test bank, follow these steps:

1. Go to www.wiley.com/go/sybextestprep (this address is case sensitive)!
2. Select your book from the list.
3. Complete the required registration information, including answering the security verification to prove book ownership. You will be emailed a pin code.
4. Follow the directions in the email or go to www.wiley.com/go/sybextestprep.
5. Find your book on that page and click the "Register or Login" link with it. Then enter the pin code you received and click the "Activate PIN" button.
6. On the Create an Account or Login page, enter your username and password, and click Login or, if you don't have an account already, create a new account.
7. At this point, you should be in the test bank site with your new test bank listed at the top of the page. If you do not see it there, please refresh the page or log out and log back in.

SYBEX
A Wiley Bra